Paul B. Kidd is a Sydney-based author, Radio 2UE talkback broadcaster, freelance *60 Minutes* researching producer and photojournalist who specialises in Australian true crime, big game fishing, adventure and humour.

Paul's articles, interviews and photographs have appeared in most major Australian outdoors and men's publications, numerous magazines and on websites worldwide.

Paul B. Kidd is a recognised authority on Australian serial killers and criminals who have been sentenced to life imprisonment, never to be released. The author of sixteen books on Australian true crime and fishing, he lives in Sydney's eastern suburbs.

Celluloid Serial Killers

The Real Monsters Behind the Movies

PAUL B. KIDD

The Five Mile Press

Published by
The Five Mile Press Pty Ltd
950 Stud Road, Rowville
Victoria 3178 Australia
Email: publishing@fivemile.com.au
Website: www.fivemile.com.au

First published 2007

Cover design by Blue Cork
Internal design and typesetting by Darian Causby/Highway 51 Design works

Printed in China

National Library Cataloguing-in-Publication data:

   Kidd, Paul B. (Paul Benjamin), 1945- .
   Celluloid Serial killers : the real monsters behind the movies.

   ISBN 9781741784725 (pbk.).

   1. Serial murderers in motion pictures. I. Title.

971.436556

For Tania, my partner and (now)
serial killer movie authority.

And, as always, my son Ben.

Author's Special Acknowledgements

Luke Anisimoff. My researcher and editor on this
and many other projects. Thanks, mate.

Many thanks to the Crisford family and staff at Dr What's, Australia's
biggest video and DVD library, 562 Oxford St, Bondi Junction, NSW.

Picture Acknowledgements

FRONT COVER
Charlize Theron as Aileen Wuornos courtesy The Kobal Collection/WireImage.com
Anthony Hopkins as Hannibal Lecter courtesy AP Photo/Ken Regan
Anthony Perkins as Norman Bates courtesy MovieStore

POSTERS/MOVIE STILLS
MovieStore: pxiv, 12, 28, 42, 68, 80, 84, 96, 110, 122, 126, 135,
156, 162, 166, 180, 188, 200, 216, 220, 230, 242, 246, 262, 266, 276,
280, 284, 288, 292
Everett/Headpress: pp132, 136, 372, 390
Capital Pictures: pp212, 296, 308
The Kobal Collection/WireImage.com: pp146, 184, 250, 320, 332, 356
Waterfront Productions: pp346, 380
Photos 12 / Alamy: p56
First Look International: p296

BLACK AND WHITE PHOTOS
Aside from acknowledgements below, all black and white pictures have been sourced by the
author. The author takes full responsibility for the copyright responsibilities attached to the use
of these photographs.
p71 Edward Gein, 51-year-old farmer, Wautoma court, Wisconsin, USA,
20 November, 1957. Image: © Bettmann/Corbis
p87 Albert DeSalvo escorted into Middlesex County Superior Court, Cambridge, Massachusetts,
January 31 1968. Image: © Bettmann/Corbis
p99 Accused murderers Martha Beck and Raymond Fernandez, Bronx County Court,
New York, USA, 14 June 1949.
Image: © Bettmann/Corbis
p192 Henry Lee Lucas in Williamson County prison, Texas, USA, 1 January 1979.
Image: © Daemmrich Bob/Corbis Sygma
p269 David Berkowitz, Hulton Archive/Getty Images.
p311 Jeffrey Dahmer, Photographer Eugene Garcia, AFP/Getty Images.
p323 Aileen Wournos testifying during a murder trial in 1992.
Image: © Daytona Beach News Journal/Corbis Sygma
p336 Angelo Buono arrives at Criminal Court, Los Angeles, California, USA, 22 October 1979.
Photographer Clarence Leino. Image: © Bettmann/Corbis
p337 Kenneth Bianchi in Bellingham, Washington in November 1978.
Image: © Bettmann/Corbis
p359 Bradley John Murdoch, Newspix/News Ltd.
p384 Mug Shot of Albert H Fish, December 13, 1934.
Image: © Bettmann/Corbis

Every attempt has been made to trace and acknowledge copyright.
Where an attempt has been unsuccessful, the publisher would be pleased to hear from
the copyright owner so any omission or error can be rectified.

CONTENTS

INTRODUCTION

Serial killers in the movies are nothing new. They have been around since the year dot. Well, from 1931 anyway. But we didn't know them as serial killers way back when – they were mass murderers or repeat killers. To the best of my research the term 'serial killer' was never used in a movie until James Woods said it in 1988 in an obscure, yet terrific thriller titled *Cop*.

But it wasn't until three years later in *The Silence of the Lambs* that the term 'serial killer' became deeply etched into the modern vernacular when we met Hannibal Lecter, Buffalo Bill and the FBI profilers who hunted them. The serial killer movie craze had begun. From then on there were more serial killer movies made than had been made in the previous 60 years.

The original intention of *Celluloid Serial Killers* was to write only about movies based on real serial killers. For example, although the names and most of the circumstances were changed, there has never been a doubt that the first movie in this book, *M*, was based on the murders of German child serial killer Peter Kürten. But in the second chapter, *Shadow of a Doubt*, it isn't widely known that Alfred Hitchcock's team based their screenplay on a story by Gordon McDowell, who in turn was inspired by real-life 'merry widow murderer' Earle Leonard Nelson. The title of *The Boston Strangler* is a dead give-away: it is based on the murders of the real-life Boston Strangler, Albert DeSalvo. All the movies are different, but they are all based – one way or another – on a real-life serial killer.

But the more I researched serial killer movies that were inspired by real-life killers, the more I realised that there were also many fabulous movies out there that were in no way based on real events, but were still worthy of a critique in the best interests of serial killer movie fans. *Copycat*, *Jennifer 8* and *The Bone Collector* come to mind.

This created a problem. I didn't want to turn *Celluloid Serial Killers* into a reference book of every serial killer movie ever made. It was originally meant to be a book of serial killer movies based on real characters, no matter how good or bad the movie was, as well as the real story of the associated serial killings. Now the book was going to include serial killer movies that, although fictional, were credible to a degree and entertaining at the same time. But not all of them fell into that category. Some had to go.

So in case you're wondering where your favourite movie is, it may be deemed not good enough for my book. It may be one that didn't make the cut: *No Way to Treat a Lady* (1968), *Black Widow* (1987), *Kiss the Girls* (1997), *Switchback* (1997); *The Diary of a Serial Killer* (1999), *Twisted* (2004), *Taking Lives* (2004) and *Suspect Zero* (2004) all fell into that category.

So this is the result: 45 chapters, more than two-thirds of which are based on some degree of fact. The others are credible and entertaining fictional serial killer movies which, at least to my knowledge, are not based on a real-life killer.

Some of the very best movies ever made feature serial killers – *The Silence of the Lambs*, *Psycho*, *Se7en* and *M* are in the Internet Movie Database (IMDB) Top 100 Movies. I hope my book introduces you to many more.

Paul B. Kidd, Sydney, Australia
pkidd@bigpond.com.au

Celluloid Serial Killers

And in the beginning there was …

(1931)

DIRECTED BY FRITZ LANG
SCREENPLAY BY THEA VON HARBOU AND FRITZ LANG

FEATURING
Peter Lorre as Hans Beckert
Gustaf Gründgens as Schränker
Ellen Widmann as Frau Beckmann
Inge Landgut as Elsie Beckmann
Otto Wernicke as Inspector Karl Lohmann
Theodor Loos as Inspector Groeber

Fritz Lang's *M* is the only foreign-language movie in this book. And for good reason. It was the first serial killer movie ever made. It is a masterpiece of film noir. And it was digitally remastered in 2004 and is readily available throughout specialist DVD outlets.

M is a fictionalised account of the real-life murders of German child killer Peter Kürten, who terrorised Düsseldorf throughout the late 1920s and into 1930. Kürten was a shadowy character who materialised as if from nowhere; he killed and then disappeared. Parents lived in fear of their children being abducted, raped and murdered.

The creepy lead character Hans Beckert (Kürten) is portrayed by Peter Lorre in his first major role. And perhaps *M* was responsible for typecasting Lorre as a villain because he went on to play some of the most memorable baddies in movie history – the courier-murderer Ugarte in *Casablanca* and the treacherously gay Joel Cairo in *The Maltese Falcon* come to mind.

But neither the wonderful cast, which includes the exceptional Gustaf Gründgens, nor the real-life murderer Kürten, is the star of *M*. Rather it is the masterful direction of Fritz Lang that takes the honours. He uses cinematography and lighting effects to create a murderous atmosphere. Check out the cigar smoke-filled rooms that today would have the movie shut down by the Anti-Cancer Council!

Lang takes the viewer on a mesmerising journey as he tells the story of the chase for the psychopathic child killer who ultimately experiences retribution not at the hands of the law, but from Düsseldorf's underworld, which had been put out of business when the cops locked the neighbourhood down for the hunt.

This plot is to die for (literally) and its masterful villains ensure an extraordinary cinematic experience. The film would be claimed as a masterpiece if it had been made yesterday, let alone more that 75 years ago.

The real story of the serial killer Peter Kürten is horror beyond belief. Given the advances in science and crime scene investigation it could never happen now. But postwar Germany was the perfect setting for a fiend of Kürten's capacity. He killed at will and, because of his perfectly normal appearance, could disappear into a crowd in a heartbeat.

Peter Kürten: The Vampire of Düsseldorf

If ever in the history of serial murder there was an example of a tortured childhood creating a serial killer, then it would have to be the case of one Peter Kürten or, as he came to be known throughout the world, the Vampire of Düsseldorf.

Born on 26 May 1883, Peter Kürten spent his childhood in a filthy one-room apartment in Düsseldorf with 10 younger siblings. His father was a violent drunk, having come from a long family line of alcoholism and insanity. Mr Kürten spent most of his time in a drunken stupor assaulting his children and forcing sex upon their mother in front of them. Years later Mr Kürten was jailed for three years for committing incest with Peter's 13-year-old sister.

At age nine, Kürten befriended a local dog catcher who lived in the same building. The dog catcher showed the young Kürten how to masturbate dogs to a climax and then torture them to death. That same year, while playing on the Rhine with a raft, Peter Kürten drowned a schoolfriend. When another student dived in to rescue the drowning lad, Kürten pushed him under the raft until he also drowned. Unable to prove anything, authorities could only assume that it was a terrible accident.

In his early teens Kürten spent his time at stables near the family home committing bestiality with sheep and goats. His greatest pleasure was having intercourse with a sheep while he stabbed it to death. By 16 Kürten had left home and had spent time in prison for stealing. Released from prison in 1899, Kürten moved in with a 32-year-old debauched, masochistic prostitute. He now practised his sexual cruelties – that he had as yet only inflicted on animals – on a human being, and she couldn't get enough. At 17 his education as a monster was complete. The beast had arrived. Over the next 24 years he was to spend 27 stints in Düsseldorf prisons for petty crimes.

During his years in and out of prison Peter Kürten taught himself to achieve orgasm by imagining brutal sexual acts. He became so absorbed with his fantasies of murder and butchery that he deliberately broke minor prison rules so that he could be sentenced to solitary confinement, even if it was only for a few days at a time. Here he could curl naked in a cold corner and seek relief in his own world of sadistic daydreaming.

Kürten found his first murder victim, Christine Klein, a 10-year-old schoolgirl, while he was burgling an apartment above an inn in Köln, just out of Düsseldorf on 25 May 1913. He had broken into the room on the first floor and saw the girl sound asleep on a thick feather bed. Seizing the child with both hands around her neck, he throttled her into unconsciousness and sexually assaulted her. Then, with a sharp pocket knife he had brought with him for just such an occasion, he slowly cut the child's throat from ear to ear, wallowing in the warm blood as it squirted all over him for the three or so minutes it took the child to die. Kürten locked the door behind him as he let himself out and then he went home and masturbated over the experience. The murder remained unsolved until Kürten's confession, many years later.

Kürten spent the next eight years in and out of prison for a variety of offences ranging from burglary to assault but in 1921 he seemingly put it all behind him when he married and settled down to a seemingly normal and respectable life in Altenburg. For the first time in his life he found a permanent job, as a factory worker. And, as Germany struggled to rebuild confidence in its workforce, he played his part by becoming an official in the post–World War I trade union movement.

And Peter Kürten dressed accordingly in a smart shirt and tie, Homburg hat and a stylish suit and overcoat. He looked anything but a murderer with a long criminal history. It was this guise of normality that would help him melt into the crowd and avoid suspicion in the years to come.

In 1925 Kürten was back in Düsseldorf and perhaps it was the memories of his hometown that rekindled the monster at the centre of his being. For four years he had curtailed his sinister urgings, but eventually they became too strong to resist. The civilian horrors perpetrated by Peter Kürten from the beginning of 1929 onwards are still talked about in Germany today.

On 9 February 1929 the body of eight-year-old schoolgirl Rosa Ohliger was found under a hedge in Düsseldorf. Rosa had been stabbed 13 times, petrol had been poured all over her body and she had been set on fire. She had been savagely stabbed about the vagina, and the seminal fluid covering her underwear indicated that she had been masturbated over as she lay dead or dying. In his later confession to the murder Peter Kürten said: 'When that morning I poured petrol over the child Ohliger and set fire to her, I had an orgasm at the height of the fire.'

A week earlier a man had attacked a woman named Frau Kühn in broad daylight. He had grabbed her by the jacket lapels and stabbed her repeatedly about the stomach and chest, inflicting 24 wounds, none of which were fatal, before running off and leaving her for dead. In his later confession Kürten told police: 'The place where I attacked Frau Kühn I visited again that same evening twice and later several times. In doing so, I sometimes had an orgasm.'

Five days after the murder of Rosa Ohliger, a 45-year-old man named Scheer was found stabbed to death on a road in nearby Flingern with 20 knife wounds to his chest and head. The day after the attack Kürten returned to the scene of his crime. He struck up a conversation with one of the detectives on site, who had no reason to think that he was, in fact, talking to the offender.

Then there was quiet for six months until a series of stranglings and stabbings warned the police that the madman was back. On 21 August, in the suburb of Lierenfeld, on three separate occasions people were stabbed late at night while walking home. Each victim had been acknowledged with a 'good evening' by a well-dressed man who tipped his hat and then lashed out at them with a knife. Although all of the wounds were very deep and possibly life threatening, no-one actually died.

Just two days later, at around 10.30 on the night of 23 August, at the crowded annual fair in the town of Flehe, two foster sisters, five-year-old Gertrude Hamacher and 14-year-old Louise Lenzen, were walking home hand-in-hand. A well-dressed man in a hat followed them from a short distance. He stopped the children and asked whether Louise 'would be very kind and get some cigarettes for me? I'll look after the little girl'.

As Louise ran back to the fair to get his cigarettes, he picked little Gertrude up in his arms and throttled her to death, before taking his time in cutting her throat with a razor-sharp pocket knife. When Louise returned a few minutes later with his cigarettes, Peter Kürten dragged her off into the bushes, where he strangled her and cut off her head.

The following day a teenage servant girl, Gertrude Schulte, was savagely attacked by a man who tried to rape her. 'I'd rather die than have sex with you,' she screamed, as Kürten tried to rip her clothes off. 'Die then,' he said as he pulled out a knife and stabbed her in the chest. Fortunately, the lass survived the attack to describe her assailant as a well-dressed man in in his 40s who wore a hat and an overcoat.

By now the monster had a name – the Vampire of Düsseldorf – which, in fact was far from the truth, given that while Kürten had committed the most terrible crimes imaginable, he hadn't actually taken to drinking the blood of his victims as is the way of fictional vampires. But, technicalities aside, the name stuck and Germans held their breath for the next attack. They didn't have to wait long.

In September a teenager named Ida Reuter was raped and battered to death. A month later, on 12 October, another servant girl, Elizabeth Dorrier, was raped and beaten to death. On 25 October, two Düsseldorf women, Frau Meurer and Frau Wanders, were bashed in separate attacks in broad daylight by a smart, well-dressed man carrying a hammer. Both survived.

As the attacks and murder toll mounted, Düsseldorf locals could be forgiven for comparing the crime wave with those of London's Whitechapel killer, Jack the Ripper, in 1888. But Jack the Ripper specialised in disembowelling prostitutes. This monster's specialty was children and young women. And, as if to prove his point, on 7 November the Vampire of Düsseldorf took his next victim, five-year-old Gertrude Albermann, to a disused factory where he sexually assaulted, strangled and then stabbed the child 35 times. Two days after Gertrude had disappeared, the local *Freedom* newspaper received a letter from the vampire telling them exactly where to find her body.

From February to May 1930 there was a succession of strangulation and hammer attacks, but none were fatal. With most of Düsseldorf's police force on the hunt for the vampire, it's not hard to understand why there was public outcry about his evasion of police. It seemed as though he could come and go as he pleased, killing and bashing to his heart's desire – if he had a heart. Perhaps it was this invisibility that was the reason he was called the vampire. By the end of May the streets of Düsseldorf were empty after dark.

The capture of Peter Kürten was more by luck than clever detective work. On 14 May 1930 a young unemployed housekeeper, Maria Budlick, was waiting for a train at Düsseldorf railway station when a man approached and offered to take her to a reputable girls' hostel and pay for her to stay there the night. After a while the man led her off the brightly lit streets and into a park. Maria had heard the stories about the murderer and refused to leave the lit footpath. The man took her by the arm and as he insisted that he go into the park with her, another man appeared on the scene and asked if the girl was all right. The man let go of Maria and fled, leaving her with her rescuer, Peter Kürten.

Maria told Kürten that she was unemployed and had no money and was grateful for his offer to stay at his place but, when they arrived at a room he rented, and that his wife didn't know about, on the Mettmanner Strasse, she refused to have sex with him and asked if he could find her somewhere else to sleep. Kürten took her by train to Worringerplatz, where he took her deep into the woods. She offered no resistance when he forced himself on her, and in this case it was a smart thing to do. Later Kürten confessed that if she had offered the slightest resistance he would have killed her. He would live to regret that he hadn't.

Afterwards Kürten took Maria back to the train and, making sure that no police were about, gave her enough money for a ticket and to stay in a hostel for the night. Kürten made sure that no-one saw him deposit the young girl at the tram station. As far as he was concerned that was the end of that. But it was just the beginning of the end.

On 21 May Maria Budlick returned to Kürten's room at Mettmanner Strasse with the police. She had remembered where the man lived and, after consulting friends about the rape, they had convinced her to take the police to his house. Maria positively identified the tenant, whose name they established as Peter Kürten, the man who had assaulted her. Quick to realise what was going on, Kürten fled the scene before police could arrest him.

At this stage there was absolutely nothing to link Kürten with the vampire murders. But he knew that what he had done to Maria Budlick on top of his record as a habitual criminal would get him a minimum 15 years in jail. Without him to provide for her, his wife of 10 years, whom he loved very much, would have to live in poverty for the rest of her life.

There was a substantial reward on offer for information leading to the capture of Germany's most wanted man, so Kürten concocted a plan. He sat his wife down and confessed to every one of his crimes in detail on the condition that she give him up to police and claim the reward.

On 24 May 1930 Frau Kürten went to Düsseldorf police headquarters and told stunned investigators about her husband, the Vampire of Düsseldorf, adding that she had arranged to meet him outside St Rochus church at 3 o'clock that afternoon. By then the entire area had been surrounded and officers rushed forward with loaded revolvers the moment Peter Kürten appeared.

He held his hands in the air and said, 'There is no need to be afraid.'

The Vampire of Düsseldorf was only too happy to tell of his crimes to a succession of stenographers, who dropped out one after the other as he related the terrible things he had done to men, women, children and animals. He began at number 1 and finished at number 79, and showed great pleasure at the disgust recorded on the faces of the interviewers. His confessions went back to his schooldays, when he had drowned his two schoolmates in the Rhine.

The only person Kürten showed any compassion for was his wife. He paid high regard to her throughout the ordeal, and was remorseful that he had been unfaithful throughout their marriage. He steadfastly maintained that he was still exceptionally fond of his wife, and was desperate to ensure the reward was hers.

Charged with nine murders and seven attempted murders, Peter Kürten's trial began on 13 April 1931. Dressed in a business suit and tie, and with beautifully groomed hair, he had the look of a businessman about town. Speaking quietly, initially Kürten denied the charges and entered a not guilty plea, stating that he only signed a confession so that his wife could claim the reward.

But his statement was full of facts that only the killer could have known and Kürten was eventually broken down by the examining magistrate and, after a harrowing and especially gruesome two months, reverted to his original confession.

It was determined by the best psychiatrists in Germany that Peter Kürten was sane and 'perfectly responsible for his actions at all times'. Given that he knew what he was doing when he committed the atrocities, it left the judge to ask the obvious 'Do you have a conscience?' to which Kürten replied:

'I have none. Never have I felt any misgiving in my soul; never did I think to myself that what I did was bad, even though human society condemns it. My blood and the blood of my victims will be on the heads of my torturers. There must be a higher being who gave in the first place the first vital spark to life. That higher being would deem my actions good since I revenged injustice. The punishments I have suffered have destroyed all my feelings as a human being. That was why I had no pity for my victims.'

The jury took only 90 minutes to find Peter Kürten guilty on all counts, and he was sentenced to death at the earliest convenience. The sooner the world was rid of him the better. On 2 July 1932 the 'Vampire of Düsseldorf' butcher of men, women, children, animals and anything that breathed, went to his death by guillotine – especially erected for him in the yard of the Klingelputz prison.

But before he was despatched to wherever the most evil of evil go after they die, Peter Kürten had one last question for the prison psychiatrist. 'After my head has been chopped off,' he enquired, 'will I still be able to hear, at least for a moment, the sound of my own blood gushing from the stump of my neck?' When the psychiatrist didn't respond, Kürten tossed the question around in his head for a minute and said: 'That would be the pleasure to end all pleasures.'

SHADOW OF A DOUBT

(1943)

DIRECTED BY ALFRED HITCHCOCK
SCREENPLAY BY THORNTON WILDER

FEATURING

Teresa Wright as young Charlie
Joseph Cotten as Uncle Charlie
Macdonald Carey as Detective Jack Graham
Henry Travers as Joseph Newton
Patricia Collinge as Emma Newton
Hume Cronyn as Herbie Hawkins

Alfred Hitchcock was a brilliant director, but perhaps not quite as original as legend would have us believe. His serial killer movies were all based on real life multiple murderers, albeit very loosely. Hitchcock's favourite of his own movies, *Shadow of a Doubt*, is no exception. The film's main character, smooth-talking Uncle Charlie, specialises in murdering landladies and wealthy widows. So it's no coincidence that so did real life serial killer, Earle Leonard Nelson.

Due to his huge, powerful hands and modus operandi, Nelson was known throughout northern America and Canada as the 'Dark Strangler' or the 'Gorilla Killer'. *Shadow*'s Uncle Charlie also strangled his victims and was known as the 'Merry Widow Murderer'. There is a hint in the movie that Uncle Charlie may have had an accident and severely hurt his head as a child. Earle Nelson fell off his bike as a child and landed on his head. It was often pondered if this could have made him the way he was.

But that's where the similarities end. Earle Leonard Nelson was a huge, gruff man of rough appearance who always looked as though he was down on his luck. His calling card was that he raped his victims after they were dead. Uncle Charlie, as played by Joseph Cotten, the heart-throb of the times, was handsome, beautifully groomed and a ladies' man, who could charm the oranges off the trees – of which there were many in Santa Rosa, California, where it was filmed.

Teresa Wright plays Charlie, a pretty high-school kid who was named after her favourite uncle and has a secret crush on him. During a visit by Uncle Charlie she notices that he has become outspoken about wealthy old women, saying how useless they are to society. She grows suspicious when she sees her uncle tear an article with the blazing headline 'Who is the Merry Widow Murderer?' off the front page of the newspaper. She locates the missing story at the local library and as she reads the article it dawns on her that Uncle Charlie is the killer.

But what happens next? Surely Uncle Charlie cannot murder a child to keep his secret safe? You'll have to watch it to find out. You'll find it on DVD at rental libraries or on the internet. In the meantime, read about the real Uncle Charlie.

Earle Leonard Nelson: The Dark Strangler

The United States had more than its share of serial killers in the 1920s, the most prolific being Earle Leonard Nelson, a giant of a man who was well over six feet tall and had huge, powerful hands. For 16 months Nelson roamed the United States, killing as he went. Boarding houses and suburban homes were his specialty and he murdered and then violated as many as 30 people. Police warned that he was inhuman, that only an animal could do the things to his victims that this killer enjoyed doing. But, when retribution caught up with Earle Nelson, he was human, albeit certainly not normal.

Earle Nelson never knew either of his parents. His mother died in 1898 of syphilis when Earle was just nine months old. His father died six months later from the same disease. Nelson was raised in San Francisco by his widowed grandmother, who had two youngsters of her own. A devout Pentecostal, she raised Earle to be God-fearing and to abide by the rules of society and the Almighty. He was a handful from an early age; either hyperactive or profoundly depressed. He never cared for hygiene and manners, despite his grandmother's best efforts and he ate like a Neanderthal man; drenching his food in olive oil and, with the plate held to his face, he would slurp his meal like a caged animal.

The taunting of the other children and being called an animal didn't help matters and soon he was spending all his time alone. As well as his strange eating habits and manic depression, Nelson demonstrated a number of other peculiarities. He would leave for school dressed in clean clothes and return home in a completely different and filthy outfit. He also had a manic obsession with the Bible, though he heeded little the good words in it.

Expelled from school at the age of seven, little Nelson became a withdrawn loner with a fearful and violent temper who was forever in trouble for shoplifting. At 11 he was knocked over and almost killed when his bike clipped the back of a trolley car. He was rushed to hospital with a giant gash to his head and hovered between life and death for a week before regaining consciousness. Future psychiatrists would ponder the significance of the accident in relation to his horrific crimes, but those who watched Nelson grow into a monster believed that the seeds of evil had been sown on the day he was born.

When Nelson's grandmother died, his aunt and her husband took in the 14-year-old high school dropout. Ten years his senior, his Aunt Lillian genuinely liked him; she overlooked his eccentricities and treated him like a normal human being. Until the end, despite his reign of evil, she was the only one who stuck by him.

Nelson moved from one job to another. His childish, erratic behaviour made it impossible for an employer to put up with him for longer than a month or two. His bizarre habit of leaving home for work in his overalls and returning home in the evening in a completely different set of filthy clothes continued. His temper got worse and his Aunt Lillian became terrified of what he might do.

A compulsive masturbator with a voracious sexual appetite, Nelson was frequenting the prostitutes near Fisherman's Wharf by the age of 15. Also a heavy drinker, he disappeared for days on end on alcoholic binges. He spent whatever little money he had left on the lurid literature of the day, and conducted conversations with invisible adversaries while he walked about the house masturbating. More and more frequently he came home badly cut and battered from fights he got into when he was drunk.

Much to Aunt Lillian's relief, Nelson left home for good in the spring of 1915 and lived on his wits throughout the California area. Irrespective of where he was living, which was usually a room with meals supplied, he would disappear for days or weeks at a time. Truth be known, he was financing his lifestyle with petty crime. Caught red-handed after he had broken into a cabin, Nelson, not yet 18, was sent for two years to the toughest prison in the country, San Quentin.

Out of jail in 1917 he joined the US army under the name of Earle Ferral (his Aunt Lillian's name) but, on his first assignment, when he was ordered to stand guard out in the cold, he dropped his rifle and went AWOL in the direction of Salt Lake City. There he enlisted in the US navy as Earle Nelson. He was sent to San Francisco as a cook and lasted for a month before deserting once again.

He hung around the Bay area, enlisting once again in the military again under a false name, this time as a medical corpsman. Obviously troubled, he deserted yet again, claiming his anus was burning and, in 1918, returned to the navy, where he refused to take part in any work duties or social activities, instead spending his time quoting the Bible and predicting the Apocalypse. Naval authorities had little choice but to commit him to the Napa State Mental Hospital, which was deemed more escape-proof than San Quentin.

Not yet 20, young Nelson was in a bad way. He confessed to masturbating daily but said he had 'given it up lately'. He was an alcoholic who had allegedly been off the drink for seven months. He tested positive for gonorrhoea and syphilis, which doctors believed he was infected with before his 16th birthday. He was preoccupied with God and the Bible, which he endlessly preached. And he was obsessed with escaping, which he did twice in the 13 months he spent there, earning him the nickname 'Houdini' from the other adoring patients. Both times he was captured and returned.

In 1919, after his third escape, the authorities at Napa didn't even bother to go and look for him. They had had enough. Crazy or not they were pleased to see the back of this fruitcake. Instead they discharged him from the military and wrote down in his record that he had 'improved', even though their assessment was that he was extremely violent, insane and homicidal. They had turned their backs on what would become one of America's most evil serial killers.

Ever the loving relative, when Nelson turned up on Aunt Lillian's doorstep she took him back into her bosom, fed and clothed him and helped find him a job as a janitor at St Mary's Hospital, near San Francisco. It was there that Nelson met and fell in love with 58-year-old Mary Martin, who was the reincarnation of the grandmother he loved as a child, and who had dominated him so much in his early years. Mary worked as a bookkeeper at the hospital and lived a reclusive, religious existence.

Incredibly, despite the almost four decade age difference, Nelson proposed marriage and, even more incredibly, Mary accepted. But there was a condition: it would have to be a Catholic rites wedding. Nelson thought that was terrific. If only poor, introverted Mary had known what she was letting herself in for. She surely would have run as fast as her legs would carry her.

We can only assume that Mary entered into the marriage expecting it to be a conventional relationship – a union of equals. But that's not what mad Nelson had in mind. He forced Mary to become the bullying mother figure with him as the naughty son who must be punished. His manic changing of clothes, usually from a neat suit into something filthy – overalls from the pigsty perhaps – and his reluctance to bathe or to use table manners must have nearly sent poor Mary around the bend.

Then there was his insatiable sexual appetite. On the nights when poor old Mary couldn't handle it for the first, second or third time, he took himself in hand in the bed beside her. Given that Mary was raised a good Catholic girl who was taught that masturbation was an abhorrent sin, she lay there in shock and disgust. It was not what you would call a marriage made in heaven.

And if that wasn't enough to send Mary to an early grave, there was the possessive jealousy. Nelson boiled when Mary talked to any other man, even her brother, and became violent when he thought she was being overly friendly. It's interesting to note that most of Nelson's future victims were similar to his wife: older women, either widows or spinsters.

After a while, when Mary no longer satisfied Nelson's manic sexual desires, he looked further afield. And randy Earle had decided that if they wouldn't give it to him willingly he would take it anyway, even if it meant killing them in the process. Sadly, this would mean the demise of more than 20 women in North America as Nelson went on his murderous rampage.

Nelson's journey into serial murder was accelerated by his further descent into insanity. He suffered chronic migraine headaches for which there was no medicinal relief. During an attack at work, Nelson fell from a ladder and knocked himself unconscious. He fled from hospital after two days, his head in thick bandages. The knock seemed to further unhinge his tentative grip on sanity and now he saw visions and heard religious voices.

Separated from Mary, who had finally seen the light and given him the boot, Nelson's rage exploded in the worst possible way on 19 May 1921, when he found his first prospective murder victim playing inside her home. On the pretext of being a plumber sent to fix a leaking gas pipe, Nelson was admitted to the home of Charles Summers by his son, 24-year-old Charles Jr. In the basement Nelson found 12-year-old Mary Summers playing. It's not known if Nelson knew that the girl was there, or if she just happened to be there while he was planning how to rob the place, but he set upon her immediately and tried to strangle her.

Mary Summers fought tenaciously for her life and, hearing Mary's screams, Charles Jr rushed to the basement, bumping into Nelson on the stairs. Nelson pushed him out of the way and ran down the street, with Charles Jr in pursuit. They fought fiercely in the street and Nelson escaped, but he was arrested shortly after by police. In jail Nelson plucked his eyebrows bare with his fingernails and complained of seeing faces on the wall so he was sent to the city hospital.

Mary visited her estranged husband where she found him in a straitjacket and screaming at the faces peering at him from the wall. Police told Mary the truth about the man she had married – for better or for worse – that he was an escaped lunatic with a prison record, who was on the run from the armed forces. She decided to stick by him.

A month later Nelson faced a judge to determine if he was mentally fit to stand trial. The judge heard psychiatrists describe Nelson as 'apathetic, eccentric, noisy, destructive and incendiary'. The examining doctors warned that he was 'restless, violent, dangerous, excited and depressed' and a danger to 'wife and self' and concluded that Nelson was 'so far disordered in his mind to endanger health and person'. Deemed insane, Nelson was sent back to the Napa State Hospital to plan his fourth escape.

In Napa, Nelson was treated with an anti-syphilis drug called Salversan which seemed to calm him and for a year he was cooperative and almost appeared to be normal. But it wouldn't last.

On 2 November 1923 Nelson went over the wall and turned up at his aunt's house in the middle of the night wearing his hospital pyjamas. A terrified Lillian gave Nelson a set of her husband's clothes and told him to leave. He was caught two days later wandering the streets of San Francisco screaming incoherent gibberish.

Nelson remained in Napa for another 16 months. After serving a total of four years from the day he assaulted Mary Summers, he was released, obviously deemed sane enough to walk the streets. He went home to Mary, but within weeks he was gone.

In mid-February 1926, Earle Nelson's first victim was 62-year-old Clara Newmann who, it seemed, had let someone into her house in response to the 'room for rent' sign on the window. Her nephew who lived in the house had seen a neatly dressed man leaving the house, and had found his aunt propped up on the toilet seat naked from the waist down with her clothes pulled up around her neck. An autopsy revealed that she had been strangled and then raped after death.

Two weeks later in nearby San José a second rooming-house manageress, senior citizen Laura Beal, was murdered in identical circumstances. Her husband found his wife naked from the waist down in a vacant apartment that was for rent in their house. She had been brutally strangled with the silk belt from her dressing gown. As was the case with Clara Newmann, Mrs Beal had been raped after death.

There were few descriptions. Clara Newmann's nephew saw a 'dark stranger', and a 'sallow-faced man' was seen hurrying from Laura Beal's house around the time of the murder, but these were the only sightings of any possible offender. Quick to link the murders, the San Francisco papers dubbed the maniac the 'Dark Strangler' and warned that a madman was loose in the district. Despite many leads nothing came of it and the killings dropped off the front pages of the papers. But it was the back pages where Nelson was looking: in the section of the classifieds offering rooms to rent.

In late March 1926, Lillian St Mary was strangled to death and then raped as she showed someone a room she had for rent in her boarding house. Mrs St Mary had been strangled so violently that her bloodshot eyes were bulging from her head. Yet the man living in the room below hadn't heard a thing. Her dress was pushed up around her waist and she was naked from the waist down. Her killer had placed her hat next to her head and her neatly folded overcoat was slipped under her feet, as if to apologise that he had interrupted her on her way out. Again, the only description of the offender was that a large man had been seen in the neighbourhood around the time of the killing.

Police issued a warning to women who rented rooms to be alert, and never show a room to a man alone. Police assured a very nervous public that it would only be a matter of time before the fiend was off the streets and behind bars. It was more wishful thinking than fact, because they had absolutely nothing to go on. Not a solitary lead. The 'Dark Strangler' was in the headlines again.

With the heat on in San Francisco, Nelson moved his murderous activities south to the resort town of Santa Barbara which, in the 1920s, was far enough away that he may as well have been on another planet. For a killer with his modus operandi, Santa Barbara was the perfect killing field. It was filled to overflowing with rooming houses and private hotels where Nelson could murder and commit necrophiliac rape to his evil heart's desire.

Almost two months after Lillian St Mary was murdered in San Francisco, 53-year-old Ollie Russell, who with her husband ran a boarding house in Santa Barbara, was found dead on the mattress in a spare room in her boarding house. She had been strangled with a loop of sash cord that had been pulled so tight that it had cut through the flesh and almost severed her head. There was blood everywhere.

A boarder who had heard loud noises coming from the room said that he looked through the keyhole and saw a large man with his trousers down around his ankles laying on top of Mrs Russell and thrusting in the intercourse position. When he had finished the man pulled up his trousers and, as he headed for the door, the voyeur fled without seeing the man's face. All he could tell police was that he was huge.

On a hot day in August 1926, Stephen Nisbet returned home from work to find his 50-year-old wife crammed into the lavatory in the vacant room of the boarding house that she ran. Mary Nisbet had been murdered and suffocated with a hand towel stuffed down her throat. It was apparent that the poor woman had resisted her killer's advances and in doing so had upset him: he had violently smashed her head into the tiled floor of the bathroom and her broken teeth were scattered all over the floor. She had been raped after she was murdered.

Then the killer accelerated his killings to a level that left investigators not wondering when, but where, the next horror would take place. Beata Whithers was found strangled and raped in the attic of her boarding house. Two days later Virginia Grant was found murdered and raped in the basement of her house. A few days later Mabel Fluke was found strangled, raped in the attic crawl space of her boarding house. To add a new twist, all of the victims had also been robbed.

For the next year Nelson weaved his way across America's northwest, killing as he went and selling his victim's possessions to survive. It seemed that no amount of police warnings in the newspapers could stop people from allowing him into their homes.

Time and again people saw Nelson in his overcoat and hat but no-one could come up with a positive ID that would alert anyone who knew him to help the police. It was as if Nelson was invisible and could kill as he desired. By the end of 1926, the Dark Strangler had killed 14 women and an eight-month-old baby, who unfortunately happened to be on the murder scene.

Nelson fled eastward, stopping in Iowa, Kansas City and then Philadelphia, where he murdered a 60-year-old woman. He then moved on to Buffalo, New York, Detroit and finally Chicago. By now Nelson had claimed more than 20 victims and America was closing in on him. It was time to move on to somewhere where he figured his crimes wouldn't be so well known, if they were known at all. But he figured wrong. They were waiting for him. Sadly two more people would die before they caught him.

Nelson crossed the border from Minnesota into Canada and headed straight for Winnipeg, where he took a room in

Hill's boarding house on Smith Street. The fact that Nelson never actually stayed in the room wasn't noticed for a few days. Had they noticed earlier, they would have found a body in his bed. Instead, Nelson was seen around town flashing a fat roll of notes and making himself known. The money had been stolen from a house owned by the Patterson family, after Nelson had forced himself on Mrs Emily Patterson when she was cleaning the porch with the front door open. Nelson bundled her inside, where he murdered her and raped her corpse. He then hid the cadaver under the bed for Mr Patterson to find when he got home from work. On the way out, Nelson helped himself to the family's savings.

On hearing the news of Emily Patterson's death, police immediately assumed that it was the work of the 'Gorilla Killer', as he was now known in the press. They immediately sent out every available policeman to Winnipeg to warn boarding-house owners that the killer was in town and to check out every new tenant who even remotely resembled the huge man in the overcoat and hat.

At Hill's boarding house on Smith Street, Mrs Catherine Hill said that they did have a new tenant, a lovely Christian man named Mr Woodcoats, who fitted the description of the wanted man, but they said they hadn't seen him for a couple of days. When they checked out the nice Mr Woodcoats' room they found the strangled and violated body of 14-year-old Lola Cowan, a schoolgirl who had gone missing while selling flowers on Smith Street to supplement the family income while her father recovered from pneumonia. Chances are that the trusting Lola was lured to Nelson's room on the pretext of more money for her flowers.

This time the Dark Strangler wouldn't be hard to find. His face was known to many people, including witnesses at the rooming house where he had pretended to be Mr Woodcoats.

As well as the entire Royal Canadian Mounted Police Force, he had every decent citizen in Canada out looking for him and, as an American in Canada, he stood out like the beast that he was. His description and a $1500 reward was circulated along the border back into the US, and it was only to be a matter of time.

Predictably, Nelson was eight kilometres from the US border when the law caught up with him. When he stopped in a general store in Wakopa to buy food, he was recognised by both the owner and a patron who knew of the reward. Nelson surrendered immediately and was put into a rusty cell in the Killarney jail, minus his shoes, socks and belt, as was the law. Left alone he picked the double lock on the cell door with a piece of wire and escaped, only to be captured a few hours later bumming a cigarette from a local.

As well as the locals, a parade of more than 40 witnesses made the trip from the States to positively identify Nelson. But against all odds, Nelson maintained his innocence. He was indicted for murders in San Francisco, Portland, Detroit, Philadelphia and Buffalo. But that aside, there was no way that Canada was going to let him get away with murdering two of their own. He would be tried first in Manitoba, Canada, which at the time still had the death penalty. The only way Nelson would make it back to the States would be in a box.

A parade of detectives from all over America appealed to Nelson to help them with their unsolved murders that were most likely the work of the Dark Strangler. He refused, professing his innocence and godliness and declined to get himself hanged just to help investigators close case files.

Nelson was officially linked to 22 murders, beginning 20 February 1926 and ending with the murders of Lola Cowan and Emily Patterson on 9–10 June. Averaging slightly more than one murder per month, the actual dates are much more clumped. There were five murders between 1 June and 10 June 1926, but none between mid-August and mid-October 1926. There were, however, several homicides where the modus operandi was very similar to Nelson's, but without enough evidence to formally link him to the crimes.

At his trial for the murders of Lola Cowen and Emily Patterson, Nelson pleaded not guilty on the grounds of insanity and the defence used his family in an attempt to prove his bizarre behaviour was obviously the work of a madman. Surely no sane human being could murder women and have sex with their corpses? The court heard from one family member after another telling of Nelson's bizarre life and habits, and the times spent in and out of lunatic asylums. It was indeed a disturbed life.

But the jury was having none of it. After hearing all the witnesses and an eminent psychiatrist tell the court that he had found Nelson to be a 'constitutional psychopath', but legally sane nevertheless, it took them less than an hour to return a guilty verdict and the judge sentenced the prisoner to death by hanging. Nelson appealed, but the high court of Manitoba disagreed and ordered the execution to go ahead immediately.

On the day before his execution, Nelson met with the family members of his two Canadian victims, including Lola Cowan's mother, but refused to admit his guilt. On 13 January 1928, he went to the gallows peacefully, protesting his innocence to the end. His final words were that he had made peace with god. But it is extremely unlikely that Nelson ever met his god. Instead he would have gone straight to hell to spend eternity with the worst of the worst.

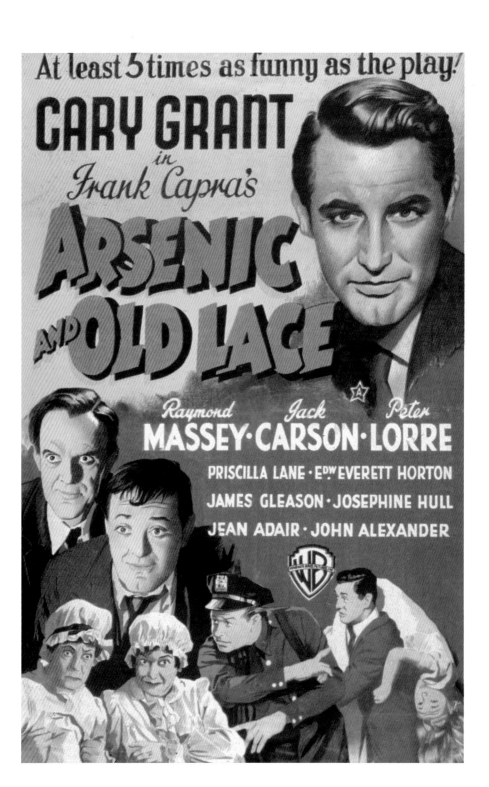

ARSENIC AND OLD LACE

(1944)

DIRECTED BY FRANK CAPRA
SCREENPLAY BY JULIUS J EPSTEIN

FEATURING

Cary Grant as Mortimer Brewster
Josephine Hull as Aunt Abby Brewster
Jean Adair as Aunt Martha Brewster
Raymond Massey as Jonathon Brewster
Peter Lorre as Dr Herman Einstein
Priscilla Lane as Elaine Harper
John Alexander as Theodore Brewster

An uproariously funny comedy about serial murder? You'd better believe it. Unlike other murder movies that claim to be 'black comedies', there is nothing very black about the 1944 *Arsenic and Old Lace*. It is unashamedly a murderfest aimed to make you laugh. And given that it was based on Joseph Kesselring's 1941 smash hit Broadway play of the same name, there was never really any doubt that it was also going to be a huge hit at the box office.

The film was directed by comedy genius Frank Capra. Hollywood heart-throb Cary Grant plays the lead, Mortimer Brewster, an avowed bachelor and drama critic who has just married the girl next door. He takes her to Brooklyn to meet his loving aunts, Aunt Abby and Aunt Martha, played by Josephine Hull and Jean Adair, who had the same roles on Broadway.

And here the fun begins. While preparing to leave for his honeymoon, Mortimer discovers the body of a vagrant and assumes that his eccentric brother Teddy, who thinks he's Theodore Roosevelt, has killed the man. Mortimer confronts his aunts about the cadaver to find that they have been committing what they consider charitable acts: inviting in and poisoning old men who are lonely and miserable and have no family. By now the body count is up to 12 and they are all buried in the basement.

The sinister Raymond Massey appears as Mortimer's psychotic other brother Jonathon, who has just escaped from an asylum for the criminally insane. The equally foreboding screen villain of the time, Peter Lorre, appears as the mysterious plastic surgeon Dr Einstein, who changed Jonathan's appearance while he (Einstein) was drunk and modelled Jonathon's new face on a monster out of a horror movie. I ask you, how could you miss with a plot like that? After all these years it is still terrific fun.

And while *Arsenic and Old Lace* wasn't based on any living person, there is a very sinister and real life black side. Many believe that the movie was the inspiration for a series of serial murders in Australia, which began in mid-1947 when a 57-year-old Sydney grandmother began poisoning her friends and relatives. Though it will never be known for sure if this was the case, the similarities make it worthy of inclusion in this chapter.

It really is one of those rare cases where a murder didn't inspire a movie, rather a movie inspired the murders.

Granny Grills: Thallium and Old Lace

Like Australia's two most notorious female serial killers before her, Martha Rendell and Martha Needle, Caroline Grills' chosen method of dispatching her victims into the next life was poison. But while the murderous Mistress Rendell used hydrochloric acid to dispose of her lover's children, and Mrs Needle chose arsenic to do away with her whole family, Caroline Grills' preference was the relatively new poison of the time, the very deadly toxic metallic substance, thallium.

Thallium had been popular in Europe for many years as a rat poison, but it didn't show up in Australia until the early 1940s. It proved to be extremely effective in the eradication of the ever-increasing hordes of rodents that invaded the eastern states of Australia leading up to and throughout the war years.

And as thallium was readily available in New South Wales without the purchaser having to record their name and address on a poisons purchase register, as they had to in other states, it occurred to the outwardly loving, caring and highly regarded Caroline Grills that thallium could also be used for getting rid of unwanted humans.

At first 'Aunt Carrie', as Caroline Grills was affectionately known by her many loved ones, killed for greed. After that it was apparent that she killed because she enjoyed it. And her specialty was murdering those around her, her relatives by marriage.

Born Caroline Mickelson in 1890, she was just 17 when she married Richard William Grills and their happy and loving union produced four sons who, in turn, gave them many grandchildren.

Grills' first association with thallium was around 1947 when the couple lived in a house in Goulburn Street in inner Sydney and the area became infested with large rats. The local council recommended the popular Thall-rat, which could be brought over the counter anywhere for a few shillings. When Caroline Grills saw what a devastating effect it had on the giant rodents, and on the other rats that feasted on their dead friends, she wondered if it might have the same effect on a couple of humans who were stopping her from getting what she wanted.

Grills' career as a murderess began in mid-1947 when she murdered her stepmother, 87-year-old Mrs Christina Louisa Adelaide Mickelson, who had married her widowed father 11 years earlier.

When Grills' ex-seaman father died, his will gave Christina a life tenancy in the comfortable family house in the fashionable Sydney suburb of Gladesville, where they had lived together.

The will also stated that when Mrs Mickelson passed on, the house would go to his daughter, Caroline Grills. Anxious to move out of the rat-infested dwelling in Bathurst Street and into the luxury of the family home which she believed was rightly hers, Caroline decided to give dear old Christina, who looked like living forever, a little nudge along the road to eternity.

One afternoon when she was visiting her stepmother at Gladesville, Caroline slipped a healthy dose of Thall-rat in her afternoon tea and, after convulsing so violently that the family doctor had to be called, she was ushered to bed where she conveniently passed away during the night. Due to Christina Mickelson's ripe old age there were not considered to be any suspicious circumstances and no autopsy was held. She was cremated days later.

Having had such an effective result with the Thall-rat, Caroline Grills waited for a few months before she applied its toxic ingredients to her next victim, 84-year-old widow Mrs Angelina Thomas. Mrs Thomas had formed a lifelong friendship with Caroline Grills' husband Richard. Mrs Thomas had partly raised Richard and he had lived with her at her cottage at Leura in the magnificent Blue Mountains, in Sydney's far west.

Mrs Thomas made no secret of the fact that when she died, her 'foster son' Richard and his charming wife Caroline would inherit her house. Caroline was very close to Angelina Thomas and would often make the long journey from Sydney to the Blue Mountains to visit and would never go empty handed, always taking along a freshly baked cake or some other goodies for afternoon tea.

After one of Caroline's visits on 17 January 1948, Mrs Thomas took a turn for the worse and passed away, leaving her house to her beloved Richard and his wife Caroline.

Having murdered two elderly women for greed, and inheriting everything she would ever need to live a long and comfortable life without the risk of ever being suspected of murder, it is hard to understand why Grills went on killing. She lived in a big, comfortable family home in fashionable Gladesville, had a 'weekender' in the picturesque Blue Mountains, her husband Richard had built up a successful real estate business and she was surrounded by a large, loving extended family of four sons, their spouses and grandchildren and many relatives by marriage accumulated along the way.

With no apparent motive for the following murders and attempted murders, the only possible reason the Crown could come up with at her trial was that Grills murdered 'for the thrill she got from watching the effect of the poison and knowing that she alone in the world knew what was causing the symptoms and suffering'.

Grills' next victim was her husband's brother-in-law, 60-year-old John Lundberg. A healthy and extremely fit ex-seaman, he fell ill and his hair started to fall out while on holidays with Richard and Caroline Grills at Woy Woy on the New South Wales central coast. After the doctor had visited and was at a loss to explain the mysterious ailment, Caroline took it upon herself to nurse the man back to good health, but his condition deteriorated, he lost his sight and his mind started to wander before he lapsed into a coma and died on 17 October 1948.

Incredibly, doctors could see nothing unusual about the circumstances surrounding the death of the healthy and athletic John Lundberg and he was cremated almost immediately without an autopsy.

On 15 October 1949, just a few months after the death of John Lundberg, Grills' sister-in-law, Mrs Mary-Anne

Mickelson, died after a long illness during which her hair fell out and she lost her sight. During her illness she had been lovingly cared for and spoon-fed by Grills.

In 1951, Mrs Eveline Lundberg, Grills' sister-in-law and the widow of the late John Lundberg, became seriously ill. Her hair started to fall out, she began to lose her vision, suffered agonising cramps in her legs and lapsed into fits of depression.

Mrs Lundberg's daughter, Christine Downey, and her husband John, often got together with Eveline and Grills for a game of bridge, during which Caroline would make endless cups of tea and serve cakes and pikelets and other home-cooked goodies she always so thoughtfully brought with her.

The sickness lingered on until 1952 when Eveline Lundberg was almost completely blind and had to be admitted to full-time care where, under the watchful eye of the nurses and not Grills, who had gone out of her way to call in each day while she was at home, started to make a speedy recovery.

With Eveline Lundberg now safely in hospital and out of reach, Caroline turned her attention to the Downeys at their weekly card games, and administered to them, as she had done with Eveline Lundberg, just enough thallium to make them ill but not kill them. In no time they both experienced impaired vision and sudden hair loss along with cramps and bouts of nausea.

Incredibly, suspicions were still not aroused. It was another event entirely which made them think that caring Aunt Carrie might be a little bit more than just a doting, kindly old relative who kept the tea cups topped up and their tummies filled with sumptuous home-cooked goodies.

What raised the Downeys' suspicions was the arrest and trial of a Sydney housewife, Mrs Yvonne Gladys Fletcher, in

September 1952. Gladys Fletcher was the victim of repeated drunken bashings by her second husband, Bertram Henry Fletcher, who on one occasion punched her in the face so savagely that she had to be taken to hospital for a blood transfusion.

In his employment as a rat catcher for a company in Newton in Sydney's inner west, Bertram Fletcher had access to any amount of deadly thallium-based rat poison. He had brought some home to keep the Fletcher household free of the pesky rodents. What Bertram Fletcher couldn't possibly know was that he was providing the ingredients for his own death.

Family friends became suspicious when Bert Fletcher died in 1952 in similar circumstances to those of Yvonne Fletcher's previous husband, department store cleaner, Desmond Butler, who had died after a long illness in July 1948. They notified police, who exhumed the remains of Fletcher and found traces of thallium.

Police then exhumed the remains of Des Butler and, even though he had been in the ground for four years, his body contained enough traces of thallium to charge Yvonne Fletcher with double murder. She was convicted and sentenced to life imprisonment.

But it wasn't the trial or conviction of Yvonne Fletcher that aroused the Downeys' suspicions that they were being poisoned by doting Aunt Carrie. It was the symptoms of the deaths of Desmond Butler and Bertram Fletcher that caused them to sit up and take notice. Both victims had suffered a long, mysterious illness during which time they had lost their vision, their hair had fallen out, they experienced agonising cramps in their arms and legs and they had become vague about what was going on around them. They were bedridden up until they eventually died in horrible pain.

Christina and John Downey visited police and told them of their suspicions.

Under police supervision, the Downeys' went about their lives as if nothing unusual was going on, while the detectives set about gathering evidence against the suspected old poisoner. The Downeys' gathered food supplied by Aunt Carrie and samples of the tea she poured out. All proved to be negative.

Until 20 April 1953. The Downeys had brought Christina's mother Eveline, now totally blind, home from hospital and, as she was sitting on the verandah enjoying the sunshine, Caroline Grills called in and made a fuss of her by making up a fresh brew of tea and serving up some homemade pikelets and strawberry jam that she had lovingly prepared at home.

As Grills returned from the kitchen with a cup of tea for the blind old lady, John Downey saw her reach into her pocket and sprinkle something into the cup.

While Christina diverted Caroline's attention, John swapped cups of tea and put the contents of the suspect cup into a jar for the government analyst. The trap had been sprung. As expected, analysis of the tea proved that it was laced with thallium, as were the tasty morsels Caroline Grills had brought with her.

Caroline Grills was arrested shortly after and, when it was discovered that there were traces of thallium in the pocket of the dress she had been wearing the day she called in on the Downeys, she was charged with the attempted murder of Eveline Lundberg.

The two bodies of her victims, which hadn't been cremated, those of Angelina Thomas and Mary-Anne Mickelson, were exhumed and were found to contain traces of thallium.

Caroline Grills was charged with four murders and three counts of attempted murder of Eveline Lundberg and John and Christina Downey.

The case against the jovial, tiny, bespectacled, 63-year-old grandmother who everyone called 'caring Aunt Carrie', first caught the public's attention in August 1953, when the Sydney City Coroner, Mr EJ Forrest conducted an inquest into the death of Mrs Christina Mickelson and found that there was sufficient evidence that Caroline Grills should be committed for trial.

But the Crown elected instead to try her for the much more recent attempt on the life of Mrs Eveline Lundberg because they felt they had a much stronger case.

The trial of Caroline Grills opened to a packed courthouse in Sydney's Central Criminal Court on 7 October 1953 before Justice Brereton, who had earlier ruled that the prosecution could use evidence from all of the other poisoning cases with which Caroline Grills had been charged.

Mrs Grills seemed to find much to be happy about in the confines of the courtroom and laughed and joked with police and her defence lawyers as the proceedings got under way. It would appear then, as it would all the way through the trial, that she was trying to give off the air that such a happy and harmless old lady couldn't possibly hurt anyone. It was a ploy that would be easily seen through.

The Crown case was represented by Mr CV Rooney QC, who stated that Mrs Grills had become 'a practised and habitual poisoner who had lost all sense of feeling'. Mr Rooney then proceeded to itemise each piece of incriminating evidence against the defendant – from the traces of thallium found in the exhumed remains of Mrs Christina Mickelson, through to the irrevocable proof that she had laced blind Eveline Lundberg's tea on the afternoon of 20 April 1953.

Caroline Grills' only defence was an indignant denial of the charges against her and a continually smiling, 'innocent little old granny' persona presented to the jury and public gallery. When she was placed in the witness box by her defence council, Mr Frank Hidden, she admitted that she had used rat poison that contained thallium over the years, but denied ever putting it in anyone's drink, adding coyly as she looked at the jury, 'Why on earth would I want to do such a thing as that?'

Caroline Grills had a flimsy excuse for every situation she was cross-examined about and, in his address to the jury, Mr Hidden went to great lengths to point out that Mrs Grills was a kindly housewife to whom people always went in times of trouble and whose main pleasure in life was doing good.

He emphatically pointed out there was an absence of motive in the alleged attempted murder of Mrs Lundberg and there was no direct link with his client and the poisoning. He further pointed out that Mrs Grills was a person of excellent character and who went around helping people and never visited her friends empty-handed.

'If she has committed these crimes,' Mr Hidden concluded, 'there can be no more treacherous or violent poisoner in history. All the historic cases of murder and attempted murder are prompted by motives of revenge, lust or gain. In these cases there is no question of revenge, of sexual motive or of gain.'

In his summing up, Justice Brereton did little to hide his sentiments and told the jury that thallium was a diabolical, inhuman and cowardly weapon which destroyed its victim's faculties, led to blindness and possibly death. Use of poison, he pointed out, displayed no particular smartness or cleverness. It was as easy, he said, to administer poison to a blind woman as it was to steal pennies from a blind man.

Justice Brereton drew attention to the number of thallium poisonings in the Grills family circle in recent years and pointed out that Mrs Grills was a common factor every time. No other person, living or dead, had a link with all of the victims.

In one of the shortest deliberations in history in a murder trial, the jury was gone a mere 12 minutes before they returned with a verdict of guilty to the charge that Grills administered thallium to her sister-in-law, Mrs Eveline Lundberg, with the intention of murdering her.

Seemingly unmoved by the verdict, Grills drummed her fingers on the dock's rail and her face tightened as she heard the verdict. Asked if she had anything to say, the old woman frowned and simply said: 'I helped to live, not to kill.'

Justice Brereton then said before he announced her sentence: 'The jury has found you guilty and I agree with its verdict. The evidence disclosed that under the guise of friendship and loving kindness, but with apparently motiveless malignity, you administered poison to Mrs Lundberg, condemning her at least to a life of blindness and possible death. You are hereby sentenced to death.'

There was an audible gasp through the courtroom as the judge passed the ultimate sentence. Her husband Richard reached out and touched her on the arm and called out to her softly – 'Carrie' – as Grills was escorted away by the policewomen guards.

In April 1954, Grills appealed against her conviction in the Full Supreme Court on the grounds that the evidence in the other poisonings she had been charged with should not have been admissible. It was dismissed unanimously.

Predictably, the death sentence was commuted to life imprisonment and 'Aunt Thally', as she was now affectionately known within the confines of Long Bay Jail, settled down to a life of handing out motherly advice and being a shoulder to cry on for the many lost souls she would encounter in her new home.

Her long-suffering husband, Richard, visited her every week and took along as many relatives as the visitors list would allow. From all reports Aunt Thally was always a tower of strength and never once gave the slightest indication that she was upset by her incarceration. She gave the impression that even though she had been dealt a bad hand, she still had to make the most of it.

On 6 October 1960 Grills was rushed to Prince Henry Hospital next to Long Bay Jail, with peritonitis following the rupturing of a gastric ulcer. She died an hour later.

And Mrs Eveline Lundberg, the kindly lady who for no apparent reason had been poisoned by Grills and wound up blind and incapacitated as a result, spent her days sitting in the sun on her daughter's verandah in Great Buckingham Street, Redfern. Towards the end of her tragically shortened life Mrs Lundberg told a reporter: 'She made my life a purgatory. But I'm not bitter. What's the use of being like that.' A short time later she died in a Western Sydney nursing home.

MONSIEUR VERDOUX

(1947)

DIRECTED BY CHARLES CHAPLIN
SCREENPLAY BY CHARLES CHAPLIN

FEATURING

Charles Chaplin as Henri Verdoux
Mady Correll as Mona Verdoux
Allison Roddan as Peter Verdoux
Robert Lewis as Maurice Bottello
Audrey Betz as Martha Bottello
Martha Raye as Annabella Bonheur

If you like Charlie Chaplin as the little tramp, then chances are you will hate *Monsieur Verdoux*, just like most of America did when it was released in 1947. This ostensible comedy, about a French dandy who robs and murders wealthy women and burns their bodies in his incinerator, was just too much for Charlie's fans to take. It didn't help that *Monsieur Verdoux* was released at a turbulent time in Charlie's life, a time when he was accused by Senator Joseph McCarthy of being a communist and by the FBI chief, J Edgar Hoover, of conducting 'un-American activities'. Charlie's headlining paternity suit with Hollywood starlet Joan Barry, which kept the papers and courts busy until 1946, didn't help either. All of Charlie's dirty laundry – including his preference for teenage girls – was hung out to dry.

The upshot of all this scandal – whipped up by the venomous gossip columnist, Hedda Hopper, who hated Charlie with a passion because he wouldn't pander to her – meant that *Monsieur Verdoux* was picketed at the cinemas and banned altogether in some states. The few critics game enough to review it – themselves in fear of being aligned with Chaplin – panned it unmercifully. 'A woeful lack of humour or dramatic taste ... It is a pity to see so gifted a motion picture craftsman taking leave of his audience,' said the *New York Herald Tribune*. A 'comedy of murders' was the catch-cry. It was Chaplin's only failure at the box office and it cost him a fortune. These days it is hailed as a masterpiece of black comedy, which was way ahead of its time.

Monsieur Verdoux is taken from an original idea by Orson Welles. It is based on the real-life murders of the modern day Bluebeard, Henri Landru, in Paris during and after World War I. Chaplin plays a dapper little ex-bank clerk who murders his conquests to support his incapacitated family.

Verdoux murders 13 times and gets away with it, but number 14, played by Martha Raye, refuses to die, even though she has no idea that her lover is trying to knock her off. Verdoux decides to try a new poison and opts to try it first on a prostitute, who he calculates won't be missed. Instead, the hooker tells him a sob story and he gives her some money and lets her go.

Years later, when Verdoux has fallen on hard times and his wife has died, he again meets up with the hooker. She is now the mistress to a multimillionaire and she repays the favour. Soon after, Verdoux is captured and found guilty for his crimes. He argues in court that he is but an 'amateur' compared with the profiteers and munitions manufacturers of the war.

If anyone in the world could have made the murderous Verdoux a pathetic yet lovable character with whom the audience could sympathise, you would think it would be Charlie Chaplin. But he doesn't. And that's where it falls down.

The story of the real-life Bluebeard, Henri Landru, is much more interesting.

Henri Landru: The Modern Bluebeard

Henri Landru certainly did not look like the type of man capable of romancing more than 300 women and then swindling them out of their life savings. He was bald, thin and short in stature, and sported a thick, extremely unattractive brownish-red beard. His eyebrows were equally bushy and his eyes peering through gave the impression of a bush animal hiding behind a hedge. Henri Landru was not a good sort.

Nevertheless, women fell under the spell of the dapper little second-hand furniture dealer and after they had handed over their every franc, paid the ultimate price for their generosity. In the end Landru murdered 10 of the women he took under his spell and, in doing so, became known as the modern-day Bluebeard.

The original Bluebeard was a figment of the imagination of Charles Perrault and was first published as a fairytale in 1697. It is the story of a violent nobleman with a bushy bluebeard who was feared far and wide for his erratic behaviour. He had been married seven times, but his wives had all disappeared and no-one knew what had become of them. As a result the local ladies gave him a giant miss.

Not one to be put off easily, Bluebeard called upon his neighbour, a squire, and asked to marry one of his daughters. The girl was terrified but, in time, she came to love him, accepted his hand in marriage and went to live with him in his magnificent chateau. Soon after their marriage Bluebeard informed his wife that he had to go overseas on a business trip. He gave her the keys to the house, which included a small key to a room that he forbade her from entering.

Naturally, Bluebeard's new wife couldn't resist the temptation and opened the door of the forbidden room to find the floor a river of blood and her husband's seven previous wives mutilated and hanging from the walls. Terrified she prepared to flee, but as she locked the door behind her, she dropped the key in the blood. She couldn't wash the stains off the key, no matter how she tried.

Her husband arrived home unexpectedly and, seeing the blood on the key and realising that she had disobeyed his orders, flew into a violent rage. As he chased her, sword in hand to cut off her head, she hid in the tower with her sister and cringed in the corner as he tried to bash the door down.

Just in time their two brothers arrived and, as Bluebeard was about to administer the fatal blow, they killed him.

Bluebeard had no living heirs except his wife, and she inherited his mansion and vast fortune. As in true fairytale tradition all ended happily and she used the money wisely to help her family.

The real-life Bluebeard had no such privileged lifestyle. Henri Landru was born into a working-class family in 1869. His mother kept the house and looked after the children, while his father worked as a fireman in the furnaces of Paris' Vulcain Ironworks. There was no indication in his early life that young Henri would grow up to be France's most notorious serial killer. He attended a Catholic school where he was a bright student, but he left at age 17 to pursue a career in engineering. He was then drafted into the army where he reached the level of sergeant before he was discharged with distinction four years later.

Although he was no oil painting, young Henri had the gift of the gab and, when it came to chatting up the ladies, his intelligence put him in a league of his own. After a multitude of conquests, in 1891 he seduced his beautiful cousin, Mademoiselle Remy, who gave him a daughter and, two years later, they were married. With the money he had saved over the years Landru went into business with a friend. This friend, a clerk, fled with all his cash leaving the Landru family penniless.

This was the turning point in Henri Landru's life. The betrayal of his trusted friend turned him from an honest man with a distinguished army record, who was a deacon and choir member of his local church, into a thief and unscrupulous criminal who built up a second-hand furniture business with the proceeds of crime. His modus operandi was simple. Newly widowed middle-aged women who were forced to sell their worldly possessions through his shop were also persuaded to invest what little money they had left for their future in one of his shonky investments. When the unfortunate women wanted to know where their money was, they were threatened with violence and told if they went to the police they would be killed.

It seemed as though Landru had found his niche in life. However, in 1900 he was sentenced to two years in jail for fraud. His wife and four children were waiting for him when he got out. But it had become a way of life. Over the next 10 years Landru was in and out of prison seven times, with sentences ranging from a few months to three years.

It was in 1908 that he engineered the scheme that would bring about the demise of many innocent women and cost him his life on the guillotine. That year, while Landru was serving a sentence for fraud in Paris, he was taken to the town of Lille to stand trial for another fraud, in which he was alleged to have placed a classified advertisement in a newspaper seeking an affluent companion for a well-to-do widower, with intention of marriage should the liaison prove to be a loving one. Having found the right applicant, Landru persuaded the 40-year-old widow to part with a 15,000-francs dowry, in exchange for some counterfeit deeds to blue-chip property. The unfortunate widow was left destitute, and sought recompense through the courts. While the widow may have had a victory in getting Landru another three years on top of his existing sentence, by the time he was released all of her money was long gone.

Out of prison just before World War I, Landru was alone and penniless. His father had committed suicide over his son's disgrace and his wife had taken his children and left him. His mother had died in 1910. For the next few years he roamed the countryside, living off petty crime to survive. By the start of the war, he was up to his old tricks. In 1914, the following advertisement appeared in the Paris newspapers: 'Widower with two children, aged 43, with comfortable income, serious and moving in good society, desires to meet widow with a view to matrimony.'

Such an offering among the misery and doom of depression and war stood out like a beacon of hope to the many single and widowed women of Paris and they flocked to his door.

After screening the applicants, Henri Landru, posing as wealthy engineer, Monsieur Diard, welcomed into his rented home a 39-year-old widow, Madame Cuchet, and her 16-year-old son, Andre. The last time Madame Cuchet and Andre were seen alive was in January 1915, soon after they and the dapper Monsieur Diard had moved into a country villa in Vernouillet. Soon after their arrival Landru opened a bank account with 5000 francs. He claimed that the money was part of his inheritance from his father (who had died penniless), but you wouldn't need a degree in brain surgery to work out that the money came from Madame Cuchet.

Landru's next victim was a wealthy Argentine widow named Madame Laborde-Line, whose hotelier husband had recently died and left her a bundle. She gushed to friends that she had found the love of her life, a charming engineer from Brazil, and they planned to marry as soon as they could make the necessary arrangements. For the time being they moved in together. Soon after, the engineer from Brazil (whom former neighbours later positively identified as Landru) personally came back and collected her furniture, of which he sent some to their villa and the rest to a garage in Paris. Madame Laborde-Line was last seen in July 1915, when she had arrived at the villa with her two dogs, just six months after Madame Cuchet and her son had vanished.

A month later victim number three, Madame Guillin, a 51-year-old widow, was last seen at the villa of the mysterious Brazilian engineer. And then, just a few months later, a Madame Heon visited Vernouillet and disappeared without a trace.

To date all of the missing women had similar traits. They were either wealthy or had access to money, were widowed or divorced and they all allowed Landru to either remove them from their immediate families or at least distance them from their loved ones.

It is impossible to say how many more women Henri Landru killed before he murdered 19-year-old Andree Babelay, a servant girl who disappeared in early 1917 while on her way to visit her mother. Babelay was totally out of character of Landru's victims. She was young, poor – it seems all she had to offer was her youth. Like all of Landru's victims, he was the last person she was seen with.

Soon after Babelay disappeared Landru left Vernouillet to live in a rented villa in Gambais, where he had a huge cast-iron oven installed in the kitchen. In this villa Landru courted Madame Buisson, a wealthy widow, who moved in with him. She disappeared in April 1917.

In September 1917 Madame Louise Leopoldine Jaume, a wealthy widow Landru had been courting for a few months, disappeared without trace. It was around this time that Landru's new neighbours in Gambais noticed toxic black smoke pouring from a chimney in his villa.

Then 38-year-old Annette Pascal vanished in the spring of 1918, while having a relationship with Landru, and, in late 1918, Marie Therese Marchadier, a well-known and highly respected entertainer, disappeared after she had struck up a relationship with Landru when he visited her home to value her furniture for sale.

It appears that there were at least 10 women, one teenage boy and two dogs who had disappeared after last being seen with Landru, yet not at any time had police been suspicious of his activities. In the end it would be two victims' families that would bring him to justice.

The lack of police attention was due to Landru's painstaking efforts to assure his victim's families their loved ones were alive and well. Two friends of Madame Guillin, who had disappeared in August 1915, had received postcards from Landru, explaining that Guillin was unable to write herself. Landru forged a letter from Madame Buisson, who had disappeared in April 1917, to her dressmaker, and another to the concierge of her Paris apartment. In another letter Landru represented himself as the attorney of Madame Jaume, his second last victim who was in the middle of divorcing her husband. He successfully closed her bank accounts and transferred the money into an account of his own. But he was about to come unstuck.

Two years after Madame Buisson met Landru, her son, who was living with his aunt, passed away. Naturally the family wanted to contact his mother and tell her of the tragedy, but they were unable to find her. Then her sister remembered that Buisson had told her of her intention to run away to Gambais with a 'Monsieur Guillet'. She wrote to the mayor of Gambais, seeking help in locating either Buisson or Monsieur Guillet. The mayor replied that he knew of neither and suggested that she should meet up with the family of another woman, Madame Collomb, who had also vanished in Gambais under similar circumstances.

At this stage no-one had any way of knowing that Madame Collomb had disappeared after meeting Landru there in early 1917.

As it turned out, the tenant of the villa was not Monsieur Fremiet, the supposed fiancé of Buisson, but a Monsieur DuPont. However, when the police went to the villa they could not find Landru or any of the aliases he was allegedly living under. One ray of hope was that while the villa was unoccupied, it had recently been lived in.

Mademoiselle Lacoste, Buisson's sister, was not discouraged. Having once met Monsieur 'Fremiet' she would pick his distinct features anywhere. She began combing the streets of Paris near the villa looking for him. In 1919 her patience paid off when she spotted Landru coming out of a clothing store and she followed him to the Rue de Rochechouart where he lived under the name of Guillet with his mistress. The police were called and Landru was taken into custody.

But what to do with him? Indeed he had a terrible record for all sorts of things and, yes, women were missing after last being seen in his company, but he couldn't be charged with murder without a body. There wasn't a skerrick of evidence to convict him of murder, and Landru wasn't talking.

With Landru in custody, police returned to Gambais and searched the villa thoroughly. All they found was the remains of two dogs. They searched his old villa at Vernouillet and came up equally empty. All the police had to hold him on was a cryptic ledger, where Landru had methodically recorded his ill-gotten income and his spending. It turned out to be a treasure trove of missing people. Every one of the missing women got a mention, plus a few others who had gone missing without saying a word to either family or friends. But where were their bodies?

Smug in the misguided belief that he couldn't be convicted of murder without a body, Landru maintained his silence and defied them to charge him. What he didn't know was that such a conviction was indeed achievable under French law. The police just kept on with the investigation in the knowledge that sooner or later, in one way or another, Landru would lead himself to the guillotine. And he did, through his precise bookkeeping.

For two years Landru sat in jail in silence as detectives investigated the disappearances of his many victims. Piece by piece they gathered information and found that every women in his ledger of death had met Landru through his advertisements in Paris. The ledger also recorded when Landru had purchased train tickets from Paris to Gambais for his partner and himself, his was a return ticket and the lady's was one way.

The gardens in the villas at Gambais and Vernouillet were turned over many times, but produced nothing. Investigators tried to link Landru to acids and other chemicals found at the villas, but came up empty. Then the neighbours at Gambais told of the noxious fumes that often poured from the kitchen chimney. Jackpot.

Among the ashes in the stove Landru had installed shortly after his arrival in Gambais, police found a mountain of evidence that included human bones and metal fasteners of the kind worn on clothes of French women of the time. Bluebeard had disposed of his prey in the furnace, but not everything was destroyed. How he killed them was still a mystery because even after being confronted with the evidence, he was still not in a talkative mood. But finally it was clear what had happened to Madame Collomb, Madame Buisson and as many as nine others. Two years after his arrest and following thousands of hours of detective work, Landru was charged with 11 counts of murder.

Bluebeard, as Landru was now known to the press and a baying public, was sent to trial in November 1921. For the murderer it was not a good situation to be in: French justice was not exactly justice at all, and the system weighed heavily against the defendant. This system was put together in the mid-1800s and anyone on trial had to prove themselves innocent, rather than the law prove them guilty. The Crown prosecutor was the head judge of a panel of three judges and he could interrogate the prisoner in the dock as viciously as he desired. The victim's relatives were allowed to bring a suit for damages during the trial, and their counsel could question the accused and take him to task before the jury.

Things weren't looking good for Bluebeard. He stuck to his guns and challenged the Crown's right to have him in court in the first place, given that they didn't have a single body. His defence refused to answer questions and instead asked for proof of murder, insisting that all of the prosecution's evidence was circumstantial.

Day after day he stood up to the withering attack of accusations that it was him and only him who had cold-bloodedly murdered at least 11 people and burned their bodies. He said he had nothing to say and that it wasn't up to him to prove himself innocent, but for the police to prove him guilty.

Landru's defence didn't go down well with the jury and, after 24 days of testimony, it took them just two hours to decide that Bluebeard was guilty as charged. As well as being notoriously against the defendant, French justice was also notoriously swift: two months after his conviction a guard walked into his cell and said that the following day he was getting his head cut off.

On 25 February 1922 Henri Landru was brought to the guillotine. Unlike his life, his execution was uneventful. Before he knelt under the blade he presented his lawyers with some framed paintings created while in prison. Unfortunately he didn't tell his lawyers to pull the frames apart because inside there was a full written confession of all of his crimes and how he had disposed of the bodies. It was not discovered until almost half a century later.

Landru declined a condemned man's right to prayers, rejected the traditional glass of brandy and the right to make a statement. The unmistakable clunk of the guillotine announced the beast was dead and a huge roar that could be heard for miles emanated from the crowd gathered outside the prison.

THE FLESH AND THE FIENDS

(1959)

DIRECTED BY JOHN GILLING
SCREENPLAY BY JOHN GILLING AND LEO GRIFFITHS

FEATURING
Peter Cushing as Dr Robert Knox
Donald Pleasance as William Hare
George Rose as William Burke
June Laverick as Martha Knox
Renee Houston as Helen Burke
Dermot Walsh as Dr Geoffrey Mitchell

Few murderers could be more depraved than William Burke and William Hare: the Bodysnatchers. They started off exhuming coffins and carting off the freshly dead contents, before moving on to murdering complete strangers, all for money. And they spent their proceeds on prostitutes and drink. Yet, because they sold the bodies to an eminent doctor for medical research, it could also be said that their sins paved the way for medical science and saved future lives.

The drunken buffoon Burke is played by George Rose, and the cunning Hare is brilliantly portrayed by Donald Pleasance. You'll find out exactly how clever Hare was at the end of the story. And it would be fair comment to say that Pleasance's performance steals the show.

Dr Robert Knox is played by the distinguished Peter Cushing and gets the star billing. The good doctor's part is pumped up to break the monotony between murders – a movie that just went from one exhumation to the next, and from one suffocation murder to another would make for pretty boring viewing – so Peter Cushing gets his name at the top of the credits. Besides, he was a pretty big star at the time.

Given its story-line, you could be forgiven for thinking that *The Flesh and the Fiends* is a horror movie; in fact, it is good-quality drama that sticks to the grisly facts and is historically correct. Dr Knox's ideas were decades ahead of 1825 Scotland and, against the wishes of the medical establishment and the church, he needed dead bodies to carry on his work. If this meant dealing with the devil, or in this case the devil's disciples, to get the bodies, then so be it. As far as Dr Knox was concerned, the still-warm corpses that Burke and Hare kept bringing to his back door in the middle of the night all died from natural causes. But, in the end, Dr Knox's association with Edinburgh's most despised killers ruined his career.

Burke and Hare: The Bodysnatchers

In business, demand for a product always creates a line of supply. And if that demand is for human cadavers, why rob graves when it's easier to smother a live victim for a fast dollar? At least that was the line of thought employed by murderous Irish duo Burke and Hare, who were responsible for 16 killings between them in 19th century Scotland.

A medical boom was under way in the Great Britain of the early 1800s and a growing number of students were joining medical colleges. With more classes in anatomy training, the demand for cadavers in good condition soared. Naturally, it wasn't long before enterprising villains started plundering the nation's graveyards, digging up bodies and delivering them mostly unquestioned to medical colleges in exchange for cash. And while it must have been obvious something was amiss to those who paid for the cadavers, the number of students ready to hand over good money in hard times no doubt made it easy to turn a blind eye.

William Burke was 36 years old when he and his partner in crime started to supply Edinburgh's medical colleges with bodies. He had already served seven years in the army. He had been married and had two children, though he left them behind in Ireland. In Scotland, he worked variously as a labourer, baker and cobbler and met a local named Helen McDougal. Helen had left one husband and was involved in a de facto relationship with another with whom she had two children. McDougal and Burke left them behind and moved around before they settling in Edinburgh, doing odd jobs to survive.

Around the same time William Hare also migrated to Scotland looking for work. Later described as a brutal man with a leering face and the countenance of an idiot, after a time he, too, settled in Edinburgh, where he found a room at a cheap boarding house in the West Port area. The house was run by a man named Logue, whose wife, Margaret, was also Irish. After Logue passed away in 1826, Burke was on hand to offer the widow support. But it wasn't long before he was sharing more than comfort with her, and the new lovers were soon running the boarding house together.

On their first day in Edinburgh, Burke and Helen McDougal met Margaret Hare, who suggested they come back to the boarding house she ran with her de facto husband. The pair soon moved in as tenants, sharing a love of alcohol with the Hares, but little else. The foursome fought frequently. Indeed, the only other thing the group had in common was a desire to make fast, easy money. In November 1827 fate showed its hand when an elderly pensioner, a war veteran and lodger at the boarding house named Donald, got sick and died. He owed £4 in rent at the time, and Hare hatched a plan to retrieve the cash.

Burke and Hare removed Donald's body from its coffin before the authorities came to collect it. They filled the coffin with bark until it weighed about the same, then sealed it up again. Once the coffin was taken away, they set off to find a buyer for their fresh cadaver. They were pointed in the direction of Professor Robert Knox's classroom, where one of his assistants showed interest in the corpse. The pair were told to return with the body after dark. When Burke and Hare arrived that night they were lugging a large sack. Knox's assistants checked out the sack's contents and gave the men £7. On the way home they discussed what a tidy little earner they'd stumbled across.

A few days later another of Hare's boarders, a man named Joseph, got sick. Joseph's illness wasn't serious, and the man owed no rent, but the lure of quick cash proved too strong for Burke and Hare. They plied Joseph with glass after glass of whisky until he passed out. Then they covered his nose and mouth, asphyxiating him while he remained unconscious, before transporting the corpse to Knox's classroom.

It was a method the pair would rely on for almost a year. With no telltale marks to indicate a murder, it appeared their victims had passed away while sick or drunk. What the men did know, though, was that they were on to a good thing financially, and it wasn't long before they were looking beyond Hare's boarding house for bodies.

Elderly pensioner Abigail Simpson had made her way into Edinburgh one February day in 1828 to collect her government allowance. Returning home, she ran into Hare, who suggested she come to his boarding house for a drink. Burke was waiting, and the trio proceeded to drink well into the evening, by which time it was easy to persuade Simpson to stay the night. Unfortunately for Burke and Hare, their own inebriation saw them pass out before they could murder the old woman. The next morning, however, was a different story.

Waking up disorientated and hungover, it wasn't hard for Simpson to be convinced that another whisky would help. When another drink followed soon after it wasn't long before the pensioner was asleep once again. This time Burke and Hare wasted no time smothering her, and cramming her body into a wooden chest. They took it to Knox's classroom, where the professor himself remarked how fresh the corpse was. The men received £10 for their effort.

It wasn't long before they had blown all their blood money on alcohol. Luckily for them, another of Hare's boarders became sick and was despatched in the same manner as Joseph had been, weeks earlier.

The next victim appears to have been scouted by Margaret Hare when she took an old lady she had met in the street back to the boarding house and began pouring her whisky. The lady kept drinking, and after a while Margaret suggested she take a rest. When she eventually decided that a nap was indeed a good idea, Margaret summoned Burke and Hare, who murdered the woman in her sleep and delivered her to Knox.

The next murder saw the pair taking a greater risk. It was the morning of 9 April when Burke saw 18-year-old prostitutes Mary Paterson and Janet Brown preparing for their day with a fortifying whisky or two at a local drinking establishment. He invited the girls back to his brother's house for breakfast where, after several more whiskies, Mary fell asleep while sitting at the table. Janet, however, showed no sign of doing the same, so Burke took her to another tavern. But Janet's drinking seemed to have no physical effect on her. The pair had returned to Burke's brother's house for yet more whisky, when Helen McDougal showed up. Finding her de facto husband with two prostitutes, a fight ensued. Janet tried to leave, but Burke tried to convince her to stay. She left, but promised to return once Burke's irate partner had gone. When she returned, though, Mary Paterson was nowhere to be found and Janet was told she had gone out with Burke. The prostitute left the house, no doubt saving her own life. By this time, of course, Mary was dead.

Predictably, it wasn't long before the money Burke and Hare received for Mary's body was squandered on alcohol, and the pair soon had their eyes on a female beggar named Effie. Burke invited the old lady back to the boarding house, plied her with booze, and then, after she had fallen asleep, murdered her and took the corpse to Knox for their £10 pay-off.

The murderers must have felt invincible by now, and their actions seem to confirm their confidence. Coming across two police officers taking a drunk woman to lock-up one morning, they stepped in, lied that they knew the woman and would happily take her home themselves. Instead, they killed her and delivered her body to Knox.

Their next victims, an old woman and her deaf grandson, strangers in the city, met their fate in June after they met Burke on the street and asked him for directions. Burke, presenting himself as a good samaritan, offered to take them to their destination, but suggested stopping at his home first, where the woman and child could rest. The grandmother agreed, and, once at the boarding house, she was soon drunk. Soon she was dead. The young boy, meanwhile, was left with Helen and Margaret in another room. But the child was becoming anxious. He hadn't seen his grandmother for a while, and he had no idea where he was. With the youngster becoming more agitated, Burke took matters into his own murderous hands, breaking the child's back over his knee. The bodies of both victims were then delivered to Professor Knox, netting Burke and Hare £16.

At this stage things began to get complicated for the team. Burke and Helen decided to visit some of her relatives out of town. Beforehand, Margaret had suggested that they kill Helen. Burke refused, but it can't have been good for team spirit. Indeed, it wasn't long after they returned from their holiday that Burke and Helen moved out of the Hares' boarding house and into a different one nearby. A further bone of contention was that Hare had been busy in the cadaver trade while Burke was away.

Nonetheless, it didn't take long for the crew to get back to business. Their first new victim was a woman named Ostler, who visited Burke's new lodgings for a party. The next was a relative of Helen's who was visiting the city. After that came another close call, when Hare invited Mary Haldane, an elderly prostitute who was well known in the area, to his boarding house for a drink. Following their by now well-worked routine, Burke joined them and they plied Haldane with grog until she fell asleep. Haldane then had the life smothered out of her and her corpse delivered to Professor Knox to be dissected in the name of science. The problem for Burke and Hare, though, was that Mary Haldane had been seen with Hare, and when her daughter, Peggy, became concerned about her mother's absence she visited the boarding house, where she was greeted by Margaret and Helen. Strong words were exchanged, with the women explaining that neither Mary Haldane, nor any other prostitute, would ever be allowed to enter the boarding house. As the argument became more heated, Hare arrived and told Peggy her mother had visited the house earlier, but had left shortly afterwards. Hare then defused the situation the way he knew best – he gave Peggy a drink, and made sure the alcohol kept coming until she too passed out and became more product for Knox's students.

Burke and Hare's next victim was also a popular identity in their area. Known to many as Daft Jamie, 18-year-old James Wilson was one of the West Port region's more eccentric characters. Homeless, his end came when he was walking the neighbourhood in search of his mother. Instead, he found Hare, who took him back to the boarding house, where they were joined by Burke. Then the whisky came out and, although James didn't indulge as much as previous victims, he eventually fell asleep anyway. The pair smothered him and set about collecting their £10 fee from Knox.

Even though several of Knox's students recognised James when he was presented in anatomy class, Knox firmly denied that it was the boy, and began dissecting the body immediately. James' mother was also asking around, questioning everyone she could to find her son, but for the time being it appeared Burke and Hare were in the clear. Of course, their luck couldn't hold forever.

On the morning of 31 October 1828 Burke was starting the

day with a whisky at a local tavern when an elderly Irish woman started making small talk with other patrons. Noticing the woman's thick accent, Burke bought her a drink and asked about her heritage. It turned out she came from the Irish town of Innisowen, and that her name was Mary Docherty. Burke laughed and told Mary his mother was also a Docherty, and was from the same town. He added that there was every chance the pair were related. From that point, Burke had no trouble convincing the old woman to come back to his house.

Once there, Helen made a big show of welcoming Mary, and Burke convinced her to stay the night. Another couple rooming there at the time, James and Ann Gray, joined in the celebrations, then went to the Hares' boarding house to spend the night, agreeing to come back for breakfast the next day. But the revelry continued even after the Grays left, with the sound of dancing and drinking continuing. Then, at around midnight, a neighbour heard an argument between two men, as well as a woman screaming out that a murder was taking place. The neighbour went looking for a policeman, but couldn't find one. He went back to the room from where he had heard the cries emanating, but all was quiet and he thought no more of it.

The Grays returned the next morning, but Mary Docherty was nowhere to be found. Helen was quick to explain that the elderly lady had started making advances towards Burke, so she had been forced to ask her to leave. The Grays accepted the story. But when Ann Gray later went to retrieve a pair of her socks from near a spare bed, Burke erupted, telling her to get away from there at once.

Later that night, both Burke and Helen left the room and Ann took the chance to see what was near the bed that Burke was so keen on her not seeing. Peering under the bed's frame she saw an old woman's corpse. The couple ran from the room, but stumbled across Helen. The Grays told her they had seen the body beneath the bed. They asked what Helen knew about it. Helen said she would pay them £10 a week if they kept their find a secret, but the Grays went off to alert the authorities.

Realising that everything was starting to fall apart, Helen and Margaret raced to warn Burke and Hare, who cleared the room and got out before the police arrived. Still, a neighbour told the investigating officers that two men had been seen earlier carrying a heavy chest from the room. While the authorities were still at the scene, Burke and Helen returned to their residence and asked what was going on. The police decided to question them separately. Burke told the officers Docherty had left the house at 7 o'clock that morning. Unfortunately, when asked the same question, Helen said Docherty had left at 7 o'clock the night before. The pair were taken in for further questioning. At the same time, the police received an anonymous tip-off that led them to the classroom of Professor Knox. Docherty's body was still there. Helen and Burke were put in prison. The Hares soon joined them.

In the days that followed, the authorities started looking into the missing persons cases that had been mounting in the West Port district in the past year. Then in early November a local paper ran an article about the disappearances. The story was seen by prostitute Janet Brown, who went to the police to ask what was going on. They showed her items of clothing they had found in Burke's room. Janet recognised them as belonging to her friend Mary Paterson.

By now public anger was brewing and there were cries to bring all involved to justice – including Professor Knox. The only problem was there had been no witnesses to the deaths. The only evidence was circumstantial. It took a month before the investigators tried the divide-and-conquer approach. They offered Hare immunity from prosecution to testify against Burke and McDougal. Hare didn't have to be asked twice. The pair were immediately charged with killing Mary Docherty. Burke received additional charges for the murders of James Wilson and Mary Paterson.

When the trial began on Christmas Eve, the prosecution called both William and Margaret Hare, who spoke against Burke and McDougal, explaining that they were the instigators of the murders. The defence tried to shift blame away from the accused, but it took the jury less than an hour to find Burke guilty. He was sentenced to execution, but Helen McDougal managed to avoid prosecution. She later returned to the house she had lived in with Burke, but an angry crowd soon arrived, and the authorities had to be called in to get her out safely. After that incident Helen moved to England, but was again confronted by angry members of the public. She eventually moved to Australia, where she lived until she passed away in 1868.

It would be a month before Burke's death sentence was carried out. In that time he confessed to committing 16 murders, either with or without Hare's help. On 28 January 1829, Burke ascended the gallows and swung until dead.

Little is known of Margaret Hare's fate, though it is thought she moved back to Ireland.

William Hare was released from police custody in February 1829. He was last seen in the English town of Carlisle, though legend has it that he was later attacked and blinded by an angry mob and lived out his remaining days as a beggar in London.

Knox refused to speak publicly about the cadavers supplied by Burke and Hare. His house and classroom were sometimes set upon by irate members of the public, and enrolments in his classes dropped as a result of the controversy. He later moved to London to take a position at a hospital catering to cancer victims. He died in 1862.

PSYCHO

(1960)

DIRECTED BY ALFRED HITCHCOCK
SCREENPLAY BY JOSEPH STEFANO

FEATURING

Anthony Perkins as Norman Bates
Janet Leigh as Marion Crane
John Gavin as Sam Loomis
Vera Miles as Lila Crane
Martin Balsam as Detective Milton Arbogast

Everything you've heard about Alfred Hitchcock's *Psycho* is true. It is a masterpiece of suspense. It was the first movie in the serial killer genre as we know it today. The music in the shower scene actually sounds like someone being stabbed to death. And, yes, it was based on a real character. Well, sort of.

Truth be known, the 'real-life' killer on whom Hitchcock modelled Norman Bates never owned a 12-room motel on a forgotten back road complete with a big house on the hill. He was, in fact, a mild-mannered Wisconsin hillbilly named Ed Gein, who was as mad as a cut snake. On screen and in real life the only thing that Norman and Ed had in common was their obsession with dead women.

Poor Norman had a problem with his dead mum: in his mind she couldn't help herself when it came to murdering the guests. In Ed's case, it was any dead woman he could dig up.

And as if that wasn't a touch unusual, Ed used the skin from the female corpses he dug up from the local graveyard, as well as from the women he murdered, to make clothing for himself, which he wore at night when he danced in the backyard beneath the light of the moon.

And, as is the American way, Ed's nocturnal lifestyle inspired author Robert Bloch to write a book about the deranged motelier Bates, a character based loosely on Ed, on which Hitchcock based his movie *Psycho*.

Until Ed Gein came along, the civilised world had never known of such depravities. *Psycho* made Ed a household name and he became a cult hero.

Thirty-one years later, Ed was again the inspiration for another famous fictional serial killer, Buffalo Bill, in the screen adaptation of Thomas Harris' novel, *The Silence of the Lambs*. But this time the serial killer didn't have a passion for digging up dead women and playing with their private parts.

Instead, Bill was inspired by Ed's dressmaking techniques and preferred using freshly murdered women's skin, rather than satin and silks, when making garments for his winter collection.

Ed Gein inspired the two greatest serial killer movies of all time. And after you have read about his life, it won't be hard to understand why.

Ed Gein: The Real Norman Bates and Buffalo Bill

When likeable farmer Ed Gein was seen loitering around the local hardware store in Plainfield, Wisconsin, on 17 November 1957 – just after it had been robbed and its owner, Bernice Worden, had gone missing – police picked him up and decided to have a look at his farmhouse. Inside,

ED GEIN

Ed's home was like a rubbish tip. Rotting garbage and piles of junk almost up to the ceilings made it physically impossible to walk through the house, let alone stand the stench of rotting food.

With his torch beam in the darkened kitchen, sheriff Arthur Schley caught what he thought was a skinned deer hanging from a butcher's hook in a beam in the ceiling. The head had been removed and the carcass was slit open and had been gutted. It didn't strike him as unusual because it was deer season. But closer inspection revealed that the 'deer' was, in fact, a headless butchered corpse. The missing woman, 50-year-old Bernice Worden, mother of his deputy, Frank Worden, had been found.

But the body of Bernice Worden was merely the beginning. As dazed police fossicked through the grisly mess of Eddie Gein's existence, they realised that they had stumbled into a chamber of horrors. Ed's soup bowl was a scooped-out human skull. His rubbish bin was made with human parts covered with skin, as were the lampshades throughout the house. Ed's belt was made of human nipples, and numerous shrunken female genitalia were kept in a shoebox. His favourite armchair was made of human remains and scattered about were human noses, a head and a heart.

But the prize of them all was the suit made completely out of human skin.

The second of two male children, Edward Theodore Gein was born on 27 August 1906 in La Crosse, Wisconsin, to polar-opposite parents: a weak-willed, violent and mostly unemployed alcoholic named George, and a domineering, overtly religious mother named Augusta. Ed Gein would go on to become one of the world's most notorious and most deranged killers; the benchmark to which all others would be measured. A man whose acts were so sickening that they still shock and repulse today, inspiring endless movies, books – and nightmares.

Ed's brother, Henry, was seven years older, and the boys' parents were opposites. Augusta, a Lutheran, raised the children according to the strict teachings of the Bible, or at least the way she interpreted it. Alcohol was evil, and women, she stressed, were immoral and would only lead her boys to eternal damnation if they were to succumb to their natural urges. Afternoons were filled with Bible readings, mostly from the Old Testament, and in the Gein household, Augusta's word was law. George barely got a look in. When it came to the boys' upbringing, his opinion meant nothing. Indeed, Augusta would have divorced the man she saw as a no-hoper if it wasn't considered a sin by the church.

In 1914 the Gein's moved to the more rural base of Plainfield, Wisconsin, where they lived on a farm, far from neighbours and the temptations of the city. Ed's only contact with the outside world was at school, where his progress could best be described as average. The one field in which he was proficient was reading, where he could at least indulge his already burgeoning imagination, escaping from the restraints of his home life, however briefly. It's little wonder that the youth had few friends, with his peers seeing him as shy and rather soft, an object of ridicule. All this time, he did whatever Augusta said – hers was the final word.

Unfortunately, Augusta's love wasn't borne of a caring, nurturing personality. She chastised and berated her offspring whenever she was displeased with them, which was nearly all the time. She never missed a chance to point out that they were headed down the same dead-end path as their useless father. As the boys grew into young manhood, their only company was each other.

George Gein passed away in 1940, and the boys were forced to work a variety of jobs, such as handyman work and babysitting, to bring in money. The people of Plainfield saw the pair as honest and hard working, and Ed especially enjoyed looking after the young children of the town, finding them easier to relate to than his peers who taunted him.

By this time, Henry was growing concerned about how attached Ed seemed to their mother, and there were times when he would openly speak his mind. The younger Gein had trouble understanding this. In Ed's eyes his mother was a bastion of righteousness. How could Henry not see her in the same glowing light? Either way, Henry would soon be out of the picture, in rather suspicious circumstances.

On 16 May 1944 a fire started burning up the rural landscape around Plainfield, its flames growing closer and closer to the Gein farm. Ed and Henry went out to fight the blaze. The pair went in separate directions and, when night fell, Ed could no longer see Henry. Once the last glowing embers were finally extinguished, Ed's concern mounted.

He contacted the local police and told them his older brother had gone missing. The authorities organised a search party, but were somewhat surprised when Ed was able to lead them straight to the brother he had reported as missing. They were even more surprised that Henry was dead, lying on a section of ground that the fire hadn't reached. There was also bruising about his cranium.

Still, even though the situation seemed suspicious, the authorities ruled out foul play, mainly because they doubted that the quiet, young Ed would have it in him to murder anyone. After all, he was just a harmless youth. The county coroner looked into the case and filed the cause of death as asphyxiation. The Gein family was now down to just Ed and his dear mother, but that would soon change, too.

Augusta Gein died on 29 December 1945 after her body was ravaged by a series of strokes. Ed was now alone. He stayed on at the farm, though, living off what money he was able to earn from his odd jobs around the town. Heartbroken at the loss of his beloved matriarch, he even boarded off the rooms of the house that she frequented the most, keeping the living room, parlour and upstairs section as a virtual shrine to her. They would stay that way for several years, a time capsule of better times, while Ed used a small room off the kitchen as his bedroom.

Understandably, Ed grew lonely after Augusta's death, and he started to develop strange habits. He would stay home alone reading magazines devoted to death and adventure, Nazis and headhunters, as well as books about human anatomy. He also started to make regular night-time visits to the Plainfield cemetery, and learnt, from the magazines he read, the process behind such macabre rituals as shrinking heads and exhuming bodies.

Unknown to the parents of the children he was babysitting, Ed often regaled the youngsters with his newfound knowledge. When he did read something more normal, like the local newspaper, he would dwell on the obituary section, looking specifically for news about the deaths of women.

In hindsight, it's perhaps not difficult to predict what might happen next.

Having led a confined existence, it's little surprise that Ed had never had intimate contact with a female. But now he began to visit the fresh gravesites under the cloak of night and dig up the recently buried women, peeling off their skin and wearing it over his own. Still, when the police later caught up with Ed, he stressed that he had never had sex with any of the corpses, citing the rank smell of decay as his main reason.

Intrigued about female body parts, Ed began to collect them from the cadavers he exhumed. Along with breasts and vaginas, he also had various preserved heads. Before long, stories started to spread through Plainfield. A boy who Ed sometimes cared for claimed that the strange man had shown him shrunken heads. When two other men visited the farm and saw the same thing, it only added credence to the young chap's tale.

Still, the stories remained rumour and conjecture; it was as if the townsfolk chose not to take them seriously. After all, who would keep real human heads in their house? Even when locals would joke with Ed about the heads in his house, he'd smile and say he kept them in his room. At the time no-one thought it was more than a slightly distasteful joke.

Then, in the late 1940s, just a few years after Augusta Gein passed away, the Wisconsin police noted an increase in the number of missing persons reports. These unsolved cases continued to mount through the 1950s. The authorities first became concerned when eight-year-old Georgia Weckler didn't arrive home from school on 1 May 1947. Despite a wide search involving police and townsfolk, the young girl was never found. With little evidence to go on, except for tyre tracks belonging to a Ford found near where Georgia went missing, the police had no leads, and the case was soon closed. Six years later, 15-year-old Evelyn Hartley went missing from La Crosse, where she had been babysitting. Alarm bells first rang when her father tried to phone the house where she was working, but got no answer. He drove over and looked through the window, but could only see one of her shoes and a pair of glasses on the floor. He looked round the residence for a way to get in, and eventually found himself at a basement window around the back, where he saw drops of blood.

After making his way inside and seeing that a struggle had taken place, he called the police, who immediately searched the area. They soon found further signs of a struggle, including more blood and Evelyn's other shoe, and a wider search of the region was quickly organised. Even though the young girl was nowhere to be found, items of her clothing turned up not far from the highway leading out of town.

It wasn't just young girls going missing, though. Victor Travis and Ray Burgess were on their way deer hunting in November 1952 when they stopped off at a Plainfield drinking establishment. They were never seen again. Despite a large-scale search, no sign of their bodies or car was found.

The next disappearance happened two years later when Plainfield tavern owner Mary Hogan went missing from her bar. Police found an empty bullet casing inside, as well as blood leading outside into the car park.

With no leads and no fresh cases, investigations into the disappearances wound down – until store clerk Bernice Worden went missing in November 1957. By this time the authorities had come to suspect Ed. They searched his shed and were shocked and disgusted to find Worden's decapitated corpse hanging by the ankles. Closer inspection revealed that she had been shot in the head at close range, with the mutilations occurring after she had died.

A search of Gein's house revealed the variety of gruesome atrocities that would be shocking even in a graphic horror movie. The investigating officers were understandably repulsed. Ed was taken to Wautoma County jail to be interviewed, and his property was excavated in the hope of finding a sign of those persons who had gone missing through the previous decade.

Despite the overwhelming evidence, Ed tried to maintain that he was innocent. But that charade ended the next day when – despite claiming to have difficulty remembering the details due to being in a daze at the time – Ed revealed how he had murdered Worden. Even though he stated that he couldn't remember shooting the woman, he said he could recall dragging her body and the cash register from the store and taking them to his house.

As for the various body parts littering his residence, Ed admitted to stealing them from the local cemetery, explaining that he dug up recently deceased middle-aged women who he believed resembled his mother. He would then take the bodies home in his Ford and tan their skins. Still, Ed insisted that the only murder he had committed was that of Bernice Worden.

His story changed after a few days of questioning, and Ed admitted that he had also killed Mary Hogan, though he again claimed to have been in a daze when he did so, and added that the shooting had been accidental.

Throughout the interrogation, Ed remained emotionless. He showed no sign of remorse or pity, even when discussing acts of grave robbing and murder. It was as if he was a small child who failed to grasp what he had actually done. As a result, there were understandable doubts about his sanity. Psychological tests were conducted and the results revealed that Ed was emotionally impaired.

After a variety of experts spoke to him and reviewed the case, he was classed as a sexual psychopath. The experts placed the blame for his condition on his upbringing and his relationship with his mother. It turned out that Ed had experienced his first orgasm at the age of 10 while watching his parents slaughter a pig. Later, once he had reached puberty, Augusta caught him masturbating while bathing. She poured scalding hot water over him before grabbing his genitals and telling him they were the 'curse of man'.

As a result of such occurrences the experts believed Ed was conflicted about his feelings towards females – he had trouble reconciling his normal, natural attraction to them with the extreme thoughts and beliefs he had been brought up with.

In the meantime, the authorities continued to search the Gein farm. They believed the various body parts recovered belonged to a total of 10 women. Ed told them that besides the two women whose murders he had admitted to, the remaining bits came from eight females he had dug up at the cemetery. Finding the story hard to believe, the authorities decided to investigate the gravesites. This, of course, caused a stir among the local community, but once the coffins were dug up, it was shown that all had been tampered with and parts, or entire bodies, were missing from the majority of graves.

By this time, news of Ed's horrific acts had spread around the world, and the press descended on the sleepy town of Plainfield, haranguing locals with endless questions about their infamous neighbour. Several of the townsfolk spoke of the shy, quiet man with the strange sense of humour. No-one could believe he was responsible for such reprehensible acts.

Gein spent 30 days being evaluated in a mental institution. The end finding was that he was mentally incompetent. As a result, he could not face trial for the first-degree murder of

Bernice Worden. He was instead committed to the Central State Hospital in Waupun, Wisconsin. His farm and belongings were also put up for auction. The people of Plainfield were mortified. Nobody wanted the Gein farm to become a tourist attraction and it surprised no-one when the house was mysteriously burnt to the ground early on the morning of 20 March 1958.

Still, several of Ed's belongings survived, including the 1949 Ford sedan that had been used to haul around the dead bodies. Bidding for the car was fierce, and it eventually went under the hammer for $760, a small fortune at the time. The successful bidder was a sideshow operator named Bunny Gibbons. He turned the automobile into a carnival attraction, charging 25 cents to anyone who wanted to view the 'Ed Gein Ghoul Car'.

Ed was institutionalised for a decade before it was decided he was fit to stand trial for the murder of Bernice Worden, and he went before a judge on 7 November 1968. It only took a week for the result to be handed down – Ed was found guilty of first-degree murder.

However, the decision was later reversed and Ed was found not guilty by reason of insanity.

He was sent back to the Central State Hospital for the Criminally Insane, where he remained for the rest of his life, spending his days reading and enjoying activities such as rug making and amateur radio. Described as a model patient who never required tranquillisers, the only disconcerting aspect to Ed's behaviour while in the hospital was the way he stared at any female with whom he came into contact.

The real-life monster who inspired so many nightmares passed away after a long battle with cancer on 26 July 1984. He was buried next to his mother, not far from the graves he had robbed, in Plainfield cemetery.

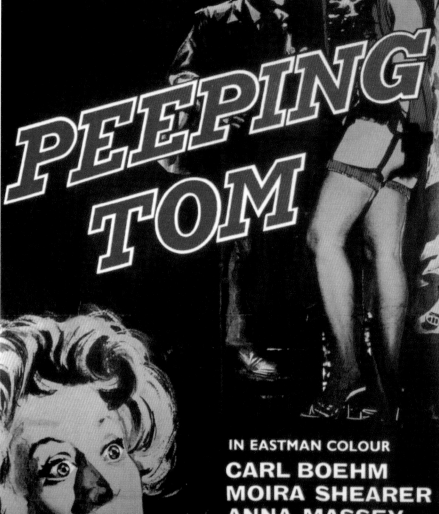

PEEPING TOM

(1960)

DIRECTED BY MICHAEL POWELL
SCREENPLAY BY LEO MARKS

FEATURING

Carl (Karlheinz) Boehm as Mark Lewis
Moira Shearer as Vivian
Anna Massey as Helen Stephens
Maxine Audley as Mrs Stephens
Brenda Bruce as Dora
Jack Watson as Chief Inspector Gregg

P*eeping Tom* signed the death warrant for the movie career of its director, the accomplished Michael Powell, considered a genius of the British theatre. Amid hideous reviews and the inevitable comparisons with Alfred Hitchcock's *Psycho*, which also came out later the same year, *Peeping Tom* was deemed an unmitigated shocker.

So they took *Peeping Tom* to America, where it got a limited run and was archived for a couple of decades until it was dug up in 1978 by a bunch of admiring directors led by Martin Scorsese and relaunched in 1979 at the New York Film Festival. Seems the world still wasn't ready for it, because it bombed again.

Scorsese was *Peeping Tom*'s greatest fan, having once said that the film, along with Federico Fellini's acclaimed *8 1/2*, contained all that could be said about directing. Scorsese is also one of Powell's most famous admirers and as a child on his way to being one of the greatest directors of all time he studied the films of the Archers', the extraordinary team of writer Emric Pressburger and director Michael Powell.

Pressburger and Powell were responsible for some of the most successful films of the 1940s and 1950s and you would think with those credentials *Peeping Tom* would be viewed in the context it was intended.

These days it has become a cult movie, lauded upon by young filmmakers, who consider it a masterpiece of the genre. Given that voyeurism and gratuitous violence are now commonplace in movies, Powell's attempt to look beyond the violence and into the hearts and minds of serial killers was way ahead of its time.

The infamous *Peeping Tom* opens with the main character Mark Lewis (Carl Boehm) following a prostitute to her room. He has a movie camera in his hand and, once inside, he sets up his camera and films the look of horror on the hooker's face as he stabs her to death with a spike he produces from one of the tripod legs. Next we find Mark in his room at home, getting off on the footage of the murder. We can only wonder how many of the audience stayed for the rest of the film, given that all this happens as the opening credits are rolling.

Mark turns out to be a stuttering loner with a manic sex drive, who works at a movie studio during the day. At night, in between being a serial killer with a fetish for home movies, he is a glamour photographer for a seedy newsagent owner who sells under-the-counter pornography.

Mark's association with a girl downstairs in his building has the viewer in constant suspense, as does the relentless taunting by one of his buxom photographic models. Both are catalysts for a bizarre triangle, and the inevitable disastrous ending.

Some critics believe that the fact that director Powell showed the audience Mark's home movies, thus making the audience voyeurs to murder, may have been the big turn-off. Others say that while Powell is endeavouring to look into the mind of a very disturbed young man and explore the reasons behind his problems, he doesn't get his message across and the audience sees only a blood-fest.

But with its rich technicolour, clever photography and excellent performances, others see it as a masterpiece, way ahead of its time.

Peeping Tom is available at some video libraries and available on DVD through the internet.

You make up your own mind.

THE BOSTON STRANGLER

(1968)

DIRECTED BY RICHARD FLEISCHER
SCREENPLAY BY EDWARD ANHALT

FEATURING

Tony Curtis as Albert DeSalvo
Henry Fonda as John S Bottomly
George Kennedy as Detective Phil DiNatale
Mile Kellin as Julian Soshnick
Hurd Hatfield as Terence Huntley
Murray Hamilton as Sergeant Frank McAfee

Between June 1962 and January 1964, 13 females were killed in their apartments in the US city of Boston, Massachusetts. All were single women, and most were living alone. All were sexually assaulted and then strangled with an item of their clothing, though there was no sign of forced entry in any of the cases. And all of the murders were attributed to the notorious Boston Strangler, even though evidence suggests two of the deaths may have come from the hands of a copycat killer.

Even today no-one has been charged with the vicious crimes, but convicted burglar and serial rapist Albert DeSalvo is generally accepted to be responsible for the murders. DeSalvo confessed to all 13 slayings, but there are still doubts about his guilt. There is also a theory that the Strangler didn't act alone. Either way, there are still a lot of unanswered questions.

Which brings us to the biggest unanswered question in movie history: whose bright idea was it to cast Tony Curtis as the Boston Strangler, one of the worst serial killers in America's history? Given that Curtis had just starred in 12 romantic comedies in a row, it must be the worst bit of casting of all time. It was probably the same idiot who cast John Wayne and his American drawl as Genghis Khan in *The Conqueror*.

At the time Tony Curtis was America's heart-throb and in the prime of his career. Nine years earlier he had starred in what many critics acclaim as the greatest comedy of all time, *Some Like It Hot*, with Marilyn Monroe and Jack Lemmon.

Six pictures earlier, Tony Curtis had the world in stitches as the Great Leslie in *The Great Race*. Then another five romantic comedies and he turns up as Albert DeSalvo, a degenerate serial rapist, murderer and necrophile who strangles 13 women, some with their own soiled underwear, and then has sex with them after they are dead.

Tony Curtis is as convincing as the Boston Strangler as Elvis Presley would have been as Hitler. This and a multitude of factual errors – and the use of the annoying 'split screen' technique, where we see as many as four screens on the main screen at any one time, all going in different directions – make this movie a disaster.

It would be best if it had never been made at all. The innocent victims should have been allowed to rest in peace rather than be remembered in this piece of tripe.

Here is the true story.

Albert DeSalvo: The Boston Strangler

The horrors of what would become known as the Boston Strangler murders began with the brutal killing of 55-year-old Anna E Slesers, a divorcee who liked classical music and kept mostly to herself. Anna had taken a bath after her evening meal and was waiting for her son, Juris, to arrive to take her to the nearby Latvian church. But when Juris knocked on the door of the apartment at 77 Gainsborough Street at around 7pm on 14 June 1962 there was no answer. Concerned, Juris forced open the locked door. He was confronted by his mother's naked body on the floor of her bathroom, the cord of her bathrobe pulled tightly around her throat in a bow, choking the life out of her. The flat had been ransacked and her purse emptied over the floor. But despite the room looking like it had been burgled, valuable jewellery and a gold watch had been left behind.

The police arrived and ascertained that Anna had been sexually assaulted with an unknown object. They surmised that what had started out as a simple random burglary turned into rape when the culprit saw the woman and became aroused. According to their original theory, he then murdered the victim so that she wouldn't be able to identify him later.

A little over two weeks later, on 30 June, 68-year-old retired physiotherapist Nina Nichols – a widow for two decades who lived a relatively solitary life – met a similar gruesome end at her apartment at 1940 Commonwealth Street in the suburb of Brighton. Once again, the room looked like it had been the subject of a robbery; Nichols' possessions were strewn randomly around the floor and all of the drawers were opened. But, as in the Slesers case, valuable items had been left behind, including a camera and cash. Nichols' watch, too, remained on her lifeless wrist.

Investigating officers noted that the victim's legs were spread and two of her own nylon stockings were tied around her neck in a bow. They also found blood in her vagina. Death was estimated to have occurred at around 5pm. It turned out that the Strangler had been very busy that day.

Almost 25 kilometres north of Nichols' apartment, the flat of 65-year-old divorcee Helen Blake had been broken into between 8am and 10am that same day. The scene was almost a carbon copy of the previous two murders, with Blake's body found face-down on her bed, her legs apart and a pair of her own stockings around her neck as a murder weapon. This time the victim's bra was tied in a bow around the neck as well, and there were signs that both her anus and vagina had been violated with an unknown object. The apartment had been ransacked, and it appeared the culprit had made off with a pair of diamond rings from Blake's fingers.

Realising that the situation was growing more serious by the day, Police Commissioner Edmund McNamara issued a warning that all women in the Boston area should exercise extreme caution and be particularly careful of strangers. An investigation was launched into known mental patients with violent tendencies, as well as regular sex offenders. But, despite their efforts, the spree of violence continued.

The next victim was 75-year-old Ida Irga, who was murdered in similar circumstances on 19 August, though her body wasn't found until two days later. Irga was lying on her back on the living room floor of her apartment, a white pillowcase knotted around her neck and her legs spread open, with her feet propped up on chairs. A pillow was placed under her bottom, and there was dried blood around her head. Again, she had been sexually assaulted with an unknown object.

Less than 24 hours after Irga's murder, 67-year-old nurse Jane Sullivan also met her fate at the hands of the serial killer, though it would be 10 days before her body was discovered. When investigators entered Sullivan's apartment at 435 Columbia Road, Dorchester, they found her lifeless body in the bathtub, with the now signature stockings tied around her neck. Blood in the hallway, kitchen and bedroom suggested she had been murdered in one of those places and her body then moved to the bathroom. There was also blood found on a broom handle, indicating it may have been used to sexually violate her, but as the body was so decomposed it was impossible to say for sure.

It would be three months before the Strangler struck again, by which time Boston was gripped by terror. The next victim was considerably younger than previous ones. Popular African-American student Sophie Clark lived only blocks away from Anna Slesers. The 21-year-old's roommates discovered the body, nude with its legs spread and three pairs of stockings around her neck. Again, there was no sign of forced entry to the apartment, but this time – unlike the previous murders – semen was found next to the body. Clark had been writing a letter to her boyfriend at the time, and there were signs that she had struggled with her attacker. Her time of death was estimated to have been 2.30pm.

Interestingly, around 10 minutes earlier, one of Clark's neighbours, Marcella Lullka, had a man knock on her door claiming to have been sent by the building's superintendent to see about painting her flat and fixing the bathroom ceiling. The man, later described as being somewhere between 25 and 30 years old, then said she had a nice figure and asked if she had ever thought of modelling. However, the woman's husband was asleep in another room and when she motioned for the visitor to be quiet, the man's demeanour changed. He quickly left.

There was a three-week period before the next body was discovered. Patricia Bissette, a 23-year-old secretary for an engineering firm, lived in the same Back Bay area as Sophie Clark and Anna Slesers. When she failed to turn up at work on New Year's Eve 1962, her boss went to her flat at 515 Park Drive. Finding it locked, he got the janitor to help him climb in through a window. There they found Bissette in her bed, with the covers pulled up over her body, as if she were asleep. Further investigation revealed that she had several pairs of stockings knotted tightly around her neck, along with a blouse. The apartment had been searched, and there was evidence that her rectum had been tampered with, as well as signs of recent sexual acts. It was later revealed that Bissette was pregnant when she was murdered.

After Bissette's death the Strangler again went to ground for a while, not striking out again until 68-year-old Mary Brown was raped and strangled in early March 1963. Two months after that, on 8 May, the body of attractive 23-year-old student and aspiring opera singer Beverly Samans was found dead at her apartment after she failed to turn up for choir practice. Her body lay on a sofa bed with her legs spread apart. A pair of stockings and two handkerchiefs were knotted around her neck, and a piece of cloth was stuffed in her mouth, with another tied around it. Her hands were also bound behind her back with one of her own scarves. She had been dead for up to three days, but there was no sign of sexual abuse. Another difference this time was that while it looked like she had been strangled, death was actually caused by four stab wounds to the throat. The knife used was found in the sink. All up, Samans had been stabbed 22 times – 18 of those were dotted around her left breast in a bullseye pattern. The police believed that because she was a singer her throat was stronger than previous victims, making it harder to strangle her.

Another quiet period followed while the authorities followed what few leads they had, including enlisting the help of a man who claimed to be a clairvoyant. But the Boston Strangler was back in business on 8 September, when 58-year-old divorcee Evelyn Corbin was found strangled by two pairs of stockings in her Salem apartment. Her nude body lay face-up on her bed, her underpants were stuffed in her mouth, and tissues smeared in lipstick and containing traces of semen were found around the bed. There was also semen in her mouth, and the flat had also been ransacked, though nothing had been stolen. On the fire escape outside her window was a fresh doughnut that could not be accounted for.

Joann Graff, a deeply religious 23-year-old industrial designer, was the next woman to die at the hands of the Strangler. Her body was found in her ransacked apartment in the suburb of Lawrence in late November. Two pairs of stockings were tied around her neck in a bow. Her vagina showed signs of trauma, and there were teeth marks on her breast. This time, at least, there were vague leads in the case.

The morning before Graff's death, a woman living down the hall from her heard a noise outside her door, before a piece of paper was slipped under it and moved from side to side. The strange paper then slipped back out and the woman heard steps walking away.

Then at 3.25pm on the day of the murder, the tenant in the flat above Graff's heard footsteps in the hall and a knock on the door opposite. He looked outside and saw a man aged around 27, wearing dark green pants with a dark shirt and jacket. The stranger asked if Graff lived in the flat he was calling on, but he didn't pronounce her name correctly. After being told he had come to the wrong flat, the stranger left. Soon after, the man heard a knock at the door below his, Graff's. He then heard the door open and shut, and assumed the woman had let the visitor in. Graff received a phone call from a friend about 10 minutes after this, but there was no answer.

The Strangler didn't strike again until the New Year, when two women returned to their flat on 4 January 1964 to find their 19-year-old roommate Mary Sullivan sitting up in her bed with semen dripping from her mouth onto her bare breasts. She had been strangled with a pair of dark stockings, over which was a pink scarf tied into a bow. Over that was a pink and white scarf that featured a floral motif. The killer had left a 'Happy New Year' card at Sullivan's feet, and the handle of a broomstick was stuck a few inches up her vagina.

With the violence in the killings escalating, Massachusetts Attorney-General Edward Brooke was put in charge of the case. He chose a friend, Assistant Attorney-General John S Bottomly, to front the task force – called the Special Division of Crime Research and Detection – investigating the

Strangler. Two months later, with no firm leads, a $10,000 reward was offered to anyone with information that would lead to the arrest and conviction of the person responsible for the 11 'official' Strangler slayings. The forensic medical experts assigned to the case believed there were differences in the murders of the younger and older victims, and attributed those of the younger women to copycat murderers.

A couple of years before the Strangler terrorised Boston, the man who would later confess to the killings, Albert DeSalvo, was responsible for a string of sex crimes in the Cambridge area. In his late-twenties at the time, DeSalvo would call on the apartments of young women and tell them his name was Johnson, and that he worked for a modelling agency. After explaining that their name had been supplied by a friend who thought they would make a good model, 'Johnson' added that the woman would receive $40 an hour for modelling evening gowns and swimsuits, adding that the job didn't entail nude work. If the woman fell for his ruse, he told them he had been sent to get their measurements, at which point he would produce a tape measure. When none of the women received a follow-up call, some phoned the authorities. The police only nabbed DeSalvo when they caught him trying to break and enter a house on 17 March 1961. He confessed to the attempted break-in, and then told them he was also the culprit who had come to be known as 'The Measuring Man'.

Investigators learned that DeSalvo was 29 years old, lived in the suburb of Malden with his German wife Irmgard Beck and their two children. He worked in a rubber factory and had several prior arrests for breaking into flats. He was ultimately sentenced to 18 months for his crimes and, with time off for good behaviour, was released two months before Anna Slesers, the Strangler's first victim, was killed.

A boastful man who many believed would later exaggerate his crimes, DeSalvo grew up with a father who regularly beat him, his mother and four siblings. As a youth he was charged with assault and battery. He served in the army from 1948 until 1956, and was arrested for fondling a young girl in 1955, though the charge was later dropped. DeSalvo also had a huge sexual appetite, and as his wife would find out, required sexual release several times daily. It was later claimed that it would take more than one woman to satisfy DeSalvo's lustful cravings. Still, those who knew him believed DeSalvo was an honest man who was devoted to his family. This would change, however, in November 1964 when he was arrested again. He had broken into a sleeping woman's apartment, held a knife at her throat, stuffed a pair of her underwear in her mouth, and then tied her limbs to the four bedposts. He then started kissing and fondling her before saying sorry and abruptly leaving. Having had a good look at the man's distinctive face, she explained what he looked like in enough detail for the police to make a good sketch of the offender. The likeness resembled DeSalvo. He was brought into the station and the woman identified him immediately. He was later let out on bail, but his photo was sent around to other police stations. A call soon came in from officers in Connecticut, who were seeking a sex offender known as 'The Green Man', because of the pants he wore. The Green Man was known to have a voracious sexual appetite. He had once violated four women in one day, all in different locations around the city.

DeSalvo was soon arrested again, and told investigators that he had assaulted as many as 300 women in four states, though many would later believe this was an exaggeration. He was sent to Bridgewater State Hospital for observation, where he soon met another inmate named George Nassar, a vicious murderer with the IQ of a genius. The pair struck up a relationship and eventually hatched a plan revolving around the reward money offered for information about the Strangler murders. The pair believed the $10,000 reward related to each individual killing – thus coming to $110,000 in total when all 11 official victims were accounted for. The pair decided Nassar should turn DeSalvo in and they would later split the reward money.

By the time an investigation had been run, the authorities had more than 2000 pages transcribed from more than 50 hours of interviews in which DeSalvo talked about what happened during the various Strangler murders. The doubts some investigators had about the confession started to become clouded as DeSalvo revealed details only the murderer could know: inconsequential matters such as a notebook found under Beverly Samans' bed, and a raincoat taken from Anna Slesers' room.

But others still had their doubts, with many experts believing DeSalvo was merely admitting to the murders to big-note himself. Indeed, the man who lived above Joann Graff, who had been face-to-face with the murderer, did not recognise DeSalvo when shown a photo of him. In the end, though, it didn't seem to matter. The Commonwealth determined that DeSalvo was indeed responsible for the Strangler murders, but this still posed another problem – his confession was inadmissible as evidence.

Nonetheless, DeSalvo faced court on 10 January 1967 for the Green Man charges. Once all the evidence was heard, it took the jury just four hours to find him guilty of all charges. He was sentenced to life in prison, and taken to Walpole State Prison, where he was stabbed to death in 1973 in suspicious circumstances. His killers have never been identified.

The cult classic

Leonard Kastle's

The Honeymoon Killers

Starring

Tony Lo Bianco

Shirley Stoler

Marilyn Chris

TARTAN VIDEO

"Excellent"

FILMS AND FILMING

THE HONEYMOON KILLERS

(1970)

DIRECTED BY LEONARD KASTLE
SCREENPLAY BY LEONARD KASTLE

FEATURING

Shirley Stoler as Martha Beck
Tony Lo Bianco as Raymond Fernandez
Mary Jane Higby as Janet Fay
Doris Roberts as Bunny
Kip McArdle as Delphine Downing
Marilyn Chris as Myrtle Young

The Honeymoon Killers is an excellent black and white biopic. It is based on a couple known as 'The Lonely Heart Killers', Martha Beck and Raymond Fernandez. Beck is a pathetically sad, grossly obese nurse who gives the impression that her idea of fun is dressing up corpses for burial. So when she meets Fernandez through a lonely hearts club, and realises that he is just as hateful and evil as she is, they embark on a series of murders that eventually sees them joined in eternity by the flick of a switch – in the electric chair in Sing Sing.

Serial killers usually act alone. England's Fred and Rosemary West, and Myra Hindley and Ian Brady, as well as Australia's Catherine and David Birnie, are three exceptions that come to mind: gruesome double acts.

For over two decades in Gloucester, Fred West and his wife Rosemary raped, tortured and murdered at least 12 young people, including Fred's daughter, Heather. They buried nine of the bodies in the backyard.

Hindley and Brady were the notorious Moors Murderers who, beginning in 1965, tortured, raped, murdered and then buried the bodies of as many as six children and teenagers on the desolate moors north of Manchester. Police found tape recordings of the children begging for their lives as Hindley and Brady tortured, sexually assaulted and then strangled them.

In 1986 Western Australia's Catherine and David Birnie buried the bodies four young women in a pine plantation on the outskirts of Perth after drugging, sexually assaulting and murdering them in the Birnie family house. Their victims ranged in age from 15 to 31. Whenever the Birnies felt like killing someone they would drive along the highways of Perth and pick up hitchhikers or other young women in need of a lift. Their victims never suspected the friendly couple until it was too late.

If you want to see a very frightening movie, with echoes of all of the above partnerships, check out *The Honeymoon Killers*. The fact that despite its age it is readily available in most big rental shops, and on the internet, proves that it is still worth watching. Recommended viewing.

Martha Beck and Raymond Fernandez: The Lonely Hearts Killers

The story of Raymond Martinez Fernandez and Martha Jule Beck is one of deception, sex, loneliness, jealousy and murder. They claimed responsibility for the deaths of several females – including the two-year-old daughter of one of their victims. Their eventual trial, which included tales of 'abnormal sexual practices' between the plump woman and the scheming Spanish man, caused a scandal in the US in the 1940s.

The couple, nicknamed the Lonely Hearts Killers, first met after a lovelorn Martha joined 'Mother Dinene's Family Club for Lonely Hearts' looking for romance. Martha – who tipped the scales at around 115 kilograms – had a long history of loneliness and depression. The letter she received just before Christmas in 1947 from Raymond Fernandez's was her only response.

Martha was born in Florida in 1919. Due to a glandular condition at an early age, she matured well before her peers. Indeed, by the time she was 10 years old she had the physique of a grown woman, and the sex drive to match. But her large body drew taunts from her peers, as well as from her own mother.

It is believed that Martha was raped by her brother when she was a young girl. When she told her mother what had happened the woman beat her and claimed that it was her own fault. As Martha grew older, her mother would drive away any males interested in her daughter with abuse and loud threats of violence. It's little wonder that by the time Martha reached her teenage years she was already a confirmed loner.

Martha studied to become a nurse and finished at the top of her class. Still, the only job she could find afterwards was at a funeral parlour, where she was in charge of preparing females for burial. It was a position far below her skill level.

She moved to California in 1942 looking for a fresh start in life and found employment as a nurse at an army hospital. She also started trawling the local bars looking for companionship among the soldiers on leave, and soon fell pregnant to one. In a massive blow to her already low self-confidence, the man attempted suicide rather than marry the overweight nurse. This drove Martha further into a deep state of depression. As a result, she decided to return to

Florida, where she told everyone she had married an officer in the navy. She even bought a ring to back up her ruse. Later she organised to receive a telegram saying that her loving husband had been killed in action.

Martha gave birth to a daughter, whom she called Willa Dean, in 1944. Just a few months later she fell pregnant to a bus driver named Alfred Beck. He married her late that year, but the couple divorced after just six months. Looking for distraction from her troubles, Martha devoured romance novels and watched endless movies, escaping however briefly into the perfect celluloid world of dashing heroes and beautiful heroines.

She started working at the Pensacola children's hospital in 1946, and put her all into the job. As a result, she was promoted to superintendent of nurses by the end of the year, but her personal life was still filled with loneliness. In a final effort to find love and romance she placed an ad in 'Mother Dinene's Family Club for Lonely Hearts', conveniently neglecting to mention that she was overweight and had two children from prior relationships.

For two weeks she waited anxiously, growing more depressed every day. Finally the letter arrived that would change her life forever.

Born in Hawaii on 17 December 1914, Raymond Fernandez's proud Spanish parents were dismayed by their boy's weak appearance. The family relocated to Connecticut on the US mainland three years later, and in 1932 Raymond moved to Spain to work on the farm of an uncle. By the time he was 20 he had grown to be handsome and strong, and he wed a local named Encarnacion Robles. He joined the Spanish merchant marines during World War II and later became a spy with the British government.

After the war, Raymond decided to return to the US to find work. His intention was to send for his wife later, but when he was travelling there by freighter, a steel hatch crashed down on his head, causing him brain damage and keeping him in hospital for months. He came out of medical care a different person – moody, irritable and prone to running off at the mouth. He eventually found himself serving time in a Florida jail for stealing clothing.

It was while incarcerated that Raymond became involved with voodoo and the occult, and he came to believe that the mystical forces he was playing with gave him ultimate power over the opposite sex. He also believed he could have sexual relations with women, no matter where they were, just by using special powers.

Once Raymond was released from prison in 1946, he lived with his sister in Brooklyn, New York, where he would often complain of headaches and stay in his room for days. Here he would compose letters to vulnerable woman in lonely hearts clubs. After instigating friendships with the women, he would steal their money or other valuable items then disappear without a trace.

Fernandez had been doing this for months before Jane Thompson came into the picture in 1947. Like the other women Fernandez was in correspondence with, Thompson was bored and lonely and, after they had exchanged several letters, the pair arranged to meet. Thompson bought them both tickets for a cruise to Spain in October, where they travelled together as if they were married, which made things a little strange when they got to La Linea, where Fernandez's real wife was still living with their two children.

Still, the threesome managed to stay civil about the situation until 7 November, when Fernandez and Thompson had an argument in their hotel room. He was seen leaving the room late at night, and Thompson's dead body was found inside the next morning. She was buried before an autopsy could be carried out, but Fernandez had already left town anyway, catching a boat back to New York where he used a forged will to claim Thompson's apartment, kicking out her mother in the process.

All this time, Fernandez had maintained contact with Martha Beck, telling her he was a rich businessman involved in import and export. He told her he had moved to America from Spain for work, and that he lived alone. He mentioned that he wanted to get married. Martha fell hard for the charming man, and wrote to him on several occasions. After a while, Fernandez asked her to send him a lock of her hair. He used it in a voodoo spell designed to make Beck find him irresistible. Then it was time for the pair to meet in person.

Fernandez caught a train to Pensacola, arriving on 28 December 1947. Martha was very impressed by the good-looking man. The fact that he also seemed interested was a huge plus in her books. The pair went back to her house where she introduced Fernandez to her children and made him dinner. That night they made love for the first time, and repeated the act several times through the next day and night.

All the while, though, Fernandez was plotting a way to relieve Martha of her money and possessions. He told her he had to return to New York for business, and that he would either come back or send for her later. Martha figured this meant he was serious about her, and she told everyone she knew that wedding bells would soon be ringing again. There was even a bridal shower planned to celebrate, but on the day it was meant to happen Martha received another letter from Fernandez. This time he explained that he didn't return her feelings. It was a crushing blow for Martha, and she tried to kill herself. After hearing what had happened, Fernandez invited her to New York, where she stayed for two happy weeks. But, as usual, the good times wouldn't last.

No sooner was Martha back in Florida than she was fired with no explanation. With her severance pay, she packed up the children and caught the next bus back to New York, landing at Fernandez's apartment on 18 January 1948. But while the Spanish con man wasn't exactly thrilled to have the woman living with him, he had to admit that he liked the care and attention she provided. Still, he wouldn't put up with having the children there, so after a week Martha left them with the Salvation Army. She would barely think about them again for three years.

Once he had settled into domesticity with Martha, Fernandez admitted all of his dodgy dealings to her. He showed her the mountain of lonely hearts letters, and told her of the women he had deceived. Martha took it all in her stride, deciding that as she had finally found happiness she would do whatever it took to cling on to it. She even decided to help Fernandez fleece his next victim. They went through the letters and photos until they came across Esther Henne in Pennsylvania.

Once they'd settled on their prey they wasted no time. With Martha posing as Fernandez's sister-in-law, they visited Henne and in less than a week Fernandez had married the lonely woman. They all moved back to the New York apartment and Fernandez was soon trying to persuade Henne to sign her insurance and pension plans over to him. She refused and soon left the flat.

Still, in that short time Fernandez managed to squeeze several hundred dollars and a car out of her. More women were lured into similar traps over the next few months, with things seeming to go smoothly for the con artists until Arkansas woman Myrtle Young fell for Fernandez's charms. The pair were married on 14 August 1948, but a jealous Martha – posing as Fernandez's sister – was determined not to let the newlyweds consummate the relationship.

Once Myrtle started complaining that Martha was even sleeping in bed with her, Fernandez drugged his latest victim, rendering her unconscious before putting her on a bus home. When she arrived back in Arkansas, Myrtle had to be physically lifted off the bus by police. She died in hospital the next day. Martha and Fernandez had pocketed $4000 for their efforts, and on their way back to New York, the pair took the opportunity to visit several women that Fernandez had been writing to, conning money off them whenever they could.

When their ill-gotten funds started to dry up, they once again cast their eyes over the lonely hearts ads. They soon found 66-year-old widow Janet Fay. Fernandez – using the name Charles Martin – spent weeks working on the deeply religious woman from Albany, New York, before she agreed to meet him. Martha and Fernandez arrived in Albany on 30 December 1948 and found a hotel to book into as man and wife.

Fernandez started his sting operation the next day, arriving at Fay's house with flowers and talking about religion. In the following days, he introduced her to his 'sister' Martha. Not long after that he proposed. Fay said yes, and quickly withdrew all of her money from local banks, a sum of more than $6000. She left Albany with Martha and Fernandez on 4 January with the intention of moving to Long Island, where Martha had already rented a flat.

After arriving at the Long Island apartment, the trio had supper and Fernandez went to bed first. What exactly happened after that is still a mystery, but Martha claims to have blacked out and come to with a dead Fay laying bloody at her feet, beaten with a hammer and then strangled with a scarf tied into a tourniquet around her neck.

The next day, Fernandez and Martha put the body into a large trunk and later buried it in the cellar of a rented house. They also typed up letters to Fay's family posing as the dead woman, explaining that she was happy and getting married and moving to Florida. They signed Fay's name and sent the letters off, not realising Fay didn't own a typewriter. Her worried family contacted the police.

Martha and Fernandez soon moved to their next victim, a 41-year-old widow and mother named Delphine Downing in Grand Rapids, Michigan. Downing was attracted to her suitor, and they were soon having sex, much to Martha's dismay. Still, the charade was going well until Downing walked into her bathroom one day and saw Fernandez without his toupee. She couldn't believe he had hidden his baldness from her, as well as the big, ugly scar on his head. Nothing 'Charles' said would calm her, but Martha eventually convinced her to take some sleeping pills. They did the job, but Downing's two-year-old daughter Rainelle soon began to cry. Martha started to choke the child, leaving bruising around the neck.

Fernandez pointed out that Downing would go to the police if she saw the marks. Then he got out a gun that had belonged to Downing's dead husband and shot the sleeping woman in the head while her daughter watched. They buried the body in the basement and spent the next two days scouring the house for money. The shocked child cried the entire time. Not knowing what to do, Martha drowned her in a metal tub and buried her in the basement next to her mother.

The smart move would have been to leave town, but instead the couple stuck around. They went to watch a film, before returning to Downing's flat to pack up their belongings. But before they could make their getaway, there was a knock on the door. Concerned neighbours had called the police. Martha and Fernandez were arrested on 28 February 1949.

They readily admitted to their crimes and signed a confession that ran to 73 pages in return for a promise that they would be tried in Michigan, where there was no death penalty, rather than be extradited to New York to face justice for the murder of Janet Fay. As it stood, there was a chance Fernandez could walk out of jail free in six years with time off for good behaviour.

The press, of course, were quick to leap on the story, and they certainly helped fuel the idea that Martha Beck and Raymond Fernandez should be sentenced to death. As a result, a deal was made with the prosecutors. Criminal charges in the Downing murders would be dropped and Martha and Fernandez would be extradited to New York to be brought to justice for the murder of Janet Fay.

The trial began before Judge Ferdinand Pecora in Bronx Supreme Court on 28 June 1949, with just one attorney, a young man named Herbert Rosenberg, representing both of the accused. The prosecutor, Nassau County District Attorney Edward Robinson Jr, called his witnesses first – these included friends of Janet Fay, as well as her landlord.

Fernandez didn't take the stand until 11 July, at which time he recanted his prior confession, explaining that he had made it only in an attempt to save his beloved Martha. Robinson, however, would not stand for the deception, and was quick to remind the court that Myrtle Young, Jane Thompson and both Delphine and Rainelle Downing were all dead after meeting the smooth, well-spoken Spanish man on the stand.

The detailed confession that Fernandez had already made was another blow to his case. Robinson read out passages in which Martha, in gruesome detail, had described Fernandez's role in the murders. The tabloids ate it up. They also relished descriptions of the lurid sexual escapades between Fernandez and his victims, including a game of strip poker he had played with Esther Henne and Martha Beck (posing as his sister-in-law). At the climax of the game, the winner of the hand would spend the night with Fernandez. Much to her delight, Martha had the best cards when it counted. By the time Martha was called to speak, public interest in the salacious trial had reached fever pitch.

When the plump woman finally took the stand on 25 July she was dressed more in keeping with a summer picnic than a life-or-death court case. She told her tale of a sad and sorry childhood, raped by her own brother and brought up longing for love. She spoke of several suicide attempts and her dreams of finding Mr Right and settling down to live a normal life.

She also admitted that she knew of Fernandez's murderous ways, and that she had helped him find his lonely victims. She sometimes laughed when explaining how easy it had been for her lover to dupe the sad, older women out of their money.

In her three days on the stand, Martha could be so graphic in the description of her sex life with Fernandez that the more pious females walked out of the room. Crowds forced their way into the court when Martha described sexual practices connected with voodoo, and police reinforcements had to be called in to battle a 'near riot'.

The trial was finally bought to a close on 18 August and the jury of 10 men and two women found both Martha Beck and Raymond Fernandez guilty of first-degree murder. Neither defendant looked at all shocked by the result. Both were sentenced to death by electric chair.

On 8 March 1950 they both received their punishment in front of at least 52 witnesses.

10 RILLINGTON PLACE

(1971)

DIRECTED BY RICHARD FLEISCHER
SCREENPLAY BY CLIVE EXTON

FEATURING
Richard Attenborough as John Reginald 'Reg' Christie
Pat Heywood as Mrs Ethel Christie
John Hurt as Timothy John Evans
Judy Geeson as Beryl Evans
Isobel Black as Alice
Phyllis MacMahon as Muriel Eady

Be prepared to meet one very scary guy in this true-life classic: necrophiliac serial killer, London's John Christie. Among the most heinous fiends who ever lived, over a 13-year period he murdered his way to the scaffold in Pentonville prison. By the time he was finally captured in 1953, John Reginald Halliday Christie had murdered seven women, including his wife and the baby daughter of one of his victims.

Christie gassed the women, strangled them and then raped their corpses.

The Christie murders case is one of the most famous in the world, but not especially for the murders themselves. Rather his notoriety stems from the fact that Timothy Evans, the dim-witted lorry driver husband of a Christie victim, Beryl Evans, and the father of the murdered baby Geraldine, was incorrectly hanged for his daughter's murder, while the real killer temporarily went free to kill again.

Richard Attenborough's performance as Christie is mesmerising. So, too, is John Hurt's portrayal of the intellectually retarded Evans: who could ever forget the spine-chilling scene in court when Evans, who had just been sentenced to death by hanging, points to Christie, the chief witness against him, and says: 'It was Christie what done it, Christie done it'.

Director Richard Fleischer strove for technical perfection, but he ran into a problem when re-enacting the scene when Timmy Evans is hanged because details of all hangings were still protected by the Official Secrets Act. To get around this problem, Fleischer secretly employed the services of the hangman, Albert Pierrepoint, who provided him with every grisly detail. Thus it was the first time that British cinema-goers got to see the real horror of a hanging.

The setting for *10 Rillington Place* is exactly where it happened: the depressing squalor of Notting Hill in postwar London. In those days it was possibly the worst bit of residential real estate on the planet. These days it's 'Millionaire's Row', and John Christie's home and killing field has long been bulldozed into oblivion.

10 Rillington Place is factual horror at it ugliest, and a truly brilliant piece of cinema. Not to be missed at any cost.

The John Christie Murders

Two separate arrests of different men in the one three-storey Victorian house in Notting Hill, London, in 1949 were later followed by two confessions of murder and two executions. But to this day there is doubt as to whether both men were actually guilty, or if one was set up by the other.

John Reginald Halliday Christie took up residence in the small, rundown ground floor apartment of 10 Rillington Place in 1938, along with his wife Ethel and their pet dog and cat. As a child, Christie would often overplay any ill health in order to garner more attention. He had been brought up in an environment that contrasted the violence his father doled out on the frail child, with the excessive love his overprotective mother showered upon him. He also had four older sisters who did their best to boss him around.

A major turning point in his life occurred at the age of eight, when Christie's grandfather died. Even though he had always been frightened of his mother's father, when Christie saw the corpse laying in its open casket, he was pleased to note that he was no longer scared of the man. After that, the young boy took to playing in graveyards.

When Christie was 10 years old, he caught a glimpse of his sister's naked thighs. The sight left the shy, inhibited child sexually conflicted. It was a feeling that would remain for the rest of his life, manifesting itself in a love–hate relationship with women. He was tempted by the pleasures of the flesh, but was unable to satisfy them. Indeed, when some of his first amorous encounters with females ended in failure, he earned nicknames among the neighbourhood such as 'Can't-Make-It-Christie'. He would be plagued by impotence for the rest of his days.

After leaving school aged 15, Christie worked as a movie projectionist. He joined the army as a signalman after World War I broke out, where he was knocked unconscious and temporarily blinded when a mustard gas shell exploded. He also lost his voice for three years, though doctors believed it was a psychiatric, rather than physical ailment.

After leaving the service, Christie found employment as a clerk, and, in 1920, married Ethel Simpson Waddington. His sexual problems hadn't abated, and Christie continued to see prostitutes after their wedding. He also changed jobs, becoming a postman. While working in this role, though, he was sent to prison for three months for stealing postal orders. Once he was released, he continued to have spates of silence. He moved to London, leaving Ethel at home in Sheffield.

When Christie was 29, he was again sent to jail, this time serving nine months for a variety of stealing charges. Once released he worked in various jobs and moved in with a prostitute, but again found himself in jail for six months after an argument with the woman ended with him taking a cricket bat to her head.

Christie continued to drift aimlessly after his release, and he was eventually incarcerated again for stealing a car from a priest. While inside, he contacted Ethel and asked if she would give him another chance. Lonely, she agreed and the couple were reunited in London in 1933, after a decade apart. But it wasn't to be a smooth ride. Christie was hit by a car and hospitalised for a while. Severe hypochondria followed, and he later signed up as a volunteer member of the War Reserve Police while World War II was brewing.

Issued a uniform and allocated the rank of special constable for Harrow Road police station, Christie was for once happy with his life. He stayed in the position for four years, and was so intent on maintaining law and order he was nicknamed the 'Himmler of Rillington Place'. Little did people know he was using his position to illicitly follow women. He even drilled a peephole through his kitchen door to keep watch on his unsuspecting neighbours.

During this time, Ethel would often visit relatives out of town. Christie seized this opportunity and began to see other women. He also developed strange sexual proclivities that would later manifest themselves in habits such as collecting female pubic hair.

Ten years after Christie and Ethel moved into the apartment at 10 Rillington Place, 24-year-old Timothy Evans and his pregnant wife Beryl, 19, rented out the flat on the top floor. It was 1948, and the couple had been married for less than a year.

A short man with a quick temper and a consuming fondness for alcohol, Evans' father had abandoned him before he was even born. He was prone to tantrums as a child, and often made up stories that cast him in a favourable light, even though his IQ was around 70. Even as an adult, the simple man could barely read.

The marriage of Evans and Beryl grew strained once their daughter, Geraldine, was born. The couple fought, often physically, and Beryl would sometimes neglect the child. What little money Evans brought in was barely enough to cover their living costs. Things only got harder in August 1949 when Beryl's 17-year-old friend, Lucy Endecott, moved in with the couple. Lucy slept in the bed with Beryl, while Evans bedded down on the kitchen floor. But Lucy eventually aroused feelings in the older man, and the pair soon moved out together, though it wasn't long before Lucy insisted he vacate their flat because Evans was just too violent for the young girl.

Back living with his wife, broke and constantly bickering, Beryl soon revealed that she was pregnant again. She tried various methods to terminate the pregnancy, and spoke to several people – including the Christies – about her desire to get an abortion.

While all this was going on, the tenant on the second floor, a man named Kitchener, went to hospital, leaving his apartment vacant for more than a month, and, on 31 October, tradesmen arrived to rip out several walls and sections of floor, as well as work on the communal washhouse at the rear of the residence.

The stage was set for murder, but there remain varying accounts as to what exactly happened. Christie later claimed that he saw Beryl Evans leaving the premises at lunchtime on 8 November with her baby, and that he never saw her again. He said that at midnight that night, though, he and his wife were awoken by a loud noise in one of the flats above, followed by what sounded like someone moving around a heavy object. With Kitchener in hospital, that left the top floor, where Evans lived with Beryl, as the origin of the noises.

The following day, Evans supposedly told the Christies that Beryl had moved back to Bristol. A day after that, he told the Christies that he was selling up and joining his wife. Except when he left town it was by train to his aunt's house in Merthyr Vale. He returned six days later, informing Christie that Beryl had left him, then he went back to Merthyr Vale.

Another version of these events has Beryl confiding in Lucy Endecott that Christie had told her he would abort her unborn child for her. Evans is believed to have heard of the plan on 1 November, and told Christie not to proceed. But Beryl was determined to go ahead with her decision. The couple later argued again when Evans found out Beryl had spent money he had given her to pay for the house on other items. Evans stormed off, not returning until later that evening.

He went to work on 7 November, at which time Beryl arranged with Christie to perform the illegal operation the next day. The couple again argued over her decision that evening. The altercation is believed to have turned physical.

The next morning, Evans left for work and the tradesmen returned at around 8am. At lunchtime, Christie went up to Beryl's room, where she panicked during the procedure. He started to hit her. Then he apparently strangled her with a cord. He may have also tried to have intercourse with her, either before, during or after the attack.

When Evans returned from work that day, Christie told him the operation hadn't worked. Evans then went into his bedroom where he found Beryl under a blanket, dead. Blood ran from her nose, mouth and vagina. Christie said that the cause of death may have been septic poisoning, before explaining that the police would probably charge both men with manslaughter if they knew what had happened. Evans agreed that they should keep quiet about the matter. The pair then carried Beryl's lifeless body into Kitchener's apartment, leaving it in the kitchen where Christie intended to later force the corpse down a drain.

At this point, Evans decided to take his daughter Geraldine to stay with his mother, but Christie believed it would cause suspicion. The next day, he told Evans he would look after the child, explaining that he would leave her with a couple he knew. Evans was to tell everyone that his wife and child were on vacation. Geraldine died the next day. It's believed Christie strangled her, then left the body with Beryl's in Kitchener's flat, but later relocated both cadavers to the washhouse, once the tradesmen had completed their work there.

He then persuaded Evans to sell his belongings and get out of town. Evans complied by returning to Merthyr Vale. But once questions about his wife and baby started to be asked, Evans crumbled and he was soon at Merthyr Vale police station saying: 'I have disposed of my wife. I put her down the drain.' He added that though Beryl was dead, he had not been the one who killed her, but that a stranger had helped his wife terminate her pregnancy using medication that had caused her death. After looking after his child for the night, Evans told the authorities, he became scared he would be blamed for his wife's death, so he put her body down a drain outside his front door by himself.

The police contacted their colleagues in Notting Hill, who went around to 10 Rillington Place. They knew Evans' story was a lie when it took three of them to remove the cover over the drain he had spoken of. There was also no body down there. Confronted with these facts, a shocked Evans changed his tune, telling them Christie had put Beryl down the drain after giving her something to abort her unborn child that had instead caused her to die herself. The authorities started looking deeper into the matter, but apparently overlooked vital evidence, such as a human thighbone in the garden at 10 Rillington Place, or the human skull Christie's dog later dug up. Still, they found something else of interest.

In Evans' flat were newspaper clippings about the then infamous Stanley Setty murder case. They also uncovered a stolen briefcase, which was cause enough to arrest him and take him to London. Christie was also bought in for questioning, as was his wife. Christie told the authorities that Evans was a liar who beat his wife.

With Beryl and Geraldine Evans still missing, the police returned to 10 Rillington Place, where they finally checked out the washhouse. Inside a sink there, they found a package containing Beryl Evans' strangled body. They then located Geraldine's body behind the door. she, too, had been strangled, and a man's tie remained around her neck. An autopsy was conducted and it was determined that Beryl had been dead for more than three weeks. There were also signs of bruising inside her vagina, though no check was conducted for semen.

Evans was soon arrested for murder, and he went on to confess that he had murdered Beryl because she kept getting the family into debt. He said they had fought and that he had hit her before strangling her with a piece of rope. Two days after that, he quit his job and killed his baby girl, strangling her with a tie and placing her body with her mother's in the washhouse. In another confession he went into more detail, but also said he had locked the washhouse behind him, which could not have been true, as the tradesmen had spent the week going in and out of the room. Many pundits believe the police led Evans through his confession, and that he was threatened with violence if he didn't admit to the murders.

Evans faced court at the Old Bailey on 11 January 1950. Christie was the main witness for the prosecution. Helping their case immensely were four separate confessions made by Evans, as well as physical evidence to back up his claims. After a trial that saw the defence try to pin the blame on Christie, it took the jury just 40 minutes to find Evans guilty. He was sentenced to death and was sent to the gallows on 9 March 1950.

After the trial, Christie fell into a deep depression that saw him lose several kilograms. He also lost his job, and, with nothing to do all day, was constantly getting in his wife's way. The pair weren't getting on, and Ethel often teased Christie about his sexual dysfunction. Around mid-December, she disappeared, and Christie told their neighbours she had gone to Sheffield, where he would soon join her. Around this time, he began to lay a strong-smelling disinfectant around the house and garden.

Come January, Christie sold his furniture and Ethel's wedding ring. With no job, he forged his wife's signature and took all the funds from her bank account. He then had his dog put down and gave his cat to the neighbours and went on the run.

Before long Ethel's naked body was discovered under the floorboards, along with the bodies of three other women in a large cavity behind recently applied wallpaper. The other three were prostitutes Hectorina McLennan, 26, Kathleen Maloney, 26, and Rita Nelson, 25. Further investigation revealed the remains of two other females in the garden. Christie later admitted to having sex with the women while he strangled the life out of them. While there is speculation he also performed necrophilia, there is no evidence, except for the circumstantial fact that he kept the corpses in and around his home long after their deaths.

Broke and with nowhere to stay, Christie was spotted by a policeman on the bank of the Thames River on 31 March 1953. Taken to Putney police station, he openly spoke about four of the murdered women found at his house, but didn't mention anything about the bodies found in the garden. When later confronted with evidence, though, he admitted to those killings as well.

Christie was put into Brixton prison while awaiting trial, where psychiatrists found him unpleasant to deal with. He also told other inmates his goal had been to murder 12 women. When authorities confronted him about the murders of Beryl and Geraldine Evans, his story wavered. At first he claimed he was innocent, then he admitted to killing the woman but not the child.

Christie faced court at the Old Bailey on 22 June 1953. He pleaded not guilty by reason of insanity. His own defence team painted a picture of a psychotic madman who didn't understand the gravity of his murderous actions. The trial was over in four days, with the jury taking just 80 minutes to find Christie guilty. He was sentenced to death and hanged on 15 July 1953.

In the subsequent years there have been public inquiries as well as several books trying to clear Evans' name and pin the blame – despite his confession – for the deaths of his wife and baby daughter on Christie. None have so far been successful, even though Christie himself at one time claimed responsibility for the death of Beryl Evans.

The last inquiry, conducted in 1965, stated that Evans had killed his wife, but that Christie had murdered Geraldine Evans and convinced Evans to keep quiet about the matter. As a result, Evans was granted a posthumous pardon of killing his little girl.

Detective
Harry Callahan.

You don't assign
him to murder cases.

You just turn him
loose.

Clint Eastwood
Dirty Harry

CLINT EASTWOOD in "DIRTY HARRY" A Malpaso Company Production Co-Starring HARRY GUARDINO · RENI SANTONI · ANDY ROBINSON · JOHN
LARCH and JOHN VERNON as "The Mayor" · Executive Producer Robert Daley · Screenplay by Harry Julian Fink & R. M. Fink and Dean Riesner
Story by Harry JULIAN Fink & R. M. Fink · Produced and Directed by Don Siegel · PANAVISION® · TECHNICOLOR® · Warner Bros., A Kinney Company

DIRTY HARRY

(1971)

DIRECTED BY DON SIEGEL
SCREENPLAY BY HARRY JULIAN FINK
AND RITA M FINK

FEATURING

Clint Eastwood as Inspector Harry Callahan
Harry Guardino as Lieutenant Al Bressler
Reni Santoni as Inspector Chico Gonzalez
John Vernon as the mayor
Andy Robinson as the Scorpio killer
John Larch as the chief

'Go ahead, make my day.'
Sorry, you lose. Although this immortal movie cliché is so often accredited to Inspector Harry Callahan in *Dirty Harry*, this character never actually said it. Well, not in *Dirty Harry*, anyway. He said it 12 years later in *Sudden Impact*.

What he did say in *Dirty Harry* has become almost as famous. As the terrified bank robber reached for his shottie – while looking up the barrel of the most powerful handgun in the world, one that could blow a man's head clean off – Harry asks: 'You've got to ask yourself one question: Do I feel lucky? Well, do ya, punk?'

This is our introduction to Harry, spoken as he bumps off a gang of bank robbers in the heart of San Francisco's CBD, his .44 magnum in one hand, a hot dog in the other. But we soon find out that *Dirty Harry* has a little more depth, and a much more interesting plot, than your average shoot-'em-up.

Frank Sinatra was originally intended to play Harry Callahan and while the Oscar winner (*From Here to Eternity*) was keen, he had to pull out of the original production because of a hand injury. The role was then offered to John Wayne who refused what would become one of the best known movie characters in history because he 'didn't want one of Sinatra's leftovers'. Paul Newman was the next to knock it back, but told the producers it would be a perfect part for a young bloke on the way up named Clint Eastwood. The rest is history. And it's hard to imagine anyone else playing the part.

What a lot of people wouldn't realise is that behind all the shoot-outs and snappy dialogue, this is a serial killer movie. The killer is never referred to as a serial killer because the term didn't come into vogue until 1988, when it first featured in a movie called *Cop*. *Dirty Harry* was released in 1971.

The character of Scorpio, who Harry pursues to the death through the streets of San Francisco, was purportedly modelled on a real-life murderer in California in 1968 and '69. Calling himself 'Zodiac', he killed five people and wounded two more over a year-long period. There is a chapter on Zodiac and the 2007 movie release of the same name on page 391.

Zodiac followed up his killings with letters to San Francisco newspapers, supplying gruesome details that only the killer could have known. He also gave cryptic clues as to when and where the next killings would be. Each letter was signed by a symbol of the zodiac: a cross superimposed on a circle. And so *Dirty Harry*'s Scorpio torments the city of San Francisco, with demands for money and threats to kill more randomly chosen members of the community.

This is one of the great serial killer movies. The plot is terrific, with lots and lots of action, and the dialogue is oh, so cool. The actors are perfect, especially Andy Robinson, who plays one of the most hateful villains you will ever see, and then, of course, there's Clint.

Even after all this time it isn't dated. And, if you've seen it before, it's still as good as the first time.

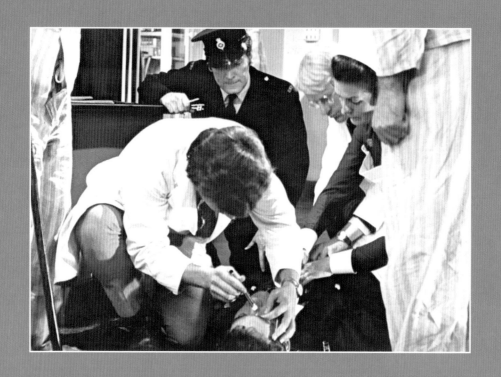

FRENZY

(1972)

DIRECTED BY ALFRED HITCHCOCK
WRITTEN BY ANTHONY SHAFFER

STARRING
Jon Finch as Richard Ian Blaney
Alec McCowen as Chief Inspector Oxford
Barry Foster as Robert Rusk
Billie Whitelaw as Hetty Porter
Anna Massey as 'Babs' Milligan
Bernard Cribbins as Felix Forsythe

It had been 12 years since Alfred Hitchcock made *Psycho* – he was obviously waiting for the right idea before he embarked on another serial killer thriller. Two series of serial murders took place during the 1960s, and these were the inspiration for what would become another Hitchcock classic – *Frenzy*.

In Boston, USA, from 1962 to 1964, a heinous fiend named Albert DeSalvo raped and strangled 13 women in their homes. DeSalvo's victims ranged from young students to elderly women. The killer's calling card was that he tied a neat bow beneath the victim's chin with the murder weapon, which was usually their underwear or a bathrobe cord. He became known as the Boston Strangler.

Then, in London, throughout 1964 and early into 1965, the naked bodies of six prostitutes were found either floating in the Thames or lying in public areas very close to it. The murders were undoubtedly the work of the same monster. The press were quick to dub him 'Jack the Stripper'.

In the same fashion as the *Boston Strangler* and *Jack the Stripper*, the elusive killer in *Frenzy* also leaves a 'signature' in that he strangled his victims with a necktie. A succession of naked victims of the Necktie Killer are found in the Thames and all over London. An innocent man is accused of the murders and the hunt is on for the real killer.

But it is the Hitchcock brand of black humour that gives *Frenzy* its class. The dialogue at dinner between the ever-so-proper police inspector and his wife is priceless. He explains the day-to-day developments of the grisly Necktie Murders while she dishes him up equally gruesome meals she has learnt in her home-cooking classes. This is definitely a film not to be missed.

For full story of the Boston Strangler murders, turn to page 87.

Jack the Stripper

Jack the Stripper's career began on 2 February 1964, when a Thames boatman discovered the body of a naked woman floating in the river. The cadaver was later identified as a 30-year-old prostitute, Hannah Tailford. Her stockings were wrapped around her ankles and her knickers had been stuffed deep into her mouth. Her autopsy revealed that Hannah had died by drowning.

The police had much more important things to do than investigate the death of a street prostitute who could have died from any one of a hundred misadventures. After only briefly looking into the matter it was handed on to a coronial inquest. Not surprisingly, the inquest returned an open verdict in the belief that the death may have been murder, suicide or a depraved customer's sexual game that had gone too far.

On 9 April 1964 another naked body of a prostitute was found floating in the Thames, this time just 300 metres from where Hannah Tailford was found. It was the body of 20-year-old Irene Lockwood, who had also drowned. Irene was four months pregnant at the time of her death.

Then, just two weeks later, on 24 April, the body of 20-year-old prostitute Helen Barthelmy was found dumped on the edge of a football field in Brentwood. Apart from all of her clothes, four of Helen's front teeth were missing and one had become lodged in her throat. Traces of spray paint were found on her body.

Now officially a murder case with three victims, the press at first referred to the investigation as the 'Nude Murders', with the killer christened 'Jack the Stripper'. Jack didn't let the papers down. Over the next nine months three more bodies turned up – all unmistakably the same killer.

Three days after she had gone missing on 11 July 1964, the naked body of 21-year-old prostitute, Mary Fleming, was found dumped on a London street. Mary's dentures were missing and she had been suffocated or choked to death.

Then, after she hadn't been seen for a month and her friends feared the worst, the nude body of 21-year-old street-walker Margaret McGowan was found in Kensington on 25 November 1964. One of Margaret's front teeth had been prised out, as if with a pair of pliers, and there were traces of paint on her skin. She had been suffocated to death.

After last being seen alive on 11 January 1965, the naked body of 27-year-old prostitute Bridget O'Hara was found dumped in some undergrowth on the Heron Trading Estate in Acton five weeks later on 16 February 1965. Bridget's body was partially mummified having apparently been stored in a cool, dry place for over a month. She had also been suffocated to death.

It was also suspected by investigators that Jack the Stripper may have been responsible for the much earlier murders of two other prostitutes in similar circumstances. On 17 June 1959, 21-year-old prostitute Elizabeth Figg's body was found floating in the Thames wearing only a slip. It was believed she had been strangled. And on 8 November 1963, the skeletal remains of another prostitute, Gwyneth Rees, who had been missing for some time, were discovered buried in a rubbish dump. The exact cause of her death was never determined. No conclusion was reached as to whether or not their deaths were the handiwork of Jack the Stripper.

The closest police ever got to capturing Jack the Stripper was the arrest of a suspect named Kenneth Archibald who confessed to the murder of Irene Lockwood in April 1964. Archibald later retracted his confession, telling police that he had only said it because he was depressed. But police wouldn't have a bar of it and he was charged and went to trial. Archibald must have breathed a sigh of relief though, because while he was on remand awaiting his trial, the bodies kept turning up. There was little doubt that whoever had killed Irene Lockwood was also killing other women while Archibald was behind bars. Archibald was acquitted.

After the murder of Bridget O'Hara in early 1965, Jack the Stripper disappeared, leaving police no closer to catching the killer than they were a year earlier.

In his 1973 memoirs about the Jack the Stripper case *Murder Was My Business*, the head of the investigation, Inspector John Du Rose, claimed that he knew who the killer was. He wrote that he believed it to be a private security guard employed at the Heron Trading Estate, where the last victim was found.

Inspector Du Rose's suspicions were based largely on the fact that there was a paint shop on the estate to which the security guard had access and he believed the bodies were kept there before they were dumped. This would explain the paint residue on some of the victims.

Unfortunately, the unnamed suspect gassed himself to death in his kitchen soon after the last victim was discovered. He left a single line suicide note that told investigators nothing: 'I cannot go on' it said, neither admitting guilt or denying it.

Inspector Du Rose also had a theory as to how the killer came to damage some of his victim's teeth. The inspector maintained that the fact that four of the victims had damage to their teeth, and Mary Fleming had her metal plate removed altogether, was because they were all victims of prolonged oral rape. That they had all suffocated could also mean that the killer's unique method of murder was to choke his victims on his penis and then dispose of their bodies.

Whatever, it seems as though we shall never know. Unlike Alfred Hitchcock's *Frenzy*, there is no end to it all. The Jack the Stripper case remains unsolved to this day.

BURTON IS
'BLUEBEARD'

He had a way with the world's most beautiful, most seductive, most glamorous women

...he

did

away

with

them.

RAQUEL WELCH
beautiful body ...suffocated

KARIN SCHUBERT
beautiful body ...shot

**SYBIL DANNING
NATHALIE DELON**
beautiful bodies
...chandeliered

VIRNA LISI
beautiful body ...guillotined

MARILU' TOLO
beautiful body ...drowned

AGOSTINA BELLI
beautiful body...falconated

JOEY HEATHERTON   beautiful body......

ALEXANDER SALKIND presents RICHARD BURTON as "BLUEBEARD" Also starring RAQUEL WELCH with VIRNA LISI · NATHALIE DELON · MARILU' TOLO · KARIN SCHUBERT
AGOSTINA BELLI · SYBIL DANNING and JOEY HEATHERTON as "Anne" · with EDWARD MEEKS as "Sergio" · JEAN LEFEBVRE and MATHIEU CARRIERE as "The Violinist"
An EDWARD DMYTRYK Film · Original Story and Screenplay by ENNIO DI CONCINI · EDWARD DMYTRYK · MARIA PIA FUSCO · Music by ENNIO MORRICONE. Publisher:
General Music, Roma · Executive in charge of Production PIERRE SPENGLER · Executive Producer ILYA SALKIND   Produced by ALEXANDER SALKIND · EASTMANCOLOR
FROM CINERAMA RELEASING

RESTRICTED
R Under 17 requires accompanying
Parent or Adult Guardian

BLUEBEARD

(1972)

DIRECTED BY EDWARD DMYTRYK
AND LUCIANO SACRIPANTI
SCREENPLAY BY ENNIO DE CONCINI
AND EDWARD DMYTRYK

FEATURING

Richard Burton as Baron von Sepper
Joey Heatherton as Anne
Raquel Welch as Magdalena
Virna Lisi as Elga
Nathalie Delon as Erika
Sybil Danning as a prostitute
Agostina Belli as Caroline

Although he famously never won an Oscar, Richard Burton made some great movies (*Where Eagles Dare, Who's Afraid of Virginia Woolf* and *Becket* for instance), but this flesh-fest isn't one of them. We can only imagine how quickly it would have sunk into the quagmire of Hollywood turkeys had Dick not been in it at all. Complete with a funny-coloured beard, Burton plays the high camp Baron von Sepper. It's quite enough to make the mythical original Bluebeard take up misogyny.

In keeping with the fairytale, the baron kills his first six wives. But then the baron conveniently tells number seven, Anne, the only Yank, what he has done and how he did it. The viewer, meanwhile, is treated to ludicrous flashbacks. One missus wouldn't shut up, so he chopped off her head. Another laughed when he couldn't get it up, so her shot her. One died on the end of a rhinoceros tusk after she had sex with another woman. For some obscure reason, the great bearded lover sent his falcon to kill yet another. He probably bored the others to death.

Groan. By this stage you're saying who cares anyway?

The only saving grace in this debacle is Joey Heatherton, who plays Anne, and delivers her lines as if she's on crystal meth. Although you can't help but think that all the wives must have been on drugs to have had anything to do with the very suspect baron. It was obviously not the intention, but Joey is wonderful comic relief in an appalling movie that takes itself seriously. It should have been billed as a comedy without any laughs, except the embarrassing ones.

Instead of watching this trip, you would be better off finding the original *Bluebeard* fairy tale – albeit a very grim example – and reading it.

The great tragedy, of course, is that but for just a couple of halfway decent movies, it was all downhill from here on for Richard Burton. The booze, cigarettes, wives and good times got the better of him. He died in 1984 aged just 58. Judging by his performance in this clunker, it would be fair to guess that if he had his life to live again, this – and possibly marrying Liz Taylor for the second time – would be something he would give a giant miss.

Meet the maniac & his friend.

Together they make the greatest team in the history of mass slaughter in...

EATEN ALIVE!

Mardi Rustam presents a new horror classic by TOBE HOOPER, creator of "THE TEXAS CHAIN-SAW MASSACRE"

Starring NEVILLE BRAND · MEL FERRER · CAROLYN JONES as Miss Hattie
MARILYN BURNS · WILLIAM FINLEY · STUART WHITMAN as Sheriff Martin

Directed by: TOBE HOOPER · Produced by: MARDI RUSTAM · Executive Producer: MOHAMMED RUSTAM
Co-Produced by: ALVIN FAST   Associate Producers: SAMIR RUSTAM · ROBERT KANTOR · LARRY HULY

Distributed by: VIRGO INTERNATIONAL PICTURES, INC.   **R** RESTRICTED

Nominated BEST PICTURE
Academy of Science-Fiction, Fantasy & Horror Films

EATEN ALIVE

(1977)

DIRECTED BY TOBE HOOPER
SCREENPLAY BY ALVIN L FAST AND KIM HENKEL

FEATURING
Neville Brand as Judd
Mel Ferrer as Harvey Wood
Stuart Whitman as Sheriff Martin
Carolyn Jones as Miss Hattie
Marilyn Burns as Faye
William Finley as Roy

If this piece of mindless foolishness wasn't based on a true story there's no way that it would have got a guernsey in this book. Fact is, this is the thinly disguised story of Joe Ball, a serial killer who murdered his girlfriends and fed them to his pet alligators. Or so the story goes.

Given that *Eaten Alive* is set in the swamplands of Texas it comes as no surprise that the director, Tobe Hooper, also directed *The Texas Chainsaw Massacre*. In fact, some parts of *Eaten Alive* may very well have been taken out of that film.

The film is set in the dark and gloomy 'Starlite Hotel', a run-down juice joint in hillybilly Texas which is run by the murderous loner and drug addict 'Judd' (Neville Brand), a disgusting bit of work who has a huge African man-eating crocodile as a pet.

Only death lives here. When a runaway teenager turns up at the bar after being sacked from the local brothel, evil Judd tries to force himself on her, with no luck. Spurned, he bashes her up, repeatedly stabs her with a pitchfork and finally feeds her to his mammoth crocodile. And, just like when Robert Shaw was chomped on by Bruce the shark in *Jaws*, we get to see her eaten alive. Not recommended dinner time viewing. And there's more! A man is decapitated with a sickle. A family pet is eaten by the monstrous crocodile. And still plenty more gratuitous blood and guts.

While the storyline is about at tight as a bride's nightie, there is one enduring mystery to this film. How on earth did they get fine actors such as Mel Ferrer, Carolyn Jones, Neville Brand and Stuart Whitman to take part? We can only assume that with their career on the downhill slide, each was in it for the money; surely experience would have told them that Oscar opportunities were limited? It's just an awful shame that such a talented bunch of actors had to wind up in this awful tripe. But, having said that, the real 'Alligator Man' didn't have all that much going for him either.

Joe Ball: The Alligator Man

Though they occurred back in the 1930s, tales of the murders committed by Joe 'Alligator Man' Ball are still widely told in Texas today. They have become part of folklore, whispered around campfires and used to scare young children at night.

Coming into the world on 7 January 1896 in Elmendorf, Texas, a small town about 25 kilometres southeast of San Antonio, Joe was the second of eight children born to Frank and Elizabeth Ball, a successful couple who ran the local general store. A loner as a child, Joe spent much of his time exploring the rugged countryside, fishing and enjoying the fresh air and wide, open spaces. As he grew older, he became fascinated by firearms, and could often be found sharpening his shooting skills until he became an expert marksman.

Joe got the chance to put his shooting abilities to use when the US declared war against Germany in 1917. Not long after his country joined the conflict, Joe signed up for the army and saw heavy action on the frontlines of Europe. He received an honourable discharge in 1919 and returned to Elmendorf to work for his father, though he seemed to have trouble finding his place back in regular society after seeing first-hand the horrors of battle.

Joe soon quit his job at the store and, once Prohibition started in America, he drifted into bootlegging. He would haul his illegal alcohol around the region in a Model A Ford, selling it straight out of the barrel. As with many in the same field, business boomed for Joe and by the mid-1920s, he had hired an African-American helper named Clifton Wheeler. The young offsider soon found that he was doing the lion's share of the harder side of the business, and also had to put up with a drunken Joe shooting at his feet to make him dance. Still, Clifton would stay in Joe's employment for years to come.

Of course, Prohibition didn't last forever, and once it was repealed, Joe was at a loose end. He bought a small plot of land just outside Elemendorf and opened a drinking establishment that he named the Sociable Inn. The tavern featured a player piano, two bedrooms in the rear, and would sometimes have cockfighting in the main bar area. Joe got on with the majority of drinkers at his place, but soon developed a reputation as a man you didn't want to mess with.

With his tavern a success, Joe consolidated his position by adding live alligators. Seeing it as a talking point to draw in more drinkers, he dug and cemented in a pool behind the bar, put up a large fence and shipped in five alligators. As he had hoped, the attraction drew in more customers than ever before. To satisfy the drunken masses, Joe started putting on special shows on Saturdays. These involved throwing live animals, such as cats, dogs or racoons, into the alligator pit, with inevitable results.

Joe grew very fond of his pet alligators and became extremely protective of them. A story has it that a neighbour once complained about the smell of rotting meat emanating from Joe's bar. Joe is said to have pulled a gun on the man and told him in no uncertain words that it was the alligators' food making the smell. He then suggested that the neighbour himself could end up as a meal for the hungry reptiles. Not surprisingly, the man is believed to have moved away from the area soon after this incident.

Another method Joe employed to keep the customers coming back was hiring only young, attractive women. Unfortunately, none of these women seemed to stay around for very long. If Joe was ever asked about his high rate of staff turnover, he replied that the girls were transient workers looking only to turn a fast dollar and be on their way. No-one seemed to think any more of it.

Soon after meeting a woman named Minnie Gotthardt in 1934, Joe found himself in a relationship that would last for almost three years. Minnie even came to have a hand in helping him run the bar. Joe's friends had little time for 'Big Minnie', but the bar owner stayed with her, even after becoming involved with one of his young waitresses, Dolores 'Buddy' Goodwin.

Joe's relationship with Dolores was a volatile one, though. At one point he threw a bottle at her, leaving a scar that ran from her neck up to her eye. Despite this, the younger woman fell hard for Joe. But Joe's wandering eye once again got the better of him, and he started a relationship in 1937 with yet another of his employees, 22-year-old Hazel 'Schatzie' Brown. Even for a confident man like Joe Ball, trying to secretly carry on three affairs with women who worked for him was tricky.

But things got a little easier when Minnie went missing in the summer of 1937. Joe hastily informed anyone who asked that Minnie had given birth to a black baby and left town in a hurry. Still, he would come to tell Dolores, whom he married a few months later, quite a different version of events. Joe informed his new bride that Minnie hadn't run off at all. Instead, he said, he had shot her in the head and buried her in the sand at a nearby beach. Dolores thought her new husband was just joking, and she never mentioned the woman again.

It didn't matter much, anyway, as Dolores herself disappeared in April 1938, just a few months after she had been involved in a serious car accident that almost took her life. One suspicious aspect of the accident was the fact that Dolores had to have her left arm amputated. Stories were soon circulating that it hadn't been a car crash at all, but that the young bride had found herself too close to one of her husband's pet alligators.

Not long after Dolores went missing, a trifecta was completed when Hazel, too, disappeared.

Even though Joe had been closely involved with three women who went missing in a relatively short space of time, he remained untroubled and his business continued to prosper. Then, around the middle of 1938, Minnie's worried family began asking around about her. They contacted the Bexar County Sheriff's office, who spoke to Joe several times, though nothing came of their questioning. Just months later, however, another concerned family member contacted the sheriffs about another of Joe's one-time employees, 23-year-old Julia Turner. When Joe was questioned, he told the authorities that the young woman had told him she was having problems in her personal life.

With no way to prove Joe was lying, the deputies searched Julia's house, and found that all of her clothes and belongings were still there. They went back to Joe's bar, where he told them he had lent her $500. He added that the waitress was distraught, and had said she was having trouble with her flatmate. The police had no way to disprove his story.

Two other female employees of the Sociable Inn went missing over the next few months. The authorities questioned Joe for hours, all to no avail. But his apparent luck couldn't last forever.

A former neighbour of Joe's contacted the sheriffs on 23 September 1938 and told them that he had seen the bar owner slicing meat from a human body to feed to his alligators. Around the same time, another man came forward with a story involving a barrel Joe had left behind at his sister's barn. The man said the rotting stench coming from the barrel was foul, 'like something dead was inside'. But by the time investigators looked into the matter, the bad-smelling barrel was no longer there. Still, deputies John Gray and John Klevenhagen decided to ask Joe about it. They went to the Sociable Inn and told Joe they were taking him to San Antonio for further questioning. Joe thought about it for a second before asking if he could shut up his bar. Gray and Klevenhagen said that was acceptable and Joe got himself a beer while the men sat down to wait. Joe drank the beer, then opened the cash register and pulled out a .45 revolver. Just as the deputies realised what was happening and lunged to stop him, Joe Ball shot himself in the heart at point-blank range and fell to the ground dead.

Local authorities were soon swarming over the Sociable Inn, looking for clues to the disappearances, or answers as to why Joe had committed suicide so readily. They found an axe with blood and hair stuck to it, as well as rotting meat around the alligator pool. With a host of missing persons cases, and all signs pointing to Joe, Bexar County deputy sheriff John Gray told his staff to speak to Joe's handyman, Clifton Wheeler. Gray and Klevenhagen found Wheeler and drove him to San Antonio. After several hours of questioning, Wheeler told them that he had killed Hazel Brown because she had fallen for another man and had been planning to move away from him.

The next day, Wheeler took the deputies to a quiet area near the San Antonio River, about five kilometres from town, and began to dig around in the ground. It wasn't long before a foul odour erupted from the earth, along with blood. Several of the men on hand immediately vomited, the smell was so rotten. Wheeler continued to dig and soon pulled out the dead woman's legs, arms and a torso. He then pointed to an old campfire, where investigators uncovered fragments of Hazel Brown's skull, as well as teeth and her jawbone.

They asked Wheeler what had happened, and he told them that Joe had been drunk one night and ordered him to round up some blankets and more booze. The pair then drove Joe's car to his sister's house to get a 55-gallon barrel, before heading to the spot near the river, where Joe held a gun to Wheeler and made him dig a grave. The pair then opened the barrel, at which point Wheeler realised it contained Hazel Brown's corpse. Joe told Wheeler to help him cut the corpse into pieces, but Wheeler refused. But when Joe realised he was too drunk to do it by himself, he forced Wheeler to hold down Brown's limbs while he sawed them off. The smell of the lifeless body was so strong the men were forced to take several beer breaks so as not to get sick. Once they had finished dismembering the cadaver, they put the head into their campfire.

Next, the investigators asked Wheeler about Minnie Gotthardt. He told them she was pregnant and Joe thought a child would make waves in his relationship with Dolores. He had taken her to a secluded area in the town of Ingleside where they drank for a while. Then he shot her in the head. Her remains were exhumed on 14 October 1938.

Even though the authorities had more questions for Wheeler – there had been, after all, other strange disappearances connected to Joe's bar, including that of a teenage boy – but the handyman maintained that he didn't know any details about the other cases.

Still, Joe Ball doesn't seem to have been quite the monster he was first thought to be. After some effort, the authorities found Dolores Goodwin alive and well in San Diego. Another of the missing barmaids was also eventually located. On top of that, it turned out that none of the rotting meat around the alligator pool was human. Indeed, Dolores was questioned by a San Antonio newspaper in 1957 and said that he had never fed a person to his pets. She also described the bar owner and war veteran as a 'sweet, kind, good man'.

Clifton Wheeler received a two-year sentence for helping Joe Ball dispose of the bodies of Hazel Brown and Minnie Gotthardt. Joe's alligators were donated to the San Antonio zoo.

MURDER BY DECREE

(1979)

DIRECTED BY BOB CLARK
SCREENPLAY BY JOHN HOPKINS

FEATURING

Christopher Plummer as Sherlock Holmes
James Mason as Dr John H Watson
David Hemmings as Inspector Foxborough
Susan Clark as Mary Kelly
Anthony Quayle as Sir Charles Warren
Sir John Gielgud as Lord Salisbury
Donald Sutherland as Robert Lees
Frank Finlay as Inspector Lestrade
Genevieve Bujold as Annie Crook

Of all the Jack the Ripper movies *Murder by Decree* is the best. And little wonder – just have a look at the cast list. Combine these actors with superb direction, authentic sets and a brilliant screenplay, and it doesn't get much better than this. It's a winner.

The combination of Christopher Plummer's Holmes and James Mason's Dr Watson works a treat. They carry on like a pair of old queens, eating, drinking and going off to the opera together. 'Well, I'm off to bed then,' says Dr Watson. 'That's fine, I'm going to sit up alone for a while. See you in the morning,' says Sherlock. But despite no female love interest in sight, there is nothing gay about them at all. Maybe that's because there's all that butch stuff, like solving crimes and apprehending criminals.

Murder by Decree is mostly factual, however, it does subscribe to the old theory that a very prominent person was Jack the Ripper, and that the killings are a conspiracy involving an heir to high office, a prostitute, a marriage, a baby and the Freemasons.

Holmes suspects that skulduggery is afoot when the mutilated bodies of street prostitutes keep piling up and no-one has bothered to consult him. After all, he is the greatest detective in the world! He does eventually become involved when commissioned by the Citizens Committee, a group of distraught Whitechapel shopkeepers, to find the Ripper because the murders are having disastrous results on their retail businesses. Holmes agrees, only to find himself unwelcome at the next murder scene, where he is warned off and declared an amateur by the head of the investigation, Sir Charles Warren, who instructs his officers to arrest Holmes. Of course they don't.

Holmes sends the old toff Watson into the local pub to chat to some of the grubby prostitutes who were friends with the murdered women. Watson has to find out if there is anything more to the murders than the cops are letting on. He discovers that the key to the puzzle is a prostitute named Mary Kelly. She, he is told, is too terrified to even speak about her relationship with Annie Crook, a prostitute who has disappeared. Holmes sets out to track Mary and Annie down, and that's when the story really starts.

The supporting cast is a showcase of the character actors of the time: Sir John Gielgud as the uncompromising prime minister; Donald Sutherland as eccentric clairvoyant, Donald Lees; David Hemmings as the slimy Inspector Foxborough; and Anthony Quayle as Sir Charles Warren, the belligerent head of Scotland Yard who is confronted by Holmes at every turn. They are all magnificent. As are Susan Clark as the haunted Mary Kelly and Genevieve Bujold as Annie Crook, who, when Holmes eventually finds her, provides one of the most memorable scenes in the movie.

But as if all that isn't good enough, *Murder by Decree* saves the best until the last. There have been some memorable final showdowns in Sherlock Holmes movies over the years, but this is the best of all. Holmes attempts to confront the unconfrontable with a litany of allegations that could bring Britain to its knees. It is riveting theatre.

Although hard to come by, *Murder by Decree* is available for rent in selective video and DVD outlets, and available for sale on DVD on the internet through Amazon and other outlets.

Not to be missed at any price.

Jack the Ripper

No other serial killer has inspired so much interest through the years as Jack the Ripper. The knowledge that his identity still hasn't been conclusively proven adds a sinister twist to the frightening tale – the fact that such a deplorable person could get away with his evil deeds under the nose of the law.

The file was officially closed in 1892, but what is sometimes forgotten is the brutality and outright viciousness with which he attacked his five female victims. He used a strong, sharp knife with a blade 2cm in width and at least 15cm long, proving that acts of shocking cruelty and horrendous depravity are by no means a modern invention.

Jack the Ripper's first victim was 42-year-old Mary Ann 'Polly' Nichols, the daughter of a locksmith, and former wife of printer's machinist William Nichols. The pair had five children, but had broken up years earlier as a result of Polly's drinking. At the time of her death, the tired and destitute but well-liked alcoholic was making a meagre living as a prostitute.

Polly's butchered body was found shortly before 4am on Friday 31 August 1888 in Buck's Row in the respectable London neighbourhood of Whitechapel. It was a typically wet and cold morning when a man named Charles Cross noticed what he thought was a tarpaulin on the ground in front of a stable yard. When he got closer, though, he saw that the dark shape was a female body, with her dress lifted up almost to the waist. Believing the woman to either be drunk or the victim of an assault, he enlisted another passer-by to help. Together they adjusted her skirt and went in search of a policeman. Neither noticed the blood or excessive wounding Polly had suffered.

Before they could return, Constable John Neil came across the body while on his regular patrol. With his lantern he immediately saw that blood was flowing out of a neck that had been slashed from one ear to the other, while her eyes were wide open and stared blankly with the long, cold glare of death. He called out to another officer who went to get a doctor and ambulance. In the meantime, Neil canvassed the immediate area, but nobody had heard a sound.

When Dr Rees Llewellyn arrived, he noted that the body was still warm, and estimated that the woman had been dead less than 30 minutes. The two knife wounds to the neck had been fatal, slicing open the windpipe and oesophagus. The corpse was then taken to the mortuary, where it was stripped to show that the victim's abdomen had been mutilated, with long, deep and aggressive knife wounds. Dr Llewellyn made a note that there was bruising on the lower jaw.

It didn't take long for word of the grisly find to spread, and police soon knew Polly's name. Her father and husband came and identified her the next day.

Inspector Frederick George Abberline, a 25-year veteran of the police force, was placed in charge of the investigation, but it was soon clear that Polly's killer had left behind no clues. There were no witnesses, and no sign of a weapon. The best lead at the time pointed towards three men employed to slaughter horses nearby, but they had been working at the time so had a confirmed alibi.

The Ripper struck again just over a week later. His second victim was a 47-year-old homeless alcoholic and prostitute named Annie Chapman. Annie was last seen shortly after 2am on Friday 7 September 1888. She was partially drunk and looking to earn money to pay for a bed for the night. Her body was discovered shortly after 6am in the backyard of 29 Hanbury Street, Spitalfields by the resident, John Davis. Davis reported that the woman's skirt was lifted up to her hips, but said that he had heard nothing suspicious during the night.

Police surgeon Dr George Bagster Phillips was brought in to investigate. He told a later inquest that Annie's face had been swollen and her small intestines and other organs had been lifted out and were laying on the ground near her right shoulder, though they were still attached to her body. Again, this victim's throat had been cut deeply, right around the neck. It is believed that Annie was strangled until she was unconscious before the Ripper slashed her throat. After she had died, he mutilated her abdomen, and removed the upper part of her vagina and two-thirds of the bladder. Those body parts were never found. Because of the surgical precision of the cuts involved in this process, it was reasoned that the killer was familiar with anatomy.

Strangely, the murderer had removed several items from Annie's pockets and arranged them at her feet – including a piece of cloth and two combs. A leather apron was also found in the yard, and an envelope containing two pills rested near her head. The date of the London postmark on the envelope was 23 August, and it showed the words 'Sussex Regiment' on the back, while the front had handwriting on it – the letter 'M', and below that the letters 'Sp'.

The Ripper then stepped up his efforts, with another victim found on the ground of Dutfield's Yard, Whitechapel, on 30 September. With nothing on the body to identify her, it took some time for police to come up with a name. It was eventually determined that she was Elizabeth Stride, a well-liked woman who made a living cleaning rooms and sewing. She was also known to get drunk fairly often, and may have been an occasional prostitute. When her body was found there was a red rose on her jacket, though she had not been wearing one when she left her residence earlier that evening. Stride had also been seen at around 12.30am on the morning of her death, talking to a man with dark hair and a moustache. According to the witness, Constable William Smith, who had been patrolling the area, the man in question had a dark complexion and stood around 170cm tall. He carried a large parcel in his hands, and was wearing a black cutaway coat, with a white collar and tie, as well as a dark hat.

Another witness, Israel Schwartz, saw a man talking to Stride at 12.45am. The man threw Stride to the ground before calling out to another man at the other side of the road lighting a pipe. The second man then started to follow Schwartz, who ran away.

Other witnesses then came forward. William Marshall had seen Stride at around 11.45pm talking to a well-spoken man wearing a cap. James Brown also saw Stride talking to a man on the night of her murder. This sighting was at 12.45am, and Stride told the man in the long dark overcoat, 'Not tonight, some other night.'

But the authorities soon had even more on their plate: another victim turned up that same evening in a small yard known as Mitre Square, less than half a kilometre away from where Stride's body had been found. Mitre Square, at the time, was busy during the day, with several warehouses and commercial premises in the area. But it was quiet and dark at night. Regardless, Constable Edward Watkins regularly patrolled it on his nightly shift. He had been through there at 1.30am, and then again 45 minutes later. Even though there was no noise or sign of disturbance, Watkins noticed something lying in a corner. He used his lantern to see what it was and was shocked to see a female body on her back, with her skirt pulled up around her waist. He later reported that, 'I saw her throat was cut and her bowels protruding. The stomach was ripped up. She was lying in a pool of blood.'

More police were called in and a search was organised in the general vicinity. Dr Frederick Gordon Brown arrived at the scene at 2.18am and saw that the victim's stomach had been ripped open and that her face had been horribly mutilated. The body was still warm, and he estimated the time of death at around 30 minutes earlier. The wounds Brown later recalled were shocking: 'The abdomen had been laid open from the breast bone to the pubes,' he started, before explaining that the intestines had been 'detached to a large extent' and that 'about two feet of the colon was cut away'. In addition to this, her left kidney had been removed, her left renal artery attacked, and much of her womb taken out. There was a slice through her lower left eyelid, and the end of her nose had been cut off, as had an earlobe.

Given the times Constable Watkins had checked on the yard, as well as another patrolman whose beat took him past the same spot just a few minutes earlier, it seemed the killer had murdered and cut up the victim in the space of about 15 minutes.

With police swarming the area, Constable Alfred Long found a blood-drenched apron outside a building on Goulston Street, Whitechapel at 2.55am. Above the bloody garment the words 'The Juwes Are The Men That Will Not Be Blamed For Nothing' were scrawled in white chalk. The apron turned out to be linked with the Mitre Square murder. As a result, it seemed logical to assume the killer had done the writing as well. Unfortunately, before the graffiti could be photographed for later analysis, police commissioner Sir Charles Warren order it be removed so as not to inflame anti-Jewish sentiment.

Police soon determined that the Mitre Square victim had been Catherine Eddowes. As with the other women the Ripper had murdered, Kate (as she was known to friends) had a problem with alcohol. She was a friendly woman who had three children and may well have turned to prostitution at times when she had been drinking heavily.

A witness, Joseph Lawende, came forward to report that he had seen Kate talking to a man at nearby Church Passage at around 1.35am. He described the man as young and dressed in a deerstalker hat and dark jacket.

As fear swept the city, police patrols in the Whitechapel area were stepped up and prostitutes mostly stayed off the job. Sailors were questioned, as were butchers and men employed to slaughter animals. Nothing came of the investigation, though, and with the Ripper staying quiet for a month or so, things slowly started to return to normal. People started to return to Whitechapel, and as a result the prostitutes came back as well, eager to make some money. One of these, attractive Irishwoman Mary Jane Kelly, was behind in her rent and down on her luck. She, too, was partial to alcohol and had been working in London since moving there when she was 21. Described as 'tall and pretty', Mary could be a handful when drunk, but was generally regarded as a nice person when sober.

The Friday of 9 November 1888 was a festive one in London – it was the Lord Mayor's Show, and the ceremony planned to swear him in was an elaborate one. Mary had hoped to be among the large crowd on hand to cheer, but her plans weren't to be. Her landlord John McCarthy sent his assistant, Thomas Bowyer, to collect the overdue rent from Mary at her residence at 13 Miller Court that morning. What he saw shocked him enough to run back to McCarthy and summon the authorities. A police constable went around to the address and looked through a broken window. He later described what he saw as, 'A sight which I shall never forget to my dying day.' It was the Ripper's most extreme work.

According to a police surgeon, Dr Thomas Bond, brought in to survey the scene, Mary's body lay naked on the bed, the skin of her thighs and abdomen removed. Her breasts had been cut off and her abdomen emptied of its contents. Her arms had been hacked into and her face mutilated until the pretty young woman was unrecognisable. Her neck was severed down to the bone. One of the missing breasts was found under her head, along with her uterus and kidney. The other breast was located next to her right foot. Her liver rested between her feet, her lungs and spleen lay on either side of her, and her abdomen and thighs sat on a nearby table.

Whitechapel was once again thrown into shock, and the police efforts went back into overdrive. Queen Victoria herself stated that she was displeased with the way the matter had been handled, and called for the streets to be lit at night and the state of the detectives department improved. But with few leads to go on, investigating officers were at their wits end.

One promising lead came from a friend of Mary's, labourer George Hutchinson, who saw the prostitute at around 2am. She asked if he had any money to spare, but after being told no, she went on her way. Hutchinson then saw her stop to talk to a man who the authorities assume was the Ripper. The man carried a small parcel in his left hand, and placed his right arm around Mary's shoulders as they spoke. As the pair walked past Hutchinson, the man in question hung his head down with his hat over his eyes. When Hutchinson stooped to see the man's face he received a harsh glare for his troubles.

The pair then walked into another street and Hutchinson followed them and kept watch for a few minutes, until the man said something to Mary and she replied, 'All right my dear, come along. You will be comfortable.' With that the man placed his arm on her shoulders again and kissed her. After that the pair walked off and Hutchinson lost their trail when they entered a courtyard. He waited three-quarters of an hour to see what had happened, but neither Mary nor the strange man returned.

The man Hutchinson described was about 35 years old and estimated to stand 168cm tall, with dark eyes and a slight moustache. He was surly looking, and wore a long dark coat and dark felt hat. Several other witnesses came forward with reports of a similar sounding man on the same night, as well as earlier in the week.

Still, before long the cold London winter set in and all the leads police had reached nothing but dead ends. The Ripper's toll ended with five murders and, despite countless theories as to his identity, there were no more killings officially attributed to the man many consider to be history's most infamous serial killer.

(1980)

DIRECTED BY WILLIAM FRIEDKIN
SCREENPLAY BY WILLIAM FRIEDKIN

FEATURING
Al Pacino as Steve Burns
Paul Sorvino as Captain Edelson
Karen Allen as Nancy Gates
Richard Cox as Stuart Richards
Don Scardino as Ted Bailey
Joe Spinell as Patrolman DiSimone

Apart from his many magnificent movies – *The Godfather* series, *Serpico*, *The Scent of a Woman* and *Heat* – Al Pacino also made a couple that the critics roasted. As a result they didn't do very well at the box office, yet went on to become huge cult movies on video. *Scarface* was one, *Cruising* was the other.

But *Cruising* didn't become a cult movie because people liked to watch what allegedly goes on in gay bars between heavily moustached homosexual men with brightly coloured handkerchiefs hanging out of their back pockets. It became popular because it is a serial killer movie. From about 1991, particularly after the international success of *The Silence of the*

Lambs, the term 'serial killer' became part of the vernacular, and movies about them became very fashionable viewing.

But that didn't make *Cruising* a good movie.

Cruising's plot is about as skinny as a Paris model. Undercover cop Pacino is sent by his boss to investigate the serial murder of gay men. The men have been raped and then cut into pieces and thrown in New York Harbour. The opening sequence of the film shows a severed limb being lifted from the water.

There is a suspect with a motive, a man whose overbearing father couldn't face the truth about his son batting for the other team. But whether this is enough to send the suspect on a dismemberment killing spree remains in doubt as the movie plunges into a multitude of subplots and red herrings featuring just about every sexual deviance imaginable, and some unimaginable.

Even the uniformed cops aren't what they seem to be and, as we rollercoaster towards the finale, we even get the impression that our hero, who we know absolutely nothing about except that he has a girlfriend, may not only be gay, but may even be the serial killer.

But you work it out for yourself.

While accredited with being based on a 1970 novel by *New York Times* reporter Gerald Walker, there is little doubt that the infamous New York 'bag murders' also had an enormous influence on the plot (or lack thereof) of *Cruising*. In 1977 and '78, New York gays were living in terror as a series of 'bag murders' took place in which six male victims were raped, mutilated and dismembered, and their remains were wrapped in black plastic garbage bags and dumped in the Hudson River.

The grizzly body parts washed up on the New Jersey shore of the Hudson while others found their way to the shores near the World Trade Center. Items of clothing from one of the garbage bags led police to a clothing shop in Greenwich Village which catered exclusively for gays. Tattoos on one of the victims identified him as a known homosexual. As curious as it may seem, in several of the cases police could not identify the bodies nor the cause of death so they were not officially classed as homicides. Instead they became what is known as CUPPIs – Circumstances Undetermined Pending Police Investigation.

In an 'unrelated case' it seemed as though there may have been a solution to the mysterious New York bag murders when 38-year-old X-ray technician, Paul Bateson, confessed to the 14 September 1977 murder of film critic Addison Verrill. Bateson said that he met Verrill in a Greenwich Village gay bar and, after having sex at Verrill's flat, he bashed Verrill's skull in with a metal skillet and stabbed him repeatedly in the heart with a kitchen knife.

While in custody awaiting trial Paul Bateson bragged of killing other homosexual men for a 'bit of fun' and cutting their bodies up and putting the pieces in garbage bags and throwing them in the Hudson River. After lengthy interviews with Bateson about the bag murders detectives were satisfied that he was the killer, but Bateson was never charged. Technically, the New York bag murders remain unsolved to this day.

Convicted of murder on 5 March 1979, Bateson was sentenced to life in prison.

TIGHTROPE

(1984)

DIRECTED BY RICHARD TUGGLE
SCREENPLAY BY RICHARD TUGGLE

FEATURING

Clint Eastwood as Captain Wes Block
Genevieve Bujold as Beryl Thibodeaux
Dan Hedaya as Detective Molinari
Alison Eastwood as Amanda Block
Jennifer Beck as Penny Block
Marco St John as Leander Rolfe

Tightrope's Wes Block is a very unusual Clint Eastwood character. Sure he's a cop hunting down the bad guys – in this case a serial killer who murders young women – but he has an unusual trait, one which you would never imagine Clint's clean-image cop would have. He gets off having sex with prostitutes while they are handcuffed, preferably to the bed. To make matters worse for Wes, someone is following him around and strangling the women after he has finished with them.

The fact that our hero can't control his natural urges doesn't make *Tightrope* a bad movie. Far from it. It's terrific. Clint still looks the same: tweed jacket with the leather elbow patches, short back and sides, and, of course, the grimaces and twitches that never change from one movie to the next.

Wes makes up for his indiscretions by being a good father to his two young daughters, despite having broken up with his wife. She has left him for a rich bloke – who we never get to see although we know he drives a 450SL Mercedes sports, which were all the go in 1984. The Block girls also collect stray dogs, which Wes can't say no to. Of course, by now we don't care about Wes' sexual indiscretions – anyone who's kind to kids and dogs can't be all that bad.

Tightrope gives the impression that New Orleans is an endless procession of bars and brothels catering for every deviance known to man. When at last we do get out of the nude jelly wrestling and pole-dancing joints – the dives that Wes has to visit in order to questions people in connection with the killings – and he dines a love interest on a paddle-steamer over a dozen oysters and a bottle of wine, it is a welcome relief.

Then it's back to the doom and gloom and debauchery of Wes' beat. The main mystery all through the film is why would anyone be doing this to poor Wes? But the mystery is revealed soon enough and, while it's far from original, it's a good enough reason to hang in there until the gripping finale.

Clint has terrific support from Genevieve Bujold, as his legitimate love interest. You'll recognise the familiar face of Dan Hedaya, who seems to have been in every Eastwood movie ever made, as his sidekick cop. And look out for Clint's daughter, Alison, as Amanda, his movie daughter.

For the trivia buffs, this is the second of three Clint Eastwood serial killer movies in this book. The first was *Dirty Harry* back in 1972 and the other is *Blood Work* from 2002. In each of them Clint plays a completely different type of cop. In *Dirty Harry* he is the squeaky clean cop in pursuit of the San Francisco serial killer. In this film, *Tightrope*, he's the not-so-squeaky-clean cop in pursuit of a serial killer and in *Blood Work* he's a retired cop with a heart transplant in search of a serial killer. But while all of the characters are a million miles apart, and all of the plots are completely different, Clint always gets his man. We have come to expect nothing less.

Tightrope is a 'Dirty Harry' for grown-ups.

Recommended viewing.

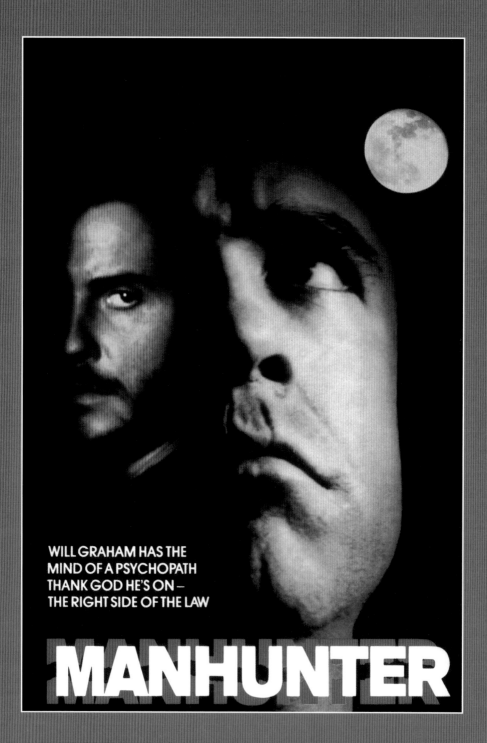

MANHUNTER

(1986)

DIRECTED BY MICHAEL MANN
SCREENPLAY BY MICHAEL MANN

FEATURING
William L Petersen as Will Graham
Kim Greist as Molly Graham
Joan Allen as Reba McClane
Brian Cox as Dr Hannibal Lecter
Dennis Farina as Jack Crawford
Tom Noonan as Francis Dolarhyde
Stephen Lang as Freddy Lounds

Say hello to the Tooth Fairy. He's a charming bit of work whose specialty is murdering entire families on the full moon. Mum, dad, kids, pets, the lot. What with the teeth and the full moon you could be fooled into thinking this is some sort of a vampire movie, but it certainly isn't – even though the serial killer does leave giant teeth marks on his victims with his abnormally large choppers.

But that's not what the plot is all about. *Manhunter* was adapted from Thomas Harris' 1981 international best seller *Red Dragon*, the novel before *The Silence of the Lambs*. It's the tale of how the FBI serial killer catcher Will Graham, played by

William L Petersen – who went on to bigger success as Grissom in *CSI* – is brought out of retirement to catch the Tooth Fairy before he kills another family. Will's claim to fame is that he caught Dr Hannibal Lecter in the first place and, if he could catch him, he can catch anyone. Trouble is, Will's just got back on track after Lecter messed badly with his brain and he wonders if he's up to doing it again. He is.

Manhunter is one of the truly great serial killer movies. It introduces us to serial killer profiling for the first time, something that was new back in 1986. These days it is what most serial killer movies are about – often more than the killers themselves.

Director Michael Mann (*Heat*) brilliantly compiled his ensemble of players and everyone seems as though they were born for the part. It's debatable if Brian Cox would have gone on to the Hannibal Lecter success that Hopkins had, but his portrayal of the insane psychiatrist is convincing and very, very scary. The almost typecast gangster, Dennis Farina, brushes up well as a cop, and is convincing as chief FBI profiler, Jack Crawford.

Mann also cleverly gives the evil villain, Francis Dolarhyde, brilliantly played by Tom Noonon, a human face, especially through his compassion for a blind girl, Reba McClane (Joan Allen). Check out the scene where they visit an anaesthetised tiger while it is having a tooth removed. It makes you want to take the Tooth Fairy by the hand and say, 'Look, we know that you murder entire families on the full moon, but that aside, let's have a crack at getting your act back on the road'. But it doesn't take long before we come back to reality with a thud.

What is disturbing is just where did *Red Dragon*'s author, Thomas Harris, get the idea of a serial killer who specialises in murdering whole families? Perhaps he concocted it himself, but there is usually a catalyst somewhere for novels of this nature. Harris said in an interview that he concocted the idea of the Tooth Fairy biting his victims from serial killer Ted Bundy, who bit the body parts of many of his victims. But at the time Harris wrote, there was no record anywhere in the world of a serial killer who killed families. The only case that had any similarities was that of the case of the Otero family murders in Kansas, seven years earlier. Here, at the start of his murder spree, a serial killer killed four members of a family. Perhaps that inspired Harris.

Here is that story.

The Otero Family Murders

DENNIS RADER

In the midafternoon of 15 January 1974, 15-year-old Charlie Otero arrived home from school in Wichita, Kansas, where he lived in a quiet neighbourhood with his devout Catholic parents and four siblings. Upon entering the house, he called out that he was home, but there was no response from anyone, not even the dog. Surprised that the usually noisy household was so quiet he looked around until he came to the bedroom of his mother and father.

There he found his father Joseph, 38, lying face down on the floor at the foot of the bed with his wrists and ankles bound together. Charlie's mother, 34-year-old Julie Otero, was on the bed tied in similar fashion, the only difference being that she had been gagged.

'My father was tied up, his eyes were bulging,' Charlie told police. 'His tongue was about bit off. My mother was on the bed. She didn't even look like my mother. And I looked at my dad. I could smell the death and the fear in the room.'

Charlie fled to a neighbour's house to get help, not realising that he had only witnessed the half of the horror. There was more to come.

The neighbour tried to call the police on the Otero home phone only to find that the line was dead. He went home to call while Charlie waited outside. When the police arrived and searched the house they found Charlie's brother, nine-year-old Joseph II, face down on the floor in his bedroom. The boy's wrists and ankles were also bound and there were three plastic bags over his head.

In the basement police discovered the body of Charlie's 11-year-old sister, Josephine, hanging by her neck from a pipe. She had been gagged and was partially nude, dressed only in a sweatshirt and socks. There was semen found on her body.

From the beginning of the investigation police were cautious in revealing the horrific details of the killings. Foolishly, some would think – but probably so as not to frighten the entire neighbourhood – police said that all four victims had been strangled to death with lengths of Venetian blind cord cut from inside the house. But this only heightened the situation given that the locals who knew the Oteros, and had been in their home, knew that there were no cords of that nature in the house. The killer must have brought his own cords, along with the plastic bags, tape, wire cutters and, more than likely, a gun to hold them at bay.

There was a madman on the loose.

Detectives found semen over Josephine, who was hanging by her neck from sewerage pipes in the basement, her feet barely touching the ground. It appeared that the killer had masturbated over the child after he had strangled her, hanged her and removed her panties. Apart from that, none of the Oteros had been sexually assaulted. Joseph Otero's watch was missing and Julie Otero's purse was rifled and dumped nearby. Outside of that, there was no evidence of a break and enter, robbery, or any sort of a struggle.

A coronial hearing into the Otero murders concluded that they were most likely killed around 9am. Police believed that while Joseph Otero was driving the three older children to school, the killer entered the house, most likely by the back door which was always left open for the dog, to find Julie Otero and her two youngest children by themselves. He most likely bailed them up with a gun, tied them up and waited until Joseph Otero came home to take the remaining two children to school.

After the murders, the killer then brazenly drove off in the Otero family car and parked it near Dillons grocery store, only a few blocks away. The Oteros' neighbours noted that it was odd that they saw a man, possibly of dark complexion, but not African-American, driving the Oteros' car from their home. But they didn't notice enough to get an accurate description of what surely must have been the killer.

With little else to go on, police pondered what on earth the Oteros must have done to warrant such brutal executions. They dug deep into Joseph and Julie Otero's past. Joseph Otero was born in Puerto Rico and emigrated to the United States, where he joined the military services. Shortly before he was murdered, Joseph had retired from the air force, where he was a well-regarded flight instructor and mechanic. Joseph Otero was in peak physical condition and was an excellent boxer. There had never been a hint of drugs or scandal of any type ever attached to his life. He was a loving husband and father, and well regarded in the community. His colleagues praised him and not one person could come up with a motive, no matter how remote, for his murder.

The same went for his beloved wife, Julie. Apart from the fact that she was put off recently from her job at the Coleman Company, it was only temporary and she was to be rehired when the company restructured and business picked up again. Julie was a loving wife and devoted mother, with lots of friends. Like her husband, after many years of training in judo she knew how to look after herself in the event of trouble.

The Otero children were also squeaky clean, never took a day off from school, and were popular among their schoolmates and had lots of friends. Like their mum and dad, all of the children trained in martial arts and knew how to handle themselves.

So how could this possibly happen? Was it a contract hit? If so, why? There was no possible reason. Was it a random killing? If so, then why a whole family? To be carried out without so much as a living witness in broad daylight required surveillance, planning and precision timing. And how could one person subdue so many people who were skilled in martial arts? That's if it was just the one killer?

Kansas police would have to wait 31 years and investigate another six murders by the same serial killer before they found out.

On 26 February 2005 Wichita police arrested 59-year-old Dennis Rader, an ordinance inspector and dog-catcher and president of the congregation at the local church. Rader was the infamous BTK serial killer the Wichita police had been hunting since he first murdered the Otero family in 1974.

After the Otero family murders Rader murdered three more women on separate occasions and, as he did, he taunted police with a barrage of letters complaining that his murders weren't getting enough publicity. Rader gave himself the nickname BTK which stood for BIND, TORTURE, KILL. In 1978, with seven murders to his credit, BTK disappeared.

Twenty-five years later Wichita police received a letter from BTK containing information about another murder in 1986, information that only the killer could have known. BTK's correspondence with the police eventually brought about his undoing and, when he was arrested in 2005, he immediately confessed to another two murders in nearby Park City, bringing his murder count to 10.

At the first day of his trial on Monday 27 June 2005, Dennis Rader pleaded guilty to the murder of 10 people. When asked by Judge Waller if he would like to make a confession – which was being televised – to the court, Rader shocked all of America by proudly going into lengthy detail about every murder he had committed. As he went on and on, prompted by the judge, it became one of the most extraordinary confessions ever caught live on television anywhere in the world.

Rader began with the murder of the Otero family. This is the amazing court transcript of his chilling confession which answered all of the questions the police had been asking for 31 years.

The Defendant:	On January 15th, 1974, I maliciously, intentionally and with premeditation killed Joseph Otero.
The Court:	All right. Mr Rader, I need to find out more information. On that particular day, the 15th day of January 1974, can you tell me where you went to kill Mr Joseph Otero?

The Defendant:	Mmm, I think it's 1834 Edgemoor.
The Court:	All right. Can you tell me approximately what time of day you went there?
The Defendant:	Somewhere between 7 and 7.30.
The Court:	This particular location, did you know these people?
The Defendant:	No, that was part of my – I guess my what you call fantasy. These people were selected.
The Court:	All right.
The Court:	You were engaged in some kind of fantasy during this period of time?
The Defendant:	Yes, sir.
The Court:	All right. Now, where you use the term 'fantasy', is this something you were doing for your personal pleasure?
The Defendant:	Sexual fantasy, sir.
The Court:	I see. So you went to this residence, and what occurred then?
The Defendant:	Well, I had – did some thinking on what I was going to do to either Mrs Otero or Josephine, and basically broke into the house – or didn't break into the house, but when they came out of the house I came in and confronted the family, and then we went from there.
The Court:	All right. Had you planned this beforehand?
The Defendant:	To some degree, yes. After I got in the house it – lost control of it, but it – it was – you know, in back of my mind I had some ideas what I was going to do.
The Court:	Did you –

The Defendant: But I just – I basically panicked that first
                   day, so –
The Court: Beforehand did you know who was there
                   in the house?
The Defendant: I thought Mrs Otero and the two kids – the
                   two younger kids were in the house. I
                   didn't realise Mr Otero was gonna be
                   there.
The Court: All right. How did you get into the house,
                   Mr Rader?
The Defendant: I came through the back door, cut the
                   phone lines, waited at the back door, had
                   reservations about even going or just
                   walking away, but pretty soon the door
                   opened, and I was in.
The Court: All right. So the door opened. Was it
                   opened for you, or did someone –
The Defendant: I think one of the kids – I think the –
                   Junior – or not Junior – yes, the – the
                   young girl – Joseph opened the door. He
                   probably let the dog out 'cause the dog
                   was in the house at the time.
The Court: All right. When you went into the house
                   what happened then?
The Defendant: Well, I confronted the family, pulled the
                   pistol, confronted Mr Otero and asked
                   him to – you know, that I was there to –
                   basically I was wanted [by the police],
                   wanted to get the car. I was hungry, food, I
                   was wanted, and asked him to lie down in
                   the living room. And at that time I realised
                   that wouldn't be a really good idea, so I
                   finally – The dog was the real problem, so

	I – I asked Mr Otero if he could get the dog out. So he had one of the kids put it out, and then I took them back to the bedroom.
The Court:	You took who back to the bedroom?
The Defendant:	The family, the bedroom – the four members.
The Court:	All right. What happened then?
The Defendant:	At that time I tied 'em up.
The Court:	While still holding them at gunpoint?
The Defendant:	Well, in between tying, I guess, you know.
The Court:	All right. After you tied them up what occurred?
The Defendant:	Well, they started complaining about being tied up, and I re-loosened the bonds a couple of times, tried to make Mr Otero as comfortable as I could. Apparently he had a cracked rib from a car accident, so I had him put a pillow down on his – for his – for his head, had him put a – I think a parka or a coat underneath him. They – you know, they talked to me about, you know, giving the car whatever money. I guess they didn't have very much money, and the – from there I realised that, you know, I was already – I didn't have a mask on or anything. They already could ID me, and made – made a decision to go ahead and – and put 'em down, I guess or strangle them.
The Court:	All right. What did you do to Joseph Otero Sr?
The Defendant:	Joseph Otero?
The Court:	Yeah, Joseph Otero, Sr. Mr Otero, the father.

The Defendant:	Put a plastic bag over his head and then some cords and tightened it.
The Court:	This was in the bedroom?
The Defendant:	Yes, sir.
The Court:	All right. Did he in fact suffocate and die as a result of this?
The Defendant:	Not right away, no sir, he didn't.
The Court:	What happened?
The Defendant:	Well, after that I – I did Mrs Otero. I had never strangled anyone before, so I really didn't know how much pressure you had to put on a person or how long it would take, but –
The Court:	Was she also tied up there in the bedroom?
The Defendant:	Yes, uh-huh. Yeah, both their hands and their feet were tied up. She was on the bed.
The Court:	Where were the children?
The Defendant:	Well, Josephine was on the bed, and Junior was on the floor.
The Court:	All right.
The Defendant:	– at this time.
The Court:	So we're – we're talking, first of all, about Joseph Otero. So you had put the bag over his head and tied it.
The Defendant:	Mm-hmm.
The Court:	And he did not die right away. Can you tell me what happened in regards to Joseph Otero?
The Defendant:	He moved over real quick like and I think tore a hole in the bag, and I could tell that he was having some problems there, but at that time the – the whole family just went – they went panicked on me, so I – I – I

	worked pretty quick. I got Mrs O –
The Court:	All right. What did you – you worked pretty quick. What did you do?
The Defendant:	Well, I mean, I – I – I strangled Mrs Otero, and then she – passed out. I thought she was dead. She passed out. Then I strangled Josephine. She passed out, or I thought she was dead. And then I went over and put a – and then put a bag on Junior's head and – and then, if I remember right, Mrs Otero came back. She came back and –
The Court:	Sir, let me ask you about Joseph Otero Sr.
The Defendant:	Senior.
The Court:	You indicated he had torn a hole in the bag.
The Defendant:	Mm-hmm.
The Court:	What did you do with him then?
The Defendant:	I put another bag over it – or either that or a – if I recollect, I think I put a – either a cloth or a T-shirt or something over it – over his head, and then a bag, another bag, then tied that down.
The Court:	Did he subsequently die?
The Defendant:	Well, yes. I mean – I mean, I was – I didn't just stay there and watch him. I mean, I was moving around the room, but –
The Court:	All right. So you indicated you strangled Mrs Otero after you had done this; is that correct?
The Defendant:	Yeah, I went back and strangled her again.
The Court:	All right.
The Defendant:	And that – And that – that finally killed her at that time.
The Court:	So this is in regards to Count Two. You

	had, first of all, put the bag over Joseph Otero's head.
The Defendant:	I don't know. I have no idea. Just –
The Court:	What happened then?
The Defendant:	I got the keys to the car. In fact, I had the keys I think earlier before that, 'cause I wanted to make sure I had a way of getting out of the house, and cleaned the house up a little bit, made sure everything's packed up, and left through the front door, and then went there – went over to their car, and then drove to Dillons, left the car there. Then eventually walked back to my car.

The whole story of the BTK serial killer
is on page 374.

COP

(1987)

DIRECTED BY JAMES B HARRIS
SCREEPLAY BY JAMES B HARRIS

FEATURING

James Woods as Detective Lloyd Hopkins
Lesley Ann Warren as Kathleen McCarthy
Charles Durning as Dutch Peltz
Charles Haid as Delbert 'Whitey' Haines
Raymond J Barry as Captain Fred Gaffney
Randi Brooks as Joanie Pratt

Based on James Ellroy's thriller *Blood on the Moon*, you couldn't be blamed for expecting big things from *Cop*; after all, it's the same bloke who wrote *LA Confidential* and *Black Dahlia*, both of which have spawned great movies in recent years. And you wouldn't be wrong. The only bad thing about *Cop* is the unimaginative title. Besides that, it's got what every serial killer movie buff has come to expect: the unsolved murders of countless (well, 16 in this story) single women dating back years, with seemingly no connection between them; a cop who's on the trail, but no-one believes his theories; finally, a connection that leads to the killer, but whose identity we don't discover until the very end. Great stuff.

And if that isn't enough to make you want to run out and rent it tonight, *Cop* holds a very special place in serial killer movie history: it is the first film in which the term 'serial killer' is actually used. This is surprising, given that the term was coined in the mid-1970s by American FBI agent and murderer profiler Robert Ressler. Until then serial killers were known as 'repeat offenders', 'thrill killers' or 'mass murderers', and their crimes were referred to as 'stranger killings'.

Ressler was in England attending a series of crime lectures at the British Police Academy. At one point the lecturer was discussing what the British police called 'crimes in series', as in a series of rapes, burglaries, arsons and murders that had been carried out by the one person. This reminded Ressler of serials he saw as a kid at the Saturday afternoon movies, where a cliff-hanger ending would lure him back the following week to see the next episode. To Ressler, the terms 'serial killer' and 'serial murder' sounded a lot better than 'series', and were an appropriate way of characterising the distinctly episodic activities of those who murdered repeatedly. Ressler began to use the term 'serial killer' at his lectures at the FBI training centre's Behavioural Sciences Unit at Quantico, Virginia. The rest is history.

After *Cop*, the term really caught on in the movies and, after 1991's *The Silence of the Lambs*, it became a permanent part of the language.

The other huge plus for *Cop* is the wonderful character actor James Woods. Without him it would be just another plot-driven movie. His performance alone is worth renting the movie. Woods is usually at his best playing a horrible bastard of some description, but in this goodie tough guy role he is more convincing than the best of them. And it's not what he does, it's how he does it. A smirk here, a knowing smile there, the convincing way he gets a stubborn witness to talk. It's giving the villains a gobful and it's how he gets in a front door with a lie. It's all terrific James Woods stuff.

Charles Durning, as the obligatory long-suffering partner who has to cover for him all the time, is well cast. As is the come-hither horn-bag, Randi Brooks, who would have made Liberace go straight.

There are a few holes in *Cop*, but who's counting? It's a racy thriller with terrific performers and a suspenseful plot.

SEA OF LOVE

(1989)

DIRECTED BY HAROLD BECKER
SCREENPLAY BY RICHARD PRICE

FEATURING
Al Pacino as Detective Frank Keller
Ellen Barkin as Helen Kruger
John Goodman as Detective Sherman
Michael Rooker as Terry
William Hickey as Frank Keller Senior
John Spencer as the Lieutenant

The last thing that boozy homicide detective Al Pacino needs, just when he's in the midst of a midlife crisis, is a serial killer who lies their naked male victims face down on the bed and puts a bullet behind their ears while the record player pumps out the old 1959 Phil Phillips 45 rpm classic 'The Sea of Love', over and over. You would think that a bullet shouldn't be necessary – after a while that tune would be enough to kill anyone.

Will the case be enough to take Al over the edge, the edge that he is already precariously balancing on? Will the stunning blonde chief suspect (Ellen Barkin) fuck him to death in a supermarket before he solves the mystery? Will his colleague, who is married to

Al's ex-wife, end up putting a bullet in him for pestering them at all hours of the night when he's fallen down the eye of a Jim Beam bottle? Will the serial killer get him?

It's almost enough to get Al off the turps, but when he teams up with another hard-drinking cop (John Goodman), that starts to seem unlikely. They lead each other through one drunken escapade after another in the pursuit of evidence to nail the *Sea of Love* killer.

Sounds corny? It isn't. It's anything but. This is racy hard-core drama at its best, and there's not a boring or cornball moment in it. And don't tell your friends who the serial killer is. Let 'em guess.

And don't believe the urban myth that was circulating after this movie was released: it was said that the cops got the brilliant idea of apprehending crooks with outstanding warrants by inviting them to a free 'Meet the Yankees' luncheon supposedly won in a local lottery. Not so. The cops thought of it first, and the movie pinched their idea. Besides, *Sea of Love* was filmed in Toronto, not New York, even though we were led to believe it was in the Big Apple.

The cast is stellar. Al Pacino is perfect as the murder investigator with a permanent hangover and John Goodman is a natural as his more sensible – though easily lead astray – sidekick. Ellen Barkin is sensational as the sultry horn bucket who could knock a bloke back and send him out humping lampposts, and Michael Rooker (*Henry: Portrait of a Serial Killer*) and John Spencer (*LA Law* and *The West Wing*) are also well cast.

If you are wondering who the little old bloke is, the one who plays Al's dad, it's the distinguished character actor of screen and stage, William Hickey. He seemed to be in everything for a while there (that's if you recognised him), and is best remembered for his Oscar nominated performance as the conniving old Don Corrado Prizzi in 1985's *Prizzi's Honour*, a prize which he should have easily won.

Novelist Richard Price originally wrote the screenplay of *Sea of*

Love for Dustin Hoffman, but Hoffman wanted too many rewrites so the lead was offered to Al Pacino. Thank God for that. It's hard to imagine Hoffman in the part of a hard-drinking cop just after the world was getting used to him as the autistic savant, Raymond Babbitt, in *Rainman*. Besides, it's a role that Pacino was made for.

Sea of Love is a powerful serial killer movie with a totally believable plot that keeps you hangin' in there until the very end.

Highly recommended.

HENRY: PORTRAIT OF A SERIAL KILLER

(1986)

DIRECTED BY JOHN MCNAUGHTON
SCREENPLAY BY RICHARD FIRE AND JOHN
MCNAUGHTON

FEATURING
Michael Rooker as Henry
Tom Towles as Otis
Tracy Arnold as Becky

If you've just had brain surgery and the doctor has told you not to strain your head by watching anything too complicated or intellectual, then this is the movie for you. A five-star no-brainer. The only thing that is halfway intelligent about *Henry* is that the movie playing on the black-and-white TV before Otis lifts it up and smashes it over a bloke's head, is *Beckett*, featuring Peter O'Toole and Richard Burton. Outside of that, it's blue-chip, wall-to-wall death and dismemberment. But, that may be your cup of tea. If so, you'll love it.

Not surprisingly *Henry* only cost $110,000 to make. What is surprising is that it took more than $600,000 at the box office – no doubt most of it coming from the good ol' boys down Texas way who watched it in open-air theatres while they swigged on the jugs and slapped their thighs to the fiddle and harmonica. Outside of that, I can't see anyone other than a mortician watching it for the sake of it. Well, at least not all of the way through.

One redeeming fact about *Henry* is that it was the first big screen movie for Michael Rooker, who plays Henry. He went on to a successful career in movies such as *Mississippi Burning*, *Sea of Love*, *JFK* and *The Bone Collector*.

Henry is allegedly the story of Henry Lee Lucas and Ottis Toole, although in the movie they are known as Henry and Otis. They are a couple of redneck scumbags who meet in a soup kitchen and while having sex decide to go on a raping and killing spree across America. Not that they are homosexual – it's just that they were brought up to think it was fine to have sex with anything that moved, irrespective of whether it was male or female, or how many legs it had.

Along the way they meet up with Otis' recently divorced younger sister Becky who, like Henry, has a hatred for her parents. Henry and Becky hit it off when she finds out that Henry was in jail for murdering his mother, who abused and humiliated him sexually. In return she tells him tales of being molested by her father. All the while Otis is attempting unsuccessfully to molest her. She (surprisingly) is disgusted. This is certainly a ménage à trois with a difference.

One night Henry and Otis rent a couple of hookers who Henry murders after sex. Murder soon becomes a way of life. One of their highlights is murdering an entire family and then getting off on their video of the killings. Another highlight is stabbing a man to death with a soldering iron and smashing the aforementioned TV over his head.

But all good things must come to an end and, when Henry

comes home unexpectedly one night to find Otis trying to rape Becky, Henry stabs him in the eyeball with a comb handle and hacks his body up in the bath. After Becky helps Henry dump the dismembered remains of her brother in the river, she realises that she has fallen deeply for Henry and they book into a motel for the night. Henry probably couldn't get it up unless she was dead. The following morning Henry leaves alone and stops down the way to unload a suitcase on the side of the road that clearly contains Becky's remains.

So if you're into shooting, incest, sodomy, necrophilia, matricide, eye-stabbing, multicide, disembowelment, rape, strangulation, dismemberment and a good old battering or two, then this is the movie for you. And if that isn't enough, then you're sure to enjoy the real story of Henry Lee Lucas, allegedly the civilised world's worst serial killers.

Henry Lee Lucas:
The Worst Serial Killer in History?

Henry Lee Lucas had a troubled upbringing. The youngest of nine children, he was born to alcoholic parents on 23 August 1936. His violent prostitute mother, Viola, was the main breadwinner of the family, selling her body to whoever had the money and desire. His father, Anderson, lost both legs after falling in front of a train while inebriated, and made extra cash selling bootleg whisky and pencils.

But to his credit, Anderson was the only person to show any affection towards Henry, and the child was devastated when he later died of pneumonia after passing out drunk in the snow. Anderson's death kick-started feelings of uncontrollable anger inside Henry, feelings that would later manifest themselves in an ugly cycle of rape, violence and

HENRY LEE LUCAS

murder, giving Henry Lee Lucas the dubious honour of being named America's most prolific serial killer, with as many as 300 victims to his name.

Henry's family lived in an overcrowded four-room shack in Montgomery County, Virginia, surviving with no power, and sharing what little food and space they had with Viola's vicious pimp Bernie, an unsavoury character with whom she maintained a sexual relationship. All 12 people slept in the one room, which meant everyone – including Anderson – had no choice but to witness Viola having sex with Bernie on regular occasions. Indeed, Henry and his brother were often punished if they tried to look away.

Forced to work from sunrise to sunset, one of Henry's regular duties as a young boy was to guard Anderson's moonshine still. Anderson would let Henry taste the harsh homemade liquor. By the time Henry was 10 years old, he was an alcoholic who drank every day.

Still, the moonshine helped numb the pain from the regular beatings his mother dished out. One time, after she had taken to his head with a wooden log, the child was knocked into a day-long coma. But the humiliation didn't stop with violence. On Henry's first day of school, Viola curled his hair and sent him to class in a dress. He endured a barrage of insults from his peers as a result.

At school, Henry displayed obvious learning difficulties. Teachers also noted that he seemed malnourished. Before long the child started to suffer seizures and would hear noises and voices in his head, no doubt a result of the regular and savage beatings he was still receiving from his mother. Compounding his troubles, an accident resulted in Henry having his left eye removed and replaced with a glass one. It's little wonder that the child constantly dreamed of growing up and venturing into the wider world, leaving the living hell of his upbringing behind him.

When Henry reached puberty at around the age of 13, he became obsessed with sex. He would trap animals to perform acts of bestiality on them, before torturing them to death. He also started to steal regularly. He later claimed, although there is no record to back it up, that he committed his first murder when he was just 14, beating a 17-year-old girl he saw at a bus stop until she was unconscious and then dragging her to a quiet area to rape her. The girl woke up screaming, at which point Henry placed his hands around her throat and choked the young life out of her.

Before long, Henry was arrested for breaking and entering and sent for a year to the Beaumont Training School for Boys in Virginia, where he made several escape attempts. The day after his release, Henry raped his 12-year-old niece. Nine months later he found himself in an adult jail, sentenced to four years in Virginia State Penitentiary on another charge of breaking and entering.

While working on a road gang in May 1956, Henry escaped, stole a car and drove to Ohio. For two months he evaded capture. He even met a girl named Stella while he was on the run. But after being caught again, Henry would not taste freedom again until September 1959, when he was released and moved to live with his half-sister Opal in Tecumseh, Michigan. He then got in touch with Stella and they decided to get married.

Unfortunately for Henry, Viola also arrived on the scene and tried to talk Henry into moving back with her. She told him she was growing old and needed someone to help care for her. Henry refused and there was a physical altercation. Stella saw what she was getting involved in and left Henry, calling off their engagement. But Henry and Viola's fight continued unabated until he stabbed her. Henry fled and Viola died two days later. The hospital records state that she passed away as the result of a heart attack, brought on by the brawl with her son.

Henry was soon caught and charged with second-degree murder. He was sent to the Southern Michigan State Prison, where the voices in his head increased, constantly taunting and teasing him. One of the voices Henry heard was Viola's, compelling him to commit suicide. He tried to do what the voices said, taking to his wrists and stomach with a razor blade on two separate occasions. As a result, he was sent to a mental institution for more than four years. While there he underwent shock and drug therapies that only made him more violent and angry.

Back in Michigan state prison in 1966, Henry studied police procedure as well as the files of other prisoners. From these he deducted that the way to avoid being captured was to cross state lines following every offence committed. Henry took note.

Because the prison system was so overcrowded, Henry was granted an early release in June 1970. He later claimed to have murdered two females that day. But he was back inside again just a year later, jailed for the attempted kidnapping of a teenage girl, as well as possessing a handgun in violation of the conditions of his parole.

Released again in August 1975, he started to make his way around the USA. On 5 December 1975 he married Betty Crawford, the widow of one of his nephews. Henry, his new wife and her three children soon moved to a trailer park, where they mainly survived on money Crawford received from social security. They moved to Texas in June 1976, then to Illinois, then to Maryland, where Crawford accused Henry of molesting her daughters. On 7 July, Henry left and continued to drift, visiting distant relatives and finding work where he could. This aimless existence lasted for a few years until he ended up in Jacksonville with no means of support.

Standing in line for food at a homeless shelter, Henry met Ottis Toole, a known bisexual, who invited him to stay at his house in the suburb of Springfield. Ottis was staying with his mother Sarah and her husband Robert, as well as his wife Novella, nephew Frank Powell Jr and 11-year-old niece Frieda Powell. Novella was soon sent to spend time with neighbours and Henry moved into the main bedroom with his benefactor.

Sarah eventually bought a new house and the ragtag group relocated. Henry found a job working in scrap metal and the backyard soon became cluttered with car parts and wrecked frames. Worryingly, Frieda and Henry started to develop a relationship, and he took to calling her Becky.

Sarah died in May 1981, and before long Henry was in jail again for car theft. Ottis was in hospital, and Frieda and Frank were returned to their natural mother, who committed suicide soon afterwards.

By 1982, Ottis and Henry were both back in Jacksonville, drinking and robbing convenience stores and small banks for fun. Keeping them in food, booze and cash, the pair also found amusement in scaring staff, often lashing out at anyone who put up any resistance. In one incident, Henry shot a female store clerk in the head then, while he stored a load of stolen beer in their car, Ottis had sex with her dead body.

Soon, these random vicious slayings were occurring with more regularity. On another occasion, while the pair drove down a Texas highway, they saw a teenage couple alongside the road. They stopped and Ottis shot the male in the head and chest nine times. Henry then repeatedly raped the female in the backseat of the car while Ottis drove them around. This, however, didn't last long, as Ottis grew angry that Henry was having relations with someone else. He stopped the car and shot the girl six times.

This cycle of escalating violence continued unabated, even when they took Frank and Frieda Powell into their care. By this time Frieda was 12 years old, and involved in a relationship with Henry. The children would wait in the car while Henry and Ottis committed brutal rapes and murders wherever their travels took them. By now the pair had settled into a pattern whereby they would kill as many as five victims in a state before crossing into the next. These murders – at times several in one day – were done for nothing more than enjoyment.

While they were living their lawless life, the pair was approached by a stranger who, after offering them a job delivering stolen cars, roped Henry and Ottis into a secret Satanic death cult called the Hand of Death. As members of the cult, they would be paid $10,000 for each contract killing they did for the group. Though the authorities have never been able to find evidence that the group existed, both men insisted that it was real.

Travelling to Miami for their induction, the men were taken to an island in the Everglades for training. There, they claimed, they were told to cut a man's throat. After the man was dead, his body was cooked and eaten by Henry, Ottis and other members of the cult in a black mass. The pair said that they were trained by the cult for seven weeks. They then set off on a mission, kidnapping children and babies that were either used in sacrificial ceremonies or sold. They also procured teenagers, who would be forced into pornography.

After a time, Henry went to California with Frieda, while Ottis remained with the cult. Alone with his young companion, Frieda became demanding, insisting the pair consummate their relationship – an act Henry was not keen to fulfil, torn as he was between lustful feelings for the girl and a desire to act as a father figure. Besides, if Henry felt like having sex, he could simply rape a random woman.

It was almost inevitable that Frieda would be lured into Henry's circle of death. The pair travelled to Beaumont, Texas, where Henry was to murder a lawyer at the request of the Hand of Death cult. After he killed the man he buried the body in a shallow grave, returning later with Frieda to unearth and decapitate it with her help. According to Henry, the act aroused Frieda so much he had little choice but to let her fondle him that night.

After this turning point, the pair started to drift around the US again, with Henry leaving a path of death and devastation in his wake. Broke and homeless, they took work where they could and relied on the kindness of strangers. Along the way Frieda found religion. It's safe to say Henry didn't join in on her conversion.

Unable to find a motel room one night in the aptly named Demon County, Texas, the tired pair could do nothing but bed down in a field just out of town. Frieda was ready to sleep in her underwear, and Henry started to drink, soon becoming heavily intoxicated. The pair then argued and Henry stabbed his 15-year-old partner in the chest before stripping and having sex with her dead body. Despite his defiling of her corpse, Henry would later admit it was the first time he'd felt remorse over his actions.

He returned to the last town they had been settled in, the tiny community of Stoneburg, Texas. Here word spread about his return and a woman who had befriended Frieda, Kate 'Granny' Rich, got in touch with Henry to ask why the young girl was no longer with him. Henry told her he would discuss the matter with her later, and offered to drive the deeply religious woman to her regular church service. He ended up stabbing her on a quiet road instead, before carving an upside-down cross on her chest and having sex with her corpse. Henry later stole a car and crossed the border, aware that he was the last person seen with the well-known woman.

It wasn't long before alarm bells were raised and a missing person report was filed for Kate Rich. A quick records check showed Henry had warrants on him for parole violations and an arrest order was issued. Henry was soon taken into custody in California, but with no body and no proof that he had killed the kindly woman, the authorities were forced to let him go. Henry wasted no time hitting the road, continuing to rape, rob and murder as he travelled. By October 1982 he was in Missouri, where he found a woman at a service station and ordered her to drive him south. The terrified woman agreed, and he later stabbed her in the neck and had sex with her corpse just off a deserted road. But his path of violence would soon come to an end.

Henry was finally apprehended back in Stoneburg, Texas by local lawman Sheriff Bill F Conway, who had been making huge efforts to nab the murderer ever since the death of Kate Rich. Conway tried everything he could to get the brutal serial killer to confess to his crimes, and on 15 June 1983 he eventually wore him down. From his holding cell, Henry wrote out a letter addressed to Conway. It read:

I have tried to get help for so long and no one will believe me. I have killed for the past 10 years and no one will believe me. I cannot go on doing this. I also killed the only girl I ever loved.

With the floodgates now open, Henry told Conway the shocking story of his trail of violence.

Henry Lee Lucas spent the rest of his life on death row in Huntsville Prison, Texas, where he died at the age of 65 of natural causes on 11 March 2001.

Ottis Toole was also caught and charged with murder. He died in jail of cirrhosis of the liver in September 1996.

THE SILENCE OF THE LAMBS

(1991)

DIRECTED BY JONATHON DEMME
SCREENPLAY BY TED TALLY

FEATURING

Jodie Foster as Clarice Starling
Anthony Hopkins as Dr Hannibal Lecter
Scott Glenn as Jack Crawford
Ted Levine as Jame 'Buffalo Bill' Gumm
Anthony Heald as Dr Frederick Chiltern
Frankie Faison as Barney Matthews

A little-known fact about this movie adaptation of Thomas Harris' international bestseller is that the horrific activities of the main serial killer, Buffalo Bill, are loosely based on the exploits of a dreadful trio of real life murderers named Ed Gein, Ted Bundy and Gary Heidnik.

Ed had a passion for wearing human skin and made clothes out of the corpses of females he had either killed or dug up, as did Buffalo Bill in this film. Eddie Gein was also the catalyst for *Psycho* and his story is on page 70.

In *The Silence of the Lambs*, serial killer Buffalo Bill, wearing fake plaster on his arm, lures a victim into his van by asking her to help him lift an item of furniture. Once in the van the victim is knocked unconscious and whisked away to Bill's dress-making dungeon to become a part of his wardrobe. This method of abduction was originally used by American psychopath Ted Bundy on some of his victims when he kidnapped, raped and murdered up to 40 female college students from 1974 to 1977. The full story of Ted Bundy is on page 298.

Which leaves us with the other terrible creature, Gary Heidnik. In Philadelphia in 1986 Heidnik kidnapped women and kept them chained up in his cellar as sex slaves, eventually murdering two of them and feeding their remains, mixed in with dog food, to the others. The description of Heidnik's cellar is similar to that of Buffalo Bill's in the movie, though, unlike Bill, Gary kept as many as five women in there at any one time, regularly beating, torturing and murdering them, until one escaped and called the cops.

These were just a few of the angles that combined to make this not only the best serial killer movie, but one the best movies of any type ever. And that's not just my opinion. The judges awarded *The Silence of the Lambs* the five top Academy Awards – picture, actor, actress, director, screenplay – for 1991, only the third movie in history to achieve such an honour. The other two were *It Happened One Night* in 1934 and *One Flew Over the Cuckoo's Nest* in 1975. It is also the only movie with a 'horror' classification to ever win Best Picture.

Jodie Foster, Anthony Hopkins, Scott Glenn and Ted Levine are brilliant in a movie that is flawless in every detail. Hopkin's Hannibal Lecter is mesmerising, especially when we get our initial glimpse of him in his cell as he meets FBI agent Clarice Starling for the first time. Hopkins won the Best Actor Oscar, despite being in the film for less than half an hour – the shortest screen appearance for any Best Actor winner.

The Silence of the Lambs came in at number 65 in the American

Film Institute's 'Top 100 Movies of All Time', with Hannibal Lecter coming in as the number one villain, and Clarice Starling as the number six hero.

And they thought *Psycho* was scary! *The Silence of the Lambs* makes that film look like the *Wizard of Oz*, and Hannibal Lecter makes Norman Bates look like Mary Poppins. And, like every classic, the older it gets the better it becomes. Have another look again soon. It's just as terrifying as the first time, even when you know the ending.

Gary Heidnik: The Real Buffalo Bill

Gary Michael Heidnik was born in November 1943 in Cleveland, Ohio. Within two years he had a younger brother, Terry, and his parents were divorced. Once he started school, he lived with his father and new stepmother, with whom he argued constantly. Making his life even more unpleasant, Gary's father was a stern man, who ridiculed the boy constantly about his bedwetting.

The constant taunts continued at school, where the other students laughed at Gary's misshapen head, the result of a fall from a tree. Before long the boy became obsessed with making money and becoming an officer in the army. He was sent to a prestigious military college to prepare, but left in his junior year, despite achieving good grades. Never really fitting into regular high school, Gary joined the regular army when he was 18, and trained as a medic in Texas, where he also became a loan shark to his fellow soldiers.

He was later stationed in West Germany but, in August 1962, he started to suffer from blurred vision, nausea and dizziness. He also showed signs of mental illness and was prescribed anti-psychotic medication and sent back to the US, where he was released with an honourable discharge and received a disability pension.

Back home, he qualified as a nurse in Philadelphia, and then enrolled at the University of Pennsylvania, where he got a job at the campus hospital. He was fired from this position, though, for sloppy work and soon found another job at the Veterans Administration Hospital near Philadelphia, training as a psychiatric nurse. But he was again dismissed.

Gary's already fragile mental state was dealt a harsh blow in 1970 when his mother committed suicide. He tried to take his own life on several occasions, and got caught up in a revolving door situation as a patient in mental institutions, where he would refuse to talk to anyone. His behaviour grew stranger as time went by. One day he attacked his brother Terry, and later said that if his brother had died he would have disposed of the body by soaking it in a bath of acid.

The sicker he became, the less Gary bathed. He also refused to take off a leather jacket, and started saluting people all the time and rolling up one leg of his pants when he wanted to be left alone.

In 1971, he decided to form his own church, and registered the United Church of the Ministers of God. He gave himself the title Bishop Heidnik. The church comprised of five members, including his retarded girlfriend and Terry. But if the church's membership was low, its bank balance wasn't. Gary used his skills in the finance world to turn an investment of $1500 into $545,000 in the space of a year, even though he was still in and out of mental care.

In 1976 Gary shot at a man who was renting a house from him. The bullet grazed the tenant's face and Gary was charged with aggravated assault and carrying an unlicensed pistol. When the house was later sold, Gary left behind boxes of pornographic magazines and a large hole dug in the basement floor.

Gary's next run-in with the law happened 18 months later, when he kept his retarded girlfriend's sister prisoner after signing her out of a mental hospital on day release. She was found in a locked room in the basement of Gary's house, where she had been raped and sodomised. As a result, Gary was charged with a variety of offences and faced trial in November 1978. Found guilty, he was bounced between mental institutions and jail until his release on 12 April 1983.

Once free, Gary Heidnik contacted a service that arranged marriage partners. He specified that he wanted an Asian virgin and was soon put in touch with a Filipino woman named Betty, who accepted his proposal and moved to Philadelphia in September 1985. Gary took her to his home on North Marshall Street, where Betty was confused to find a retarded woman sleeping in a bed she was told was hers. Still, the pair married on 3 October. But a week later, she came home to find Gary having sexual relations with three women. Betty told Gary to give her money so she could go home, but he refused. With no other choice in the matter,

Betty stayed, and it soon became normal for Gary to have other women in the house. He even made his bride watch while he had sex with them. If she complained, she was beaten.

Betty left Gary in 1986 after he beat, raped and threatened to kill her for complaining about the constant stream of women he was bringing into their house. Two weeks later, he was arrested on assault charges, which were dropped when Betty didn't show up for the preliminary hearing. After that, Gary's behaviour grew even more depraved.

On 26 November 1986, part-time prostitute Josefina Riveria was walking through a cold, rainy night in the bad part of north Philadelphia after having a fight with her boyfriend, when Gary stopped his white Cadillac Coupe de Ville and offered her a lift. The pair went to a fast-food restaurant for coffee, where Josefina noticed that the man who said his name was Gary Heidnik wore expensive jewellery but cheap, dirty clothes.

Next, Gary drove the woman to his house. They went through a kitchen which had US pennies glued over the walls and then upstairs, where Josefina was shocked to see the walls were almost covered in one and five dollar notes. Her shock continued when they reached the bedroom door and she felt Gary's hands choking her from behind. But instead of killing her, Gary handcuffed his victim and took her down to the basement. Waiting there was a dirty mattress and metal clamps which were attached to a chain attached to a large pipe on the ceiling. Gary closed the clamps around Josefina's ankles, and then glued them to her, drying the adhesive with a hairdryer. Then, after telling her to sit up, he placed his head in her lap and went to sleep.

Josefina eventually drifted off as well, and awoke to find faint rays of daylight shining into the small room. They showed that a hole had been dug up through the concrete in the middle of what was now her prison. Gary soon returned and started to dig, making the pit deeper and wider. While he was working, he told Josefina that he dreamed of fathering a large family. He added that he planned to get 10 women pregnant. Then he raped her.

The next time Gary left Josefina alone, she managed to get off one of the manacles on her ankle and pull off a cover from a window. The chain, however, kept her from getting more than halfway out. Josefina screamed, but the only person that she alerted was Gary, who came down and beat her before forcing her into the hole he had dug. With Josefina squashed into a ball, Gary then put pieces of plywood over her and weighted them down, before turning on the radio at maximum volume to muffle her screams.

When Gary finally let her out of the pit, Josefina saw a young retarded African-American woman chained to the pipe. The woman was naked except for a light top. Gary told Josefina the woman's name was Sandy Lindsay, then he left them alone. Sandy told her fellow prisoner that she had been a friend of Gary's for years, and that she had often had sex with their captor in the past.

The pair were together in their basement prison for weeks. Gary even forced Sandy to write a letter to her mother saying that she had gone away but would be in touch. Gary also raped the women frequently, beat them often and fed them rarely. Kept mostly naked, the women had to huddle together to stay warm. If they broke his rules or tried to scream for help, he would leave them suspended by one arm to an overhead beam for hours.

Meanwhile, Sandy's mother didn't believe her daughter had gone away. She contacted the authorities and said she that thought Sandy was being held against her will. She could only give the police a first name, Gary, but she also told them his address – 3520 North Marshall Street – and phone number. The investigating officer visited the address, but there was no answer when he knocked on the door and he soon forgot all about it.

In the lead-up to Christmas, Gary started looking for another member of his harem. The unlucky candidate was 19-year-old Lisa. Spotting her while she was walking to a girlfriend's house, he pulled over in his Cadillac and talked her into getting inside, then took her to his house and drugged her. Once she had passed out he raped her and took her to join the others in the basement.

Gary was still seven women short of his target, but that changed 10 days later when he brought home 23-year-old Deborah Dudley. The new arrival caused trouble immediately, though, questioning Gary's authority, which only brought her beatings and the resentment of the other captives, who were also punished for her actions.

Other things started to change around this time as well. Josefina began to act as if she enjoyed the situation, and she feigned loyalty to Gary. This inspired confidence in her captor. But Gary's sex drive was also on the rise. Not only would he have daily sex with each of his captives, he made them perform sex acts on each other while he watched. He also started feeding them dog food, beating them until they ate it.

The population of Gary's basement prison peaked on 18 January when he returned with petite 18-year-old Jacqueline, who he raped upstairs before handcuffing her downstairs with the others.

That night Gary decided to celebrate Josefina's 26th birthday, buying Chinese food and champagne for everyone. It was an obvious indication as to who his favourite prisoner was. But his good mood wouldn't last.

A couple of weeks later he caught Sandra trying to remove the plywood cover over the pit. He handcuffed her by one hand to a beam in the roof for days. During this time she refused to eat and soon had a high fever and was suffering from nausea. After a week of being force-fed pieces of bread Sandra Lindsay died. Gary carried her body upstairs and decapitated her with a power saw. He then fed parts of her body to his dog. He also ground up her flesh in a food processor and mixed it into dog food, which he fed to his animals and the girls. He kept her head in a pot on the stove, though, and later showed it to Deborah, telling her that the same thing would happen to her if she continued to cause trouble. He then opened the oven to reveal Sandra's ribcage being roasted.

Gary soon became convinced that the women were devising a plot against him. He decided to gouge the insides of their ears to deafen them, reasoning that they wouldn't be able to hear him coming. The only one of his prisoners that didn't suffer this torment was Josefina. He also started to spend more time alone with the woman who was the first of his prisoners.

As time went by, Gary's behaviour, if possible, became even stranger, and he added a new form of torture to the beatings and humiliation. After stripping the insulation from an extension cord, he plugged it into a power point and would then touch the girls' chains with the live wire in a crude version of electric shock therapy. After a while, he made this punishment even more extreme by ordering Josefina to fill the pit with water. He then drilled holes in the cover and forced the other three girls into the wet hole with their chains on. After putting the cover back on, Gary poked the wire through one of the holes, shocking the women. The second time he pushed the wire through it touched Deborah's chain directly. The shock was so strong that the woman shuddered and fell down dead in the water. He wrapped the body in plastic the next day and put it in his freezer.

After Deborah's murder, Gary made sandwiches and then told Josefina to write the time and date on a piece of paper. He then ordered her to make a written statement that she had helped him electrocute her fellow prisoner to death. This, he believed, gave him absolute control over the woman. She would never be able to tell the authorities about his actions, as she was now an accomplice. It was a turning point in what Gary believed was a growing relationship with Josefina.

After she wrote her confession, Gary removed Josefina's chains and told her to go upstairs and get changed. She had been his prisoner for four months, and this was the first time she had been fully clothed in that entire time.

Josefina was now with Gary constantly, even going shopping with him or to eat in restaurants, as well as sharing his bed. On March 22, she accompanied him to a wooded area called Pine Barrens where the pair dumped Deborah's body by some trees. The next night they went driving around to look for a new prisoner to take Deborah's place. The woman they found, Agnes, was taken back to the house and quickly stripped and chained up in the basement with the others.

On 24 March, Josefina convinced Gary to allow her to visit her family. As an added incentive, she told him that she would bring him back another prisoner. That night, Gary drove her to near her house, but as soon as he left she ran to the flat where she lived with her boyfriend, Vincent Nelson.

Vincent could hardly believe the story Josefina was telling him. The police were called and when officers John Cannon and David Savidge arrived Josefina had to show them the scars on her ankles from the chains before they were convinced her appalling tale was actually true. Gary Heidnik was arrested that night, picked up at the service station where he had arranged to meet Josefina and the new woman she had promised to bring him.

The police broke down the door at Gary's house at around 5am on 25 March 1987. After freeing the female prisoners, a search of the kitchen revealed two forearms, one upper arm, two knees and parts of thigh. The human remains wrapped and stored in Gary's fridge totalled almost 11 kilograms.

Legal proceedings against Gary Heidnik began on 23 April 1987. With lawyer Charles 'Chuck' Peruto acting for him, Gary was facing charges of murder, kidnapping, rape, aggravated assault, involuntary deviate sexual intercourse, indecent exposure, false imprisonment, unlawful restraint, simple assault and indecent assault.

Lisa was the first of his prisoners called to give evidence at the preliminary hearing, and she told her terrible tale in shocking detail. Next to take the stand was Josefina, who went further into the deaths of Sandra Lindsay and Deborah Dudley.

The court was packed when Gary's proper trial started on 20 June 1980. The accused sat emotionless while the prosecution's damning case was put forward. Admitting that his client was guilty, Peruto decided to argue that Gary was insane. It didn't work. On 30 June 1988 the jury found Gary guilty of two counts of first-degree murder, five counts of rape, six counts of kidnapping, four counts of aggravated assault and one count of involuntary deviate sexual intercourse. He was sentenced to death, and spent the next 11 years waiting on death row, where he tried to commit suicide several times. Gary Heidnik was executed by lethal injection at 10.29pm on 6 July 1999.

PRIME SUSPECT
(EPISODE 1)
(1991)

DIRECTED BY CHRISTOPHER MENAUL
WRITTEN AND CREATED BY LYNDA LA PLANTE

FEATURING
Helen Mirren as DCI Jane Tennison
John Bowe as George Marlow
Zoë Wannamaker as Moyra Henson
Tom Bell as DS Bill Oatley
John Belfield as DCS Michael Kiernan
John Forgeham as DCI John Shefford
Tom Wilkinson as Peter Rawlins

Given that *Prime Suspect* Episode 1 wasn't based on a real serial killer, or any particular series of murders or, in fact, on any actual female DCI in charge of a homicide investigation, all credit for this masterpiece of multicide must go to creator and writer Lynda La Plante.

For a work of fiction, this is a totally credible and accurate encounter of what goes on behind the scenes in a large-scale murder investigation. Having said that, we can only wonder if it would have been anywhere near as good without the magnificent cast, led by Helen Mirren in arguably the performance of her career.

Now that it is readily available for sale or rental as a DVD, this made-for-television gobsmacker more than qualifies as a serial killer movie. And what a movie it is! One of the all-time greats of its genre, it's up there with *The Silence of the Lambs* and *Se7en* as a modern classic.

When Detective Chief Inspector Jane Tennison (Helen Mirren) finally lands herself a new job in charge of a team of detectives, she finds they don't like taking orders from a woman, especially an inexperienced one.

The detectives are in the middle of investigating the brutal murder of a young woman and they battle their new leader every step of the way. Against their wishes, she persists in her line of inquiries because she believes that if she doesn't persist, the beast who did this murder will get away with it, and with lots of other brutal slayings as well.

There are obstacles for Jane at every turn. She battles the blokes who want her replaced with another bloke, and the bureaucrats who want to replace her to please the blokes. After her lover leaves her – because she's spending too much time tracking down a serial killer who may not even exist – the booze she quaffs by the vase-full seems to be the only thing that can console her.

During three and a half hours of superb filmmaking you'll find yourself jumping out of the chair to cheer Jane on through all of her dramas, and you will rejoice as she triumphantly brings the case to its riveting finale, spitting in the eye of bureaucracy. Of course, the team members who started out hating her become her best pals.

While Helen Mirren steals the show, it wouldn't be half as good if it wasn't for the performance by John Bowe as George Marlow, the persecuted serial killer suspect, and his long-suffering missus, Moyra, played by *Harry Potter*'s Zoë Wannamaker.

Prime Suspect Episode 1 has got the works required by every serial killer movie enthusiast: brilliant detective work, a serial killer in denial, crooked cops, a severely flawed main character and a trap to catch the killer to die for.

Not to be missed.

NOTE: Episode 6 in the *Prime Suspect* series deals some years later with the killer who was locked away in Episode 1 for the murders. He has had a bestseller written about him that claims he is innocent. And when the dead bodies of young women turn up one after the other, with similarities to the initial murders that only the jailed killer and the police – Jane Tennison in particular – would know about, this starts to seem likely.

Did Jane lock up the wrong villain? If not, is there a copycat killer on the loose? And, if so, how did they find out the secrets of the previous killings? It's compelling stuff and well worth a look, but not a patch on Episode 1. The big disappointment is that a different actor plays the serial killer. This one is also out on DVD.

ANDY GARCIA · UMA THURMAN
On the trail
of a serial killer
Detective John Berlin
has no clues
no suspects
And no alibi
Jennifer 8
IS NEXT
PARAMOUNT PICTURES PRESENTS A SCOTT RUDIN PRODUCTION JENNIFER EIG
ANDY GARCIA UMA THURMAN LANCE HENRIKSEN KATHY BAKER GRAHAM BECKEL KEVIN CONWAY AND JOHN MALKOVI
CHRISTOPHER YOUNG JUDY RUSKIN FILM EDITOR CONRAD BUFF PRODUCTION DESIGNED BY RICHARD MACDONAL
CONRAD L. HALL, A.S.C. EXECUTIVE PRODUCER SCOTT RUDIN PRODUCED BY GARY LUCCHESI AND DAVID WIMBU
BRUCE ROBINSON Soundtrack Available on records, CD and cassette. A Paramount Communications Compa

JENNIFER 8
(1992)

DIRECTED BY BRUCE ROBINSON
SCREENPLAY BY BRUCE ROBINSON

FEATURING
Andy Garcia as Sergeant John Berlin
Lance Henriksen as Sergeant Freddy Ross
Uma Thurman as Helena Robertson
John Malkovich as Agent St Anne
Graham Beckel as John Taylor
Kathy Baker as Margie Ross

J*ennifer 8* copped such a terrible caning from the critics on its release that all but the dedicated serial killer enthusiasts stayed away. Even the voyeurs gave it a miss when the word got out that it was a body double, and not Uma Thurman, in the full nude bosom scene. As a result, despite its blockbuster cast *Jennifer 8* only recouped just over $US11 million at the box office of the alleged $US25 million it cost to make, which, presumably, most would have gone in salaries.

Which is all such a pity as *Jennifer 8* is a pretty good movie. It has all the ingredients of a very watchable whodunit. Not brilliant, but serial killer fans will enjoy it.

Andy Garcia plays Sergeant John Berlin, a disillusioned LA homicide detective who has had enough of the big smoke and joins one of his mates on the police force of a small rural town. Almost immediately, while searching a rubbish tip for evidence, he comes across an arm. His detective know-how tells him that the worn-down fingertips indicate that the arm belonged to a young blind woman. His search of the records leads him to believe that she is the victim of a serial killer who has claimed the lives of seven other blind women in the district in recent years.

Andy's victim is code-named Jennifer – the eighth victim – hence the title.

Andy meets Helena Robertson, played by Uma Thurman, who is so beautiful that it wouldn't matter if she was blind, deaf, dumb and spoke in Swahili, Andy is a goner. Trouble is, it looks as if Uma is going to be the next victim. Andy spends the rest of the movie keeping her alive, tracking down the killer, keeping his hostile workmates off his back and staying out of jail as the prime suspect.

Pardon the pun, but Blind Freddy could tell you who the killer is about two-thirds of the way through, but that doesn't detract from the movie in any way. In fact, it keeps you hangin' in there wondering why the dude would want to do such terrible things to the less-than-defenceless victims anyway. Plus there's so much aggravation and drama happening to Andy that there isn't any time to lose interest.

The majority of serial killer movies are guilty of monumental plot blunders and *Jennifer 8* is no exception. Initially the severed hand that Sergeant Berlin finds in a the rubbish dump is identified as being that of a blind person. This is because the fingertips are worn down from reading Braille. But later on it is actually quite a significant plot detail that the owner of the hand didn't read Braille at all. Oops.

The cast of *Jennifer 8* is strong and, apart from superstars Andy, Uma, Lance Henriksen and John Malkovich – who appears late as a tough FBI agent – there are lots of familiar faces and terrific performances among the supporting actors.

Jennifer 8 may not be a great movie, but it is a great *serial killer* movie.

A TRUE AND HORRIFYING STORY.

BRIAN
DENNEHY
MARGOT
KIDDER

Loving father.
Pillar of society.
Mass murderer.

Only one man could stop him.

TO CATCH A

KILLER

Starring BRIAN DENNEHY · MICHAEL RILEY · MARGOT KIDDER and MEG FOSTER
Associate Producers TERRENCE TURNER & DAVID McAREE
Co-Executive Producer PETER FILION Co-Producer PATRICK WHITLEY
Written By JUD KINBERG Executive Producers JINNY SCHRECKINGER and JUD KINBERG
Produced by RICHARD O. LOWRY Directed By ERIC TILL

TO CATCH A KILLER

(1992)

DIRECTED BY ERIC TILL
SCREENPLAY BY JUD KINBERG

FEATURING

Brian Dennehy as John Wayne Gacy
Michael Riley as Lieutenant Joseph Kozenczak
Margot Kidder as Rachel Grayson
Meg Foster as Attorney Linda Carson
Martin Julien as Theodore 'Ted' Koslo
Scott Hylands as Sergeant Mike Paxton

If the story of John Wayne Gacy – how he got away with murdering young men and burying them under his house for years – was a novel, no-one would buy it. It is just too ridiculous to be the figment of even the most fertile imagination. But he did do it and, for a very long time, he got away with it.

Chubby Gacy posed as a harmless construction company owner and tireless social worker, who dressed up as Pogo the Clown to entertain the kiddies and raise money for local charities. All the while he was killing at his leisure. It's enough to put you off going to the circus ever again. Gacy was often publicly praised for his fundraising efforts by the local community of Des Plains, Illinois. He even received a commendation from Democrat president Jimmy Carter's wife, Rosalynn, for his contributions and time.

But behind Pogo's greasepaint and ruby lips was one of the most evil serial killers who ever lived: a man who was so persuasive that he could lure a seemingly never-ending procession of boys and young men back to his home where he would commit atrocities, before killing them during sex and burying their bodies in the crawl space beneath his house. The plausible Gacy foiled his victims, the community and the police.

The key to this film is the magnificent performance by Brian Dennehy as John Wayne Gacy. Judging from the video available of the real-life Gacy speaking from his cell on Death Row, Dennehy captures him perfectly. He is a self-assured, swaggering bully, who thinks he can get away with murder. And he did, at least until he was convicted of more homicides than anyone in US history.

Although *To Catch a Killer* was made for TV, it is available as a movie at most DVD shops, and for sale on the internet. It is highly recommended viewing: authentic and very, very real. Brian Dennehy will frighten the daylights out of you, and any teenage boys in the house.

John Wayne Gacy: The Killer Clown

Even though he would eventually be executed for the murders of 33 young men, John Wayne Gacy – described by those who knew him as generous, charming and civic-minded – will forever be more infamous for dressing up as Pogo the Clown, a character the respected and trusted community figure used to entertain local children. The image of a smiling clown who hosts large street parties but secretly

JOHN WAYNE GACY AS
POGO THE CLOWN

GACY WITH JIMMY
CARTER'S WIFE, ROSALYNN

drugs, sexually assaults and kills his male victims is shocking to the core, and sent a chill down the spine of anyone who followed the body count as the case unfolded.

Born in Chicago on 17 March 1942, Gacy was the second of three children. While his mother was a loving figure, Gacy's father was an alcoholic who would beat his wife.

Gacy was a quiet boy. At age 11 he hit his head on a swing, which caused a blood clot in his brain. Even though he suffered blackouts as a result, the problem wasn't diagnosed, and instead he was treated with medication until he was 16 years old. He was also found to have a heart condition, which would send him to hospital several times over the years.

With his grades failing, Gacy dropped out of high school in his senior year and moved to Las Vegas, finding work as a janitor in a funeral home, before going back to Chicago, where he enrolled in business college. Upon graduation, he worked for the Nunn-Bush Shoe Company and was promoted to a men's clothing outlet in Springfield, Illinois. Here his heart condition kicked in again and he started to gain weight. He was also hospitalised because of a bad back.

It was in Springfield that Gacy became involved in community groups such as the Jaycees, and he would later become their vice-president. During this time he also met co-worker Marlynn Myers, whom he married in September 1964. Marlynn's father owned several Kentucky Fried Chicken outlets in Iowa, and the pair moved there so that Gacy could learn the family business. He was a hard and enthusiastic worker, who would put in 14-hour days.

Before long, Gacy and Marlynn had a son and a daughter and they seemed to be the image of suburban bliss. But it was hard to overlook the fact that Gacy was always in the company of young boys. Rumours spread that he had begun to put the hard word on young male workers in the restaurant business. Then, in May 1968, he was indicted by a grand jury for committing an act of sodomy on teenager Mark Miller. According to Miller, Gacy had tied him up and violently raped him. Gacy contended that Miller had engaged in sex with him voluntarily for money.

Four months later, 18-year-old Dwight Andersson was arrested for assaulting Miller. He told the authorities that Gacy had hired him to beat up the boy, and Gacy was charged with the offence and ordered to undergo psychiatric evaluation. The experts found that he had an antisocial personality, but that he was fit to stand trial. Not long after the evaluation, at the age of 26, Gacy went to prison for the first time, entering Iowa State Reformatory on the sodomy charge. Marlynn also divorced him and took their children away.

Though he had been sentenced to 10 years, Gacy was paroled after just 18 months because of his good behaviour. It was June 1970 when he was released and he moved back to Chicago, where he worked as a chef and lived with his mother for four months before finding his own place at 8213 West Summerdale Avenue in the quiet Norwood Park township.

Here he soon became close to his neighbours, Edward and Lilla Grexa. But despite his outwardly friendly front, Gacy was still courting trouble. In November he was charged with disorderly conduct after he picked up a boy at a bus station and forced him to perform sexual acts. The charges were dropped, though, when the boy didn't show up for the court date.

By all appearances an upstanding member of society, Gacy romanced newly divorced Carole Huff, and married the mother of two in June 1972. Carole and her daughters moved into Gacy's house, where the Grexas were regular guests at parties and barbecues. Still, though they were all friends, the Grexas would often point out the strange smell that permeated Gacy's residence, as if an animal had died under the floorboards.

Gacy started a contracting business in 1974, called PDM Contractors Inc (standing for Painting, Decorating and Maintenance). Most of the help he hired came in the form of eager teenage boys. He started to grow more distant to Carole. They no longer had sex and Gacy developed insomnia. His personality was becoming unpredictable as well. One minute he would seem friendly, the next he would blow into a rage that would see him hurling objects around the house. Carole then started to find pornography around the house featuring naked males. It was the last straw. Gacy admitted to her that he found young men more sexually appealing than women. She filed for divorce in early 1976.

After that, Gacy volunteered his business services to the local Democratic township committeeman, Robert F Matwick. Gacy's team fixed up Matwick's headquarters, and the divorcee was nominated to the Norwood Park Street Lighting Commission. Then, in 1975 he became Matwick's secretary treasurer. But stories were already circulating.

One of the boys working with Gacy repairing Matwick's

party headquarters, 16-year-old Tony Antonucci, revealed that Gacy had made advances towards him, but had retreated when Antonucci threatened him. Weeks later, at Gacy's house, the older man tricked the boy into a pair of handcuffs, but he got out of them. A 17-year-old co-worker named Johnny Butkovich wouldn't be so lucky.

Butkovich worked for Gacy to earn extra cash to indulge his passion for car racing. But a time came when Gacy said he couldn't pay the youth what he was owed for the previous fortnight. Butkovich and two friends called around to Gacy's house hoping to intimidate the money out of him but, after a loud argument, the boys left. Butkovich drove his friends home, but that was the last they ever saw of him. He wouldn't be the last young man to go missing, though. Michael Bonnin, 17, was next, followed by 16-year-old Billy Carroll, 17-year-old Gregory Godzik and 19-year-old John Szyc, who was last seen driving in his 1971 Plymouth Satellite on 20 January 1977.

Not long after Szyc went missing, the police picked up another teenage boy driving the same make car. The youth told them to speak to the man he was living with, a man named John Wayne Gacy. But Gacy fast-talked his way out of the situation, explaining that he had bought the car off Szyc. If the authorities had have run a simple title check, though, they would have noted that the papers were signed over to Gacy 18 days after Szyc went missing.

After that close call, the next boy to disappear was 18-year-old Robert Gilroy, who was last seen on 15 September 1977 on his way to catch a bus to meet friends. An investigation was launched but nothing would come of it until a year later, when 15-year-old Robert Piest went missing.

Piest had disappeared from the pharmacy he worked at. His mother was waiting outside to take him home when the boy told her he had to talk to a man about a contracting job offer. He went back inside, but when he hadn't returned after three hours, the worried mother got in touch with the authorities. It was the beginning of the end for Gacy.

An investigation was launched, headed up by Lieutenant Joseph Kozenczak, who soon found out that a man named Gacy had made Piest the job offer. Kozenczak visited the house at 8213 West Summerdale Avenue, and Gacy later gave a statement saying he knew nothing about Piest going missing. Still, Kozenczak checked the man's record and saw that he had served time for sodomy on a teenage boy. Alarm bells rang and a search warrant was obtained for Gacy's home.

When a team of police entered the residence on 13 December 1978 Gacy wasn't home. They discovered several suspicious items, including marijuana and amyl nitrate, nylon rope, gay and child pornography, handcuffs, two drivers licences and a collection of rings, one of which had the letters 'J.A.S.' engraved on it as well as the words 'Maine West High School Class of 1975'. The team also confiscated several items of clothing they found which were obviously too small for Gacy, as well as three of his cars – a 1978 Chevrolet truck, a PDM van and a 1979 Oldsmobile Delta 88. Hair found in the boot of the Oldsmobile would later be confirmed as belonging to Piest.

When the search of Gacy's house led the police into the crawl space beneath it, they were sickened by a smell they believed to be sewage.

Gacy was brought down to the station again, but with nothing to charge him with at that time, they could only question him about Piest again and let him go, albeit with 24-hour surveillance. Police also began to question Gacy's friends, but they all seemed shocked at the suggestion that the upstanding citizen could be involved in anything illegal.

With no other options, the police booked Gacy with possession of marijuana while they waited for their experts to come back with the results on the items seized in the search of Gacy's house. The wait proved worthwhile.

It turned out that one of the rings belonged to missing teen John Szyc. Then they learnt that three former employees of Gacy's had also disappeared. When the authorities and technical experts decided to check Gacy's house once again, Gacy went into damage control, admitting that he had indeed killed someone and buried the body under his garage but, he added, it had been in self-defence. Investigators took note of his story and marked out the garage. But instead of starting their search there, they began with the crawl space below the house itself. It didn't take long to uncover the first rotting corpse.

Gacy was told of the find on 22 December 1978. Realising that he had hit the end of the road, he quickly admitted to multiple murders and confessed that most of the remains would be found buried under his house.

Gacy went on to say that he committed his first murder in January 1972. His second killing was two years later, while he was married to Carole Huff and living with her and her young daughters. His modus operandi was to trick his victims into being handcuffed, before stuffing a sock or their underwear into their mouths and raping them while holding a rope or board to their throats until they stopped breathing. The corpses would then be kept in his attic or under his bed for days before they were buried under the house. When the crawl space was reaching capacity, and the digging of shallow graves started to irritate his old back complaint, Gacy began to dump the bodies in the Des Plaines River. Two bodies were also found set in concrete under his patio.

With the killer clown safely behind bars, by the spring of

1979, 8213 West Summerdale, the killing field and graveyard for so many young men, had been reduced to ruin by the locals. They had thrown bricks at it, smashed the windows and even set fire to it. When the remains of the house were finally bulldozed, it left a conspicuous vacant block of mud and slush as a constant reminder of the buried bodies.

Still the onlookers came in bus loads to be reminded of Chicago's most terrible resident since Al Capone. It was decided that grass should be planted there as a silent memorial. But, despite there being no logical explanation for it, neither grass nor trees would grow.

The murder trial against John Wayne Gacy commenced on 6 February 1980, with prosecutor Bob Egan painting a chilling picture. In rebuttal, Gacy's lawyer Robert Motta portrayed his client as irrational and insane, unaware of the severity of his actions.

By the time the prosecution rested their case, around 60 witnesses had testified, including family and friends of Gacy's victims. Rather than trying to counter the damning evidence presented, Gacy's defence instead tried to strengthen their assertion that the killer was insane. Gacy's mother took the stand and told of the vicious beatings her husband unleashed upon the boy, while several medical experts concluded that Gacy was not in control at the time of the murders.

At the end of the trial the jury took two hours to find him guilty. He was sentenced to death and placed in Menard Correctional Center. After years of frivolous appeals, on 9 May 1994, Pogo the Clown was executed by lethal injection. That certainly took the smile off his face.

CITIZEN X

(1995)

DIRECTED BY CHRIS GEROLMO
SCREENPLAY BY CHRIS GEROLMO

FEATURING

Stephen Rea as Lieutenant Viktor Burakov
Donald Sutherland as Colonel Mikhail Fetisov
Max von Sydow as Dr Alexander Bukhanovsky
Jeffrey DeMunn as Andrei Chikatilo
Joss Ackland as Bondarchuk
John Wood as Gorbunov

Three years before Stephen Rea played the part of a Soviet super-sleuth in *Citizen X*, he played the role for which he is best remembered: the IRA volunteer in *The Crying Game* who almost dies of shock after he falls for his victim's hairdresser girlfriend, Dil, only to discover that when she lifts up her dress that Dil is really Bill.

Having recovered from that, Stephen Rea is brilliant as the real-life Russian forensic detective, Viktor Burakov. Burakov is in pursuit of Andrei Chikatilo, the worst fiend in Russia's history – and that is really saying something – who, over a 12-year period abducts and murders more than 50 victims, most of them under

17. He cuts off their body parts and eats them while they are still warm. A charming bit of work.

Unfortunately for Viktor, who is in charge of the investigation, he runs into the Russian bureaucracy machine very early in the peace. This inhibits his manhunt, especially when the prime suspect, Chikatilo, is questioned and released on the dubious grounds that he was a school teacher and a 'member of the Communist Party', and people like him wouldn't do such terrible things to Russia's children. Besides, serial killers don't exist in Russia – such a phenomenon can only be the product of the corrupt capitalist West.

With Viktor's investigation hampered at every turn, he eventually gets some help from kindly Colonel Mikhail Fetisov (Donald Sutherland) and the brilliant psychiatrist Dr Alexander Bukhanovsky (Max von Sydow). But for a while there it looks as if Viktor – if he doesn't catch the killer soon – is more likely to wind up with a bullet behind the right ear, Russia's form of capital punishment, rather than the mysterious serial killer.

While the red-tape drama between Burakov, the Board, Colonel Fetisov and Dr Bukhanovsky tends to overshadow lots of the murders, in many ways it is probably for the best: a couple of hours watching what Chikatilo did to those kiddies would be enough to send you straight to the rubber room at the local rehab.

Jeffrey DeMunn is convincing as Chikatilo. There are times when you will find yourself almost feeling sorry for the man who kills and rapes children, gouges their eyes out and then eats them. For instance in the scene with the psychiatrist, he opens up and we see for the first time what makes the pathetic monster tick.

Citizen X claimed four Emmy Awards, including Best Director for Chris Gerolmo. Sutherland won a Golden Globe and an Emmy for Supporting Actor. And justifiably so. This film is not to be missed.

But the real story of Andrei Chikatilo is as evil as it gets.

Andrei 'The Maniac' Chikatilo

Born with a misshapen head (the result of water on the brain) in a tiny Ukrainian village in 1936, Andrei Romanovich Chikatilo, the serial killer who would come to be known throughout the Russian press simply as 'The Maniac', went on to confess to a staggering 56 murders between 1978 and 1990, though there would only be evidence for 53 – 31 females and 22 males.

With his father a prisoner of war in World War II, before being sent to a Russian prison camp, Chikatilo's mother raised the boy and his younger sister on her own during times stricken with famine so severe that desperate people resorted to cannibalism. His mother told him that his own older brother had been eaten when he was 10 years old. The story was used as a warning for Chikatilo not to leave their yard.

During the Nazi occupation, Chikatilo saw dead bodies in the street, blown to pieces. He later admitted that the sight, while frightening, was also exciting to him.

He first started to fantasise about torture when he was a young, awkward boy, teased by those his own age because of his sensitive nature.

Chikatilo experienced his first sexual feelings as a teen, ejaculating in his pants while wrestling with a 10-year-old friend of his sister's. From then on he would be able to ejaculate but remained unable to gain an erection – but he would always remember the young girl's struggle, and the sense of power he felt from it.

When he was old enough, Chikatilo joined the army, and when he came home he found himself a girlfriend. But the relationship didn't last long as he was unable to make love to her. The girl told everyone about Chikatilo's dysfunction and he was deeply hurt. He started to imagine himself ripping her into pieces.

He next became a teacher and found himself in a marriage arranged by his sister. His wife was often critical of Chikatilo, which pushed him further into a fantasy world of his own design. When he was 37 years old, in 1973, his mother died, and he was soon molesting young girls, enjoying the feeling of power it gave him, unlike anything else in his life. These feelings soon manifested themselves in more extreme violence, and Chikatilo murdered his first victim – nine-year-old Yelena Zakotnova – in 1978. Unfortunately another man was arrested and executed for the crime, and Chikatilo found a new job as a machinery parts supply liaison, a position that saw him on the road often, travelling from town to town.

It was a couple of years until Chikatilo's victims started turning up in numbers. The first was mostly just bones when it was found in a forested area in southern Russia. The local authorities – the militsia – found that the decomposed body had no identifying clothing, but they determined that it was a female. There were two broken ribs and several stab wounds in the bones. It also appeared that a knife had been used to gouge out the victim's eyes.

The authorities found a missing persons report for a 13-year-old girl named Lyubov Biryuk from the nearby village of Novocherkassk. The top detective from militsia headquarters, Major Mikhail Fetisov, arrived and ordered fingerprint checks and a search of the area. They found items belonging to Lyubov and confirmed she was the victim, though the dress she wore was nowhere to be found. An autopsy revealed Lyubov had been hit from behind with extreme force using both the handle and blade of a knife. Her body suffered at least 22 stab wounds.

Less than two months later, near the train station of an industrial town called Shakhty, about 30 kilometres away, another set of bones was discovered. They belonged to an unidentified adult woman and had been there for about six weeks. Again there were multiple stab wounds and the eyes had been gouged out.

A month later another unidentified female body was found with the same wounding pattern about 15 kilometres to the south. By now it was obvious to all concerned that a serial killer was at work. Fetisov organised a 10-man task force that included 37-year-old Viktor Burakov, a hard-working second lieutenant from the criminology laboratory, who was a crime scene expert.

The task force didn't have much time to settle into their new role. That same month another female victim was found in the same area as the second body. The wounds were the same as the previous cases, though the murder had occurred six months earlier.

Burakov was soon called to the mining town of Novoshakhtinsk, where 10-year-old Olga Stalmachenok had been reported missing, last seen on 10 December 1982 travelling on a bus to a piano lesson. Olga's parents then received a disturbing postcard signed 'Sadist-Black Cat'. It said their daughter had been dumped in the forest, and that there would be 10 more victims in the next 12 months.

Olga's naked body turned up four months later, frozen in a tractor rut on a nearby farm. Burakov investigated the scene and saw that there were dozens of knife puncture marks on her skull, stomach and chest. The eyes had again been stabbed, as had the vagina.

No further bodies were found for four months, though Chikatilo was still active – the corpses were just hidden by the winter's snow. Then the remains of a 13-year-old girl who had Down's syndrome were found not far from the first dumpsite. With the death toll mounting, Chikatilo's next victim put investigators in a spin.

The body of an eight-year-old boy was found in forestland near Rostov airport in September. He had last been seen travelling on public transport, and his corpse bore the by-now telltale signs of Chikatilo's gruesome handy work. The task force couldn't believe the man they were hunting could murder so indiscriminately. It seemed anyone could be a target – young, old, male or female. But while they wondered if there was perhaps more than one person responsible for the brutal slayings, the police announced that they had apprehended the maniac.

The man in custody was 19-year-old Yuri Kalenik, but all the police had on him was the word of a friend with whom Yuri had grown up with in a home for retarded children. Nonetheless, they interrogated him for days – with no lawyer present – until he confessed to the seven murders of which the authorities were so far aware, as well as four other unsolved cases.

Burakov was brought in and, at first, agreed that Yuri was a viable suspect. But that belief dimmed after he read the confession. It was clear he had been intimidated into his admission. Burakov was wondering what to do next when another body was found.

Chikatilo's violence was escalating. The young female victim's nipples had been bitten off, and her stomach slashed open. Then, on October 20, yet another body turned up. This confirmed Burakov's doubts about Yuri's guilt – the young man had been in custody when the latest victim had been disembowelled, and other internal organs removed.

A month later, another female cadaver was found in nearby woods. Then, in early 1984, the body of 14-year-old Sergei Markov turned up near some railway tracks. There were around 70 stab marks on his neck and his genitals had been cut off. The young boy had also been anally raped, and it appeared that Chikatilo had defecated near the murder scene.

At least this murder gave investigators their first decent piece of evidence, after they found traces of semen in Markov's anus. While comparing it to the blood antigens of suspects wouldn't confirm guilt, it would at least be able to eliminate suspects.

The next victim was an 18-year-old woman who had last been seen at a bus station. Her body was found in woodland, with her eyes left intact, though a finger had been cut off. Chikatilo left more evidence behind this time, as well – a size-13 shoeprint in mud near the corpse, as well as traces of semen and blood on her clothes.

After that, Chikatilo waited until March when he stabbed and cruelly mutilated 10-year-old Dmitri Ptashnikov in Novoshakhtinsk, slicing off the tip of his tongue and penis, and again leaving behind a large shoeprint. In another breakthrough in the case, witnesses reported seeing a tall man with glasses and hollow cheeks. Another witness said they had seen a white car.

But if Chikatilo was getting sloppy, he wasn't slowing down. Lyudmila Alekseyeva, 17, was the next victim, stabbed 39 times. Then came another twist – a mother and daughter murdered together; the young girl beaten to death with a hammer, her mother stabbed with a knife.

With the authorities by now attributing 24 murders to the man they were searching for, Burakov was named head of a new task force, with around 200 staff below him. Undercover agents were posted in places the task force believed the killer was finding his victims – parks, bus and train stations. One of these officers saw a man talking to a teenage girl at Rostov station. After she got on her bus, the man moved on to another woman. This behaviour was considered suspicious enough to question the man. It was Andrei Chikatilo.

Chikatilo explained that he was in the area for business, but lived in Shakhty. He added that he had once been a teacher, and missed talking to young people, hence his conversation with the girl. The officer accepted the story and sent Chikatilo on his way. But when he saw the suspicious man again, he followed him until he sought the services of a prostitute, paying for oral sex in public, shielded only by his long coat. The officer pounced and Chikatilo was booked for indecent exposure. A search of his briefcase revealed a kitchen knife, rope, lubricant and a soiled towel.

The authorities thought they had their man, but Chikatilo was a well-regarded member of the Communist Party. Nothing in his history suggested he was a heartless murderer. He was kept in a cell for a few days anyway, but admitted to nothing more than a weakness for sex.

By now the pressure was on Burakov to come up with a killer, but Chikatilo eased back on his murder spree, with only one body turning up in the next 10 months. After that, the next murder was that of a young woman in August 1985. Then detectives in Moscow linked the murders of three young boys to the ongoing investigation – all of the victims had been raped, while one had also been decapitated. It seemed Chikatilo was back on a roll.

Indeed, the next victim was a homeless 18-year-old girl, found among trees near a bus station in Shakhty. A grey hair found between her fingers matched one found at a previous crime scene. Then Chikatilo eased back the pace of his murders again until 18 August 1985, when a woman's body was found whose wounds matched those of the previous victims, except that she had been buried with only a hand sticking up out of the dirt. Investigators now faced the possibility there were any number of unfound corpses out there under the ground.

But Chikatilo went quiet again, with no bodies turning up until 6 April 1988, when spring melted the snow to reveal a woman's body dumped near railroad tracks. Bound and stabbed, her skull had been crushed and the end of her nose was missing. Her eyes were still intact and the killer hadn't sexually assaulted her, but there was a familiar large shoeprint nearby.

It was only a month before the task force were again checking out a murder – this one was of nine-year-old boy Aleksei Voronko, discovered on 17 May in forestland near a railway station. His penis had been cut off and he had been sodomised and stabbed.

Chikatilo went through another quiet spell, and Burakov's task force wondered if perhaps their killer had died. It wasn't until April 1989 that another body was discovered. This time it was a 16-year-old boy who had gone missing months earlier. The child had been stabbed over and over again, and his genitals had been cut off. Back to his evil ways, Chikatilo's murder count kept clicking ever higher. On 11 May he kidnapped an eight-year-old boy, who he stabbed, mutilated and dumped on the side of a road. In August he murdered a Hungarian student, then came an 11-year-old boy followed closely by a 10-year-old male, whose penis he removed. The boy's tongue was also removed, apparently bitten out.

It seemed Chikatilo would never be stopped. He continued killing randomly, violently murdering a woman before attacking a 13-year-old boy in July 1990. A month later, on 17 August, he stabbed 11-year-old Ivan Fomin 42 times before cutting off his penis. Next came a 16-year-old retarded boy, stabbed 27 times and castrated. Then an athletic 16-year-old male, followed by a young women, who was beaten and cut open. Part of her tongue was also missing. But this time Burakov got the breakthrough for which he was so desperate. A man had been seen coming out of the woods where the last victim was dumped. The man was identified as 54-year-old Andrei Chikatilo, the same man questioned back in 1984. He was taken into custody on 20 November 1990. His house was searched and 23 knives were found there. When interrogated, Chikatilo maintained that he was innocent. He was held for nine days before he finally confessed.

Investigators were appalled when Chikatilo admitted that murdering his victims had given him pleasure, and that he enjoyed the taste of their blood. He then said that he found a form of 'animal satisfaction' when he ate the nipples or testicles of his victims.

He appeared in Rostov court on 14 April 1992. Bald and

looking mentally unbalanced, he was held in a large iron cage. The room was packed with the families of his many victims, who started baying for his blood the minute he was brought into the room.

Despite Chikatilo's confession, the trial dragged on for six months before the judge announced that he was guilty of five counts of molestation and 52 counts of murder. Andrei Romanovich Chikatilo was executed with a single bullet to the head on 15 February 1994.

SIGOURNEY
WEAVER

HOLLY
HUNTER

COPYCAT

One man is
copying the
most notorious
killers in history,
one at a time.

COPYCAT

(1995)

DIRECTED BY JON AMIEL
SCREENPLAY BY ANN BIDERMAN AND DAVID MADSEN

FEATURING

Sigourney Weaver as Helen Hudson
Holly Hunter as Detective MJ Monahan
Harry Connick Jr as Daryll Lee Cullum
William McNamara as Peter Foley
Dermot Mulroney as Reuben Goetz
JE Freeman as Lieutenant Thomas Quinn

Now here's a thriller with a difference. A serial killer who copies other serial killers. That's right. In this highly entertaining but somewhat dubious murder spree, we have a psychopath on the loose who is re-enacting the murders of such famous bygone American serial killers as the Boston Strangler, the Hillside Strangler(s), Son of Sam, Jeffrey Dahmer and Ted Bundy... in that order.

Our killer copies their murders down to the last detail and, in the process, terrorises agoraphobic author, lecturer and serial killer profiler, Helen Hudson, played by Sigourney Weaver, who, after almost being eaten by some of the most loathsome critters in the history of the movies in *Alien 1, 2* and *3*, has one of the most instantly recognisable terrified faces in the world. It worked a treat in *Alien*, and it works well here.

Helen's terror of going out the front door, even to get the morning paper in the hallway, is justified in that she was attacked and throttled half to death in a public toilet by demented hillbilly serial killer Daryll Lee Cullum, played passionately by the unlikely choice of crooner Harry Connick Jr. Daryll's crooked green teeth and rotten breath would be enough to make anyone stay in doors for ever for fear of getting a whiff of them again.

And even though Daryll is locked away on death row awaiting the gas chamber, Helen lives in dreaded fear that somehow he will get out of the slammer and come and attack her or, even worse, breathe on her again. Hence she lives in a barred and iron-clad fortress surrounded by a barrage of computers, an endless supply of brandy and the token gay flatmate.

There are a lot of holes in the plot that you could drive a Jumbo jet through – such as how does the serial killer keep coming and going as he pleases in and out of Helen's impenetrable fortress? But stellar performances from the cast – which includes Holly Hunter as the pint-sized cop, Dermot Mulroney as her sidekick and William McNamara as the handsome, baby-faced serial killer – as well as lots of suspense, more than make up for the gaps. It is nail-biting stuff from go to whoa.

As was so skilfully done with Buffalo Bill and Hannibal Lecter in *The Silence of the Lambs*, and also in 1986's *Manhunter* with Hannibal Lecter and the Tooth Fairy, director Jon Amiel links the serial killer on the loose, the copycat killer, with the more notorious killer in jail, in this case Daryll Lee Cullum. They have contact to ensure Daryll pops up from time to time, either making threats or giving information for promises.

The end credits begin to roll as Daryll Lee Cullum is in his cell scrawling a letter to a pal telling of his soon-to-be prized possession – a pair of Helen Hudson's soiled knickers that she promised him for some valuable information about the copycat killer. It leaves us wondering if she would honour her promise.

Either way, Harry crooning 'With Imagination, I'll Get There' will never be quite the same again.

(1995)

DIRECTED BY DAVID FINCHER
SCREENPLAY BY ANDREW KEVIN WALKER

FEATURING
Brad Pitt as Detective David Mills
Morgan Freeman as Detective Lieutenant William Somerset
Gwyneth Paltrow as Tracy Mills
R Lee Ermey as Police Captain
Kevin Spacey as John Doe
John Cassini as Officer Davis

According to a recent poll of the top 250 movies by the world's most popular movie information source, the Internet Movie Data Base (IMDB), *Se7en* came in at 38, just behind *The Silence of the Lambs* at 27 and *Psycho* at 21, making it the third most popular serial killer movie of all time. No-one could dispute that. Just like *Psycho* and *The Silence of the Lambs*, *Se7en* is a 10 out of 10; faultless in every detail.

Se7en is brilliantly scripted and superbly filmed in an unidentified American city where it rains constantly. It's not at all surprising that Richard Francis-Bruce was nominated for an Oscar for editing and that *Se7en* collected a whole bunch of other acting, writing and technical awards in America as well as around the world.

At the beginning of *Se7en* the teaming of Brad Pitt and Morgan Freeman as the cops looks like it might not work. But it doesn't take long to realise that the dialogue between the young, white, new cop and the old, black, retiring cop, particularly in some of the grisliest scenes you're ever likely to see, is one of the many highlights of a thriller that will have you eating your fingernails as you hang on for the ride of a lifetime.

Se7en wasn't modelled after a real-life murderer simply because no-one in real life could be this bizarre. *Se7en*'s serial killer, known only as John Doe (Kevin Spacey), specialises in bumping off perpetrators of the Seven Deadly Sins – gluttony, greed, sloth, lust, pride, envy and wrath – that were portrayed so graphically by Geoffrey Chaucer in *The Canterbury Tales*. But John doesn't do it by the book. In *Se7en* the punishment is distinctly different from Chaucer's.

Punishment in hell for the deadly sin of gluttony was to be force-fed rats, toads and snakes. In *Se7en* the victim is tied up at a table naked with barbed wire and force-fed cans of Campbell's spaghetti until he dies slowly of internal haemorrhaging.

Punishment in hell for the deadly sin of greed was to be boiled alive in oil. In *Se7en* the victim is forced to eat a pound of his own flesh, in reference to the greed of Shylock in Shakespeare's *The Merchant of Venice*.

Punishment in hell for the deadly sin of sloth was to be thrown into a snake pit. In *Se7en* the victim is tied to a bed and eventually dies of severe mental and physical deterioration after spending a year completely immobile while being force-fed barely enough fluids to keep him alive.

Punishment in hell for the deadly sin of lust was to be roasted alive by fire and brimstone. In *Se7en* a prostitute is bound to the bed and, at gunpoint, a man is forced to have sex with her using a strap-on phallus consisting of a huge razor sharp knife.

Punishment in hell for the deadly sin of pride was to be lashed to the spokes of a wheel until every bone was fractured. In *Se7en* a beautiful model is found dead with her nose cut off – 'to spite her face'. Her choice was suicide with a bottle of sleeping pills glued to one hand, or help from the phone glued to the other and to live with her disfigurement. She chose suicide.

Punishment in hell for the deadly sin of envy was to die by being immersed in freezing water.

Punishment in hell for the deadly sin of wrath was to be dismembered alive.

To reveal *Se7en*'s alternative punishment for envy and wrath would ruin the ending of the movie. You are just going to have to see it and find out for yourself.

Gwyneth Paltrow as Brad Pitt's wife is about the only bit of brightness in a movie that is as visually bleak as the plot. Kevin Spacey, who plays the crazed serial killer John Doe, comes into the movie very late. He refused billing on the opening credits claiming that he didn't want the audience to wait to see him in the movie and would rather that his part be a surprise and add to the suspense.

The only touch of humour comes when cops Pitt and Freeman are interviewing the manager of the sleazy brothel where the latest murder victim has been found.

'Did you see a man come in here carrying a package,' Freeman asks the man.

'Mister, *everyone* who comes in here is carrying a package,' he replies.

KILLER: A JOURNAL OF MURDER

(1996)

DIRECTED BY TIM METCALF

SCREENPLAY BY THE WRITER'S GUILD OF AMERICA

FEATURING

James Woods as Carl Panzram

Robert Sean Leonard as Henry Lesser

Ellen Greene as Elizabeth Wyatt

Cara Buono as Esther Lesser

Robert John Burke as RG Greiser

Richard Riehle as Warden Quince

If you've got 91 minutes to spare, then your time would be better spent worming the cat than watching this piece of rubbish. *Killer: A Journal of Murder* was promoted as 'the story of Carl Panzram, America's first serial killer'. It isn't, and he wasn't. Anyone could tell you that America had serial killers a long time before Panzram came along. HH Holmes, for one, comes immediately to mind.

And while the life and crimes of Carl Panzram is extraordinary in the extreme, this movie does nothing to tell us of his many serial murders, preferring instead to concentrate on his life in prison and his relationship with an Orthodox Jewish guard, who has the personality of a three-toed sloth. Even the usually brilliant James Woods in the lead role can't save this grogan.

In *Killer* we know that Carl Panzram is one bad dude. He is in the nick for robbery and, while there, he befriends a guard who takes pity on him and gets him some paper and a pencil so he can write his memoirs. So Carl tells how he wound up in the slammer. This would be terrific, except they leave out all the good bits about his career as a serial killer. There are many much more interesting stories to be told than what we see in the movie.

In *Killer* we see a kindly, trusting (and very stupid) warden allow psychopathic Carl out of jail a day at a time to go to the local library. This is all very warm and fuzzy – until Carl rapes the librarian. Then we see him bash a guard to death – one who was such a mongrel that I'm sure the cinema-going audience would have stood up and cheered. Then there's all the dramatics leading up to Carl wanting to be hanged, and the eventual hanging which, to my mind, couldn't come soon enough. Carl was a prize scumbag who boasted of killing 21 people – but we are privy to only one of the murders in the movie and even then it's only a snapshot of what happened. And, apart from a whole lot of mindless crap that goes nowhere, that's it.

What the movie doesn't tell you is that Carl Panzram really was a serial killer and rapist who murdered men, women and children. But none of this became known until he wrote his journals in jail and gave them to his friend the guard, Henry Lesser. They were published in 1960 after two crime reporters had verified that the vast majority of Panzram's claims were true.

Carl Panzram's life of crime began at eight. By the time he was 14 he had burned down the reformatory that couldn't contain him. Having been serially and forcefully sodomised since childhood, young Carl thought that was normal practise and, at 16, began raping men. By the time he went to the gallows he claimed to have sodomised more than 1000 victims at gunpoint.

Panzram committed armed robberies and burned churches across America. He stole $40,000 and a Colt .45 from the home of President William Taft, and he claimed to have shot and killed 10 men with it. At one stage Panzram bought a yacht and hired a crew, all of whom he murdered and threw into the sea. He escaped from prison and went to Africa where he murdered all of the porters he had hired to accompany him on a crocodile hunt, laughing as he fed them to the crocs. Along the way he raped and murdered a 12-year-old boy.

And that's just some of it. It gets worse. Find out the shocking truth for yourself in the following story of Carl Panzram. You certainly won't get it from *Killer: A Journal of Murder*.

The Extraordinary Life of Carl Panzram

Full of bitter hate instilled in him from a life spent mostly in a barbaric prison system where he was often beaten and raped, Carl Panzram's killing spree saw him not only terrorising victims at home in the US, but also in Africa.

Born on a remote farm in Minnesota on 28 June 1891, Panzram himself later admitted to being 'a human animal' from the day he came into the world. His cruel streak only grew stronger and meaner through the years of hardship that followed. His father left the family when Panzram was just seven years old, and he worked the hostile land with his mother, sister and five brothers, who would beat the boy whenever they saw fit, which was often, and for just about anything at all.

At the age of 11, Panzram broke into a neighbour's house and stole a pistol. When the brothers found out they beat him until he was unconscious. He was later sent to the

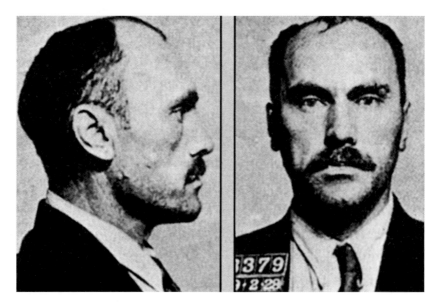

CARL PANZRAM

Minnesota State Training School for the crime, where the 300 inmates were taught to abide by the Christian ways, but were also beaten savagely by the guards. In July 1905 Panzram burnt down the schoolhouse, but later that year he managed to convince the parole board that he had changed for the better, even though inside, after the years of bashings and sexual assaults, he was a seething pool of hatred.

Panzram's mother took him home, but he continued to get into trouble at any opportunity. When he was 14, he left the farm with deep-seated feelings of resentment towards his mother. He soon found himself in Montana State Reform School for a year after being caught for burglary. Already weighing in at more than 80 kilograms, he escaped with another prisoner named Jimmie Benson in 1907 and joined the army, lying about his age easily, thanks to the fact that he had the build of an adult long before most others his age.

Panzram's military stint didn't last long, becaue he was soon caught with stolen goods while absent without leave. As a result, he received a dishonourable discharge and was sent to Leavenworth Federal Penitentiary for three years. Here, at 16, he was put in shackles and suffered the same gruelling routine as the grown men with whom he was incarcerated. Many had criminal careers longer than Panzram had been on the planet.

After the beatings he suffered in jail became regular events, he lashed out and burnt down a workshop on the prison grounds. As a result, he was chained to a 25-kilogram metal ball, and sent to break rocks in a quarry for 10 hours a day, seven days a week.

But all prison seemed to do was make Panzram angrier and stronger, his muscles rippling as a result of the tedious hours of manual labour. He was 19 when he was released in 1910. With no real prospects or plans, he drifted around, getting into trouble with the law for things such as vagrancy, arson and burglary. He set fire to churches and broke into homes. Panzram also started using the alias Jack Allen – the first of many assumed names he would take on – as he made his way through the northwest of the US. In Oregon he got arrested under that name for robbery, assault and sodomy, and was sent to jail, but escaped after a couple of months. He made his way to Idaho, where was again arrested and jailed, this time under the name Jeff Davis.

On his first night inside, Panzram started a large fire in the ramshackle jail and escaped with several other inmates, making his way to Chinook, Montana, where he was again caught for burglary. This time he gave authorities the more formal name Jefferson Davis and was sentenced to serve a year at Montana State Prison, where he was processed on 27 April 1913.

While in Montana State Prison, Panzram was reunited with Jimmie Benson, who was serving 10 years for robbery.

Benson was transferred before the pair could pull of a planned escape, but Panzram soon made his own run on 13 November 1913, though another arrest for burglary – this time under the name Jeff Rhodes – quickly saw him back inside Montana State Prison for another 12-month sentence. His daily routine at this time would be to intimidate a smaller prisoner into sodomy in the morning, then work all day, and often into the night, as the guards saw fit.

Panzram was released on 30 March 1915 and once again began to drift, committing crimes wherever he went.

He was next sentenced to seven years at the brutal Oregon State Penitentiary in Salem for larceny, under the name Jefferson Baldwin. Listing his occupation as thief, Panzram quickly grew tired of the beatings and whippings and isolation and vowed to escape once again. On New Year's Day 1916, he cursed an officer. As a result of his insolence, he was hung for 10 hours a day for two days. The harsh punishments continued, including being placed naked and chained in a dark solitary cell for 61 days with only bread and water, but with regular heavy dousing with a fire hose. While inside the unlit cell he chased and ate cockroaches for extra sustenance. After several failed attempts, on 18 September 1917 Panzram finally escaped, but was captured again just days later after a shoot out with a sheriff's deputy.

Placed in Oregon Prison again, he wouldn't taste freedom until 12 May 1918 after a daring escape that saw guards shooting freely at the fleeing inmate. Panzram decided it was best to get out of the general area, so he adopted the name John O'Leary and made his way to the East Coast, burning down churches along the way and stealing whenever and whatever he needed to survive.

He spent part of 1920 conducting a one-man crime spree in New Haven, Connecticut before shifting his activities to Manhattan's Lower East Side, where he lived on a boat called the *Akista*. Here he would sodomise, rob and murder random sailors, shooting them in the head with a stolen pistol and then dumping their corpses into the water, weighted down with rocks.

The next year, Panzram was back in jail for six months for burglary and possession of a loaded pistol. Soon after his release he was arrested again after becoming involved in a gun battle between a maritime union and the police. Instead of going to jail, though, he jumped bail and stowed away on a ship to Angola in Africa, where he found work on an oil rig. Here, in a coastal town called Luanda, he raped an 11-year-old boy before bashing him to death with a rock. He later admitted that he had hit the child until his brains were coming out of his young ears.

Weeks later, he hired six locals to take him crocodile hunting in the jungle. While there, he shot and killed all six, leaving them for the crocs.

Back in the US for the summer of 1922, Panzram once again took to drifting and ended up in Salem on 22 July, where he raped a 12-year-old boy named George Henry McMahon six times before beating him to death with a rock in a quiet area of woods. He then covered the body with branches and, noticing that two witnesses had spotted him fleeing the woods, left town for Yonkers, New York.

Using the alias John O'Leary, Panzram found a job as a watchman and started regularly sodomising a 15-year-old boy named George Walosin, but soon grew bored and made his way to Providence, Rhode Island, where he stole a boat and sailed to New Haven, where he once again spent nights stealing and raping.

In June he sailed back to Yonkers and hooked up again with Walosin, before sailing to Kingston where he planned to sell the stolen vessel. He repainted the ship and changed its name and went to town looking for a buyer. A young man expressed interest, and Panzram took him back to the boat for a few drinks. Not realising he had been chosen as a victim, the man then tried to rob Panzram, and was shot twice in the head in front of Walosin and dumped overboard for his trouble.

The pair then headed south to Newburgh, where Walosin jumped ship. Once he made his way back to Yonkers, he told the police that Panzram had raped him. The authorities caught up with Panzram in the village of Nyack on 29 June 1923 and charged him with sodomy and robbery.

Placed in Yonkers city jail, Panzram made an escape attempt a few days later, but was caught and confined in solitary. But he still had a trick up his sleeve. Convincing a lawyer named Cashin that his stolen ship was worth up to $10,000, and that he would sign it over if he could get him out of jail, Panzram was released on bail, which Cashin paid for out of his own pocket. He made a hasty getaway. Of course the ship was soon discovered to be stolen, and Cashin lost both it and the bail money he had posted.

Panzram's next stop was the quiet, well-to-do village of Larchmont, near the Connecticut state line. Here he stole the boat of a high-society doctor, but smashed it into the rocks. Broke and desperate, he broke into the train depot on 26 August 1923 and was rifling through the stored luggage when he was arrested. Bail was set at $5000 while he waited at the local lock-up. Here, he admitted that he was still wanted in Oregon, where there was a $500 reward set for his capture under the name of Jeff Baldwin. Panzram wanted to claim the money for himself.

After some legal manoeuvring, Panzram was sent upstate to Clinton Prison, also known as Dannemora. Around 15 kilometres from the Canadian border, Dannemora was the most extreme and brutal penitentiary in the US at the time, full of hardened criminals ruled over by vicious guards who treated them worse than animals. He arrived in October 1923 and was stripped, searched and relieved of his few possessions.

Within months he tried to escape, but injured his spine and broke both legs and ankles in the process. Instead of being taken to the hospital, though, Panzram was dumped on the floor back in his cell. He would not receive medical treatment for 14 months, at which time one of his testicles had to be removed. This had little effect on Panzram's behaviour, however, as he was soon caught sodomising a fellow inmate and sent to solitary. Here he hatched wild and vivid plans to murder as many people as possible by blowing up a New York bridge or dumping arsenic in a local water supply.

Five years later, in July 1928, Panzram was finally allowed to walk free from prison, though the actual walking part was a painful chore because of his crippling injuries. Fuelled by hatred and driven mad by isolation, Panzram picked up on his crime spree with renewed fervour, breaking into houses and killing at least one man during the course of a robbery. This pattern continued until he was finally taken into custody again and sent to prison in Washington. But he was far from repentant. After an escape attempt was uncovered, Panzram was taken to an isolated spot and handcuffed with his arms around a wide wooden pole. He was then wrenched upwards so that his arms were above his shoulders and only his toes were offering support on the ground. He was left in this position for a day and a half, enduring constant agony the whole time and vowing revenge on everyone involved in the torture. After the guards then beat him, he admitted to killing several young boys. He added that he had enjoyed the murders.

Once he started to confess, Panzram owned up to dozens of murders. He ended up penning a 20,000-word account of his life, listing literally thousands of crimes. In this lengthy confession, the 36-year-old blamed society and the brutality he had endured at the hands of the prison system for his criminal behaviour.

Once word of his confession got out, a warrant for Panzram's arrest arrived from Philadelphia for the choking murder of Alexander Uszacke on 26 July 1928. Then the Salem authorities brought in the two witnesses from the George Henry McMahon murder six years earlier. They were quick to identify the heavy-set tattooed man before them.

With no chance of escape or release, Panzram again wrote a letter confessing to the murder of 12-year-old George McMahon, as well as 21 other victims. He added that if he were to ever be released he would surely 'knock off another 22!'

In the face of such stunning admissions, Panzram's next court appearance on burglary and house-breaking charges seems rather insignificant. Nonetheless, he was found guilty of all counts and sentenced to 25 years in Leavenworth prison. Here he warned the warden that he would murder the first person who bothered him. It wouldn't take long for him to make good on his promise.

On 20 June 1929, Panzram used an iron bar to smash in the skull of Robert Warnke, the supervisor in the laundry where he had been assigned work detail. He then walked up to the guards and told them what he had done, before quietly returning to his cell.

Carl Panzram was back in court on 14 April 1930 for Warnke's murder. It took the jury only three-quarters of an hour to find him guilty. They didn't recommend mercy. The killer, thief and rapist was sentenced to death, and just before he was hanged at 5.55am on 5 September 1930, Panzram spat in the executioner's face and snarled: 'Hurry up, you bastard, I could kill 10 men while you're fooling around!'

THE BONE COLLECTOR

(1999)

DIRECTED BY PHILLIP NOYCE
SCREENPLAY BY JEREMY LACONE

FEATURING

Denzel Washington as Lincoln Rhyme
Angelina Jolie as Amelia Donaghy
Queen Latifah as Thelma
Michael Rooker as Captain Howard Cheney
Mike McGlone as Detective Kenny Solomon
Luis Guzman as Eddie Ortiz
Ed O'Neill as Detective Paulie Sellitto

Based on Jeffery Deaver's international bestseller of the same name, *The Bone Collector* is perfectly believable viewing, if you are prepared to overlook a couple of minor things. Firstly, the serial killer profiler, Lincoln Rhyme (Denzel Washington), is a quadriplegic ex-cop, who does all of his detective work from home. Secondly, his main forensic detective, Amelia Donaghy, was a beat cop handing out parking tickets a few hours earlier until she showed some nous when summoned to the first crime scene in the movie where she stops a train and and does all sorts of other very clever things.

It seems a demented taxi driving serial killer is trying to get Lincoln's attention by committing one murder after the other and leaving clues that only the super-sleuth can make head or tail of. And when Lincoln does follow the clues, clues that even Stephen Hawking would have trouble deciphering, he sends the cops directly to the location with brave new chum Amelia leading the way.

Guided by Lincoln on the phone, Amelia discovers some recently deceased cadavers in New York's grotty nether world. Each corpse – and several others, as it turns out, that the police captain seems to have overlooked until Lincoln got on to the case – have died a ghastly death and all have had a chunk of skin and a piece of bone taken out of a leg. All of Lincoln's ace detective work leads them to a 100-year-old book called (surprise, surprise) *The Bone Collector*. The genius Lincoln is now able to predict where and when the next murder is going to take place. I hope I haven't given too much of the plot away.

Given that the Australian director Phillip Noyce hadn't had a decent film since the classic *Clear and Present Danger* in 1994, and before that the equally good *Patriot Games* in 1992, it's hard to imagine that he went into this project lightly, even though the plot and the main character were about as far out there as it gets. Having said that, Noyce had David Fincher's 1995 serial killer masterpiece *Se7en* as a guide to how the grizzliest and darkest crime scenes set in the most appalling surroundings can work effectively.

So welcome to the world of mega-high-tech serial killer catching. And Noyce pulls it off without our hero Lincoln so much as leaving the building, given that he is confined to his special bed at home and surrounded by nurses and so much computer and surveillance equipment that his electricity bill must eat up every cent of his medical insurance.

Of the other players it was unusual to see Michael Rooker playing the part of a cop, and a nasty one at that, after being the serial killer in both *Sea of Love* and *Henry: Portrait of a Serial Killer*. It was also a change of roles for Ed O'Neill playing a cop. We all thought he was typecast forever as the malcontent husband in *Married with Children*.

On the surface it looked as if *The Bone Collector* couldn't fail, and they were right. The combination of Jolie, Washington, Noyce and author Deaver was blue chip. It took over $150 million at the box office, at a cost of $73 million to make.

The Bone Collector provided the hottest question of 1999. Would the world's two most glamorous stars get their rocks off together – in the movie – given that Denzel hadn't moved a muscle in four years, and this most likely included the one that mattered most for a liaison. Was the pouting Angelina, the sexiest woman in the world, really capable of raising the dead? You'll have to see it and decide for yourself.

JOHN **LEGUIZAMO** ADRIEN **BRODY** MIRA **SORVINO** JENNIFER **ESPOSITO**

NYC '77. Disco in the clubs. Panic in the streets.

SOS
SUMMER OF SAM

The summer of '77 was a killer...

A **40 ACRES** AND A **MULE**
FILMWORKS PRODUCTION
A **SPIKE LEE** JOINT

SUMMER OF SAM

(1999)

DIRECTED BY SPIKE LEE
SCREENPLAY BY VICTOR COLICCHIO
AND MICHAEL IMPERIOLI

FEATURING

John Leguizamo as Vinny
Adrien Brody as Richie
Mira Sorvino as Dionna
Jennifer Esposito as Ruby
Michael Rispoli as Joey T
Ben Gazzara as Luigi
Anthony LaPaglia as Detective Lou Petrocelli

If you think about it, finding an unusual angle to make a dramatic movie of substance about one of the world's best-known serial killers, Son of Sam, wouldn't be easy. Which probably explains why no-one had ever made one before *Summer of Sam*. Realistically, without a lot else going on around it, the Son of Sam story is pure documentary material.

In the summer of 1977, New York postal worker, David Berkowitz, gave himself the name 'Son of Sam', which he said he got from Harvey, his neighbour's Labrador retriever. Harvey allegedly told Berkowitz to randomly shoot and kill lots of young people. And, naturally, when the neighbour's dog tells you to do something, you do it. Berkowitz was caught via a parking violation and will never see daylight beyond the walls of the slammer where he has found God. Good.

An unconventional challenge like the *Summer of Sam* needed an unconventional director, and Spike Lee was up to the challenge. While Berkowitz goes about his grisly business throughout the movie he is not really what it's about. It's about what his murders, and the hunt for Son of Sam, are doing to New York's small Italian/American community.

The central characters go about their lives while the shadow of the murders – 'there's been another one' – hangs over their heads. A waitress, a hairdresser, a punk and a dancer in a gay club are the core of a close-knit group of families who have all grown up together and are now confronted with suspicions that Sam may be any one of them. No-one is left out. Even the local priest is suspect because he lives on his own and doesn't have to explain his whereabouts to anyone. Ritchie, one of the local kids who is a bit unusual – punk haircut, British accent, dating local sexpot Ruby – becomes the prime suspect in the eyes of a neighbourhood, in which a lynch mob mentality is festering.

John Leguizamo, in the lead as Vinny, is aggressive and vile, and it would have been of good service to the movie if Sam had shot him as well. Adrien Brody is terrific as the unfortunate Ritchie – it's hard to imagine that he's the same bloke who took out the Best Actor Oscar in 2002's *The Pianist*. Mira Sorvino is wonderful as the promiscuous Vinny's long-suffering wife, and Ben Gazzara was made for the part – albeit a very short one – as the local Mafia boss.

Summer of Sam is a tense and realistic movie that gives us an insight into a New York culture that you would never otherwise see. But the crimes of the real Son of Sam were beyond belief.

Son of Sam

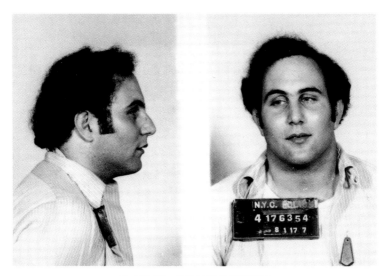

DAVID BERKOWITZ

The serial killer who came to be infamously known as the Son of Sam was born Richard David Falco in Brooklyn on 1 June 1953. He would go on to terrorise the city of New York through the mid- to late 1970s, racking up a total of six murders. As a result, he has little chance of seeing freedom again. But the Son of Sam's life was difficult from the start.

Just days after Falco was born he was put up for adoption and taken in by Nathan and Pearl Berkowitz, who gave him their surname and reversed the order of his given names. And – despite appearing to be more intelligent than most children his age – he went on to have a fairly troubled upbringing, developing a reputation as a bully.

His adopted mother passed away a victim of breast cancer in 1967, a situation that made his already strained relationship with Nathan Berkowitz even more difficult. When Nathan later remarried, his adopted son took a strong dislike to the new woman. This did little to keep him out of trouble.

In 1971, Berkowitz enlisted in the US army. Once he left
the service he became involved in the Christian religion, and
managed to locate his birth mother, Betty Broder. This wasn't
the fairytale happy ending he may have been hoping for.
Indeed, it seemed to make Berkowitz's life even unhappier.

It turned out that Betty had been married to a different man,
Tony Falco, with whom she had a daughter, when she
conceived Berkowitz to a man named Joseph Kleinman. He
tried to convince Betty to have an abortion but she refused,
and when Berkowitz was born it was Falco's name that was
placed on the birth certificate. This story had an effect on
Berkowitz, and he and his mother didn't stay in contact.

It is believed his first of a string of violent outbursts were
on Christmas Eve 1975, when he lashed out at two separate
women with a knife. Shortly after this attack, Berkowitz
moved to the New York suburb of Yonkers, around 20
kilometres north of Manhattan, and the violence escalated.

The New York summer of 1976 was hot and steamy when
the newspapers started running reports about what they were
then calling 'The .44 calibre killer', because of the make of
gun used in a horrific series of shootings. Two young women,
18-year-old Donna Lauria and 19-year-old Jody Valenti, had
the unfortunate distinction of being the first recognised
victims of the killer that would later become known as the
Son of Sam, when they were both shot while sitting inside a
parked car on the night of 29 July 1976. Lauria died as a
result of the attack, but Valenti survived. The next shooting
occurred in Queens on 23 October that same year, when 19-
year-old Carl Denaro was shot in the head while sitting in a
parked car. He also lived, as did the woman he was with.

Berkowitz's next victims – 16-year-old Donna DeMasi and
18-year-old Joanne Lomino – also lived, despite being shot while
they walked home after seeing a film on 26 November 1976.

The next shooting was on 30 January 1977, when an engaged couple felt the sting of Son of Sam's bullets while – following the killer's by-now familiar modus operandi – sitting together in a parked car. John Diel survived the attack, but his 26-year-old fiancée Christine Freund wasn't so lucky. It was Freund's death, though, that finally convinced the authorities that all the shootings were related. It was determined that the gun used in the Diel/Freund attack had been a rare .44 Charter Arms Bulldog, in keeping with the large calibre used in all the other shootings. Adding to the theory was the fact that the majority of the other attacks revolved around either young couples, or young females with long brown hair, sitting in parked cars.

The next bullet hit 19-year-old student Virginia Voskerichian as she walked through Queens on 8 March 1977. She died as a result, but the authorities determined that, once again, the shell was from a .44 Bulldog. A press conference was called two days later and the police informed the public that it appeared the same pistol had been used in all of the shootings. A task force named Operation Omega was soon set up, with 300 officers following the direction of Deputy Inspector Timothy J Dowd. Meanwhile, the press had a field day, reporting every sensational detail. The most substantial lead was the sighting of a yellow Volkswagen at the scene of one of the shootings. On top of this, thousands of owners of .44 Bulldog pistols were also questioned. The authorities believed the person they were looking for had serious issues with women. Still, at this early stage they were mostly clutching at straws. They needed a strong lead.

The next murders occurred on 16 April 1977, when 20-year-old Alexander Esau and 18-year-old Valentina Suriani were both shot and killed in the Bronx. This time, though, the killer left a hand-written note laying in the street nearby. Rambling, often incoherent, full of spelling mistakes and signed by the 'Son of Sam', it read:

I am deeply hurt by your calling me a woman-hater. I am not. But I am a monster. I am the 'son of Sam'. I am a little brat. When father Sam gets drunk he gets mean. He beats our family. Sometimes he ties me up to the back of the house. Other times he locks me in the garage. Sam loves to drink blood. 'Go out and kills' commands father Sam. Behind our house some rest. Mostly young – raped and slaughtered – their blood drained – just bones now. Pap Sam keeps me locked in the attic too. I can't get out but I look out the attic window and watch the world go by. I feel like an outsider. I am on a different wavelength then everybody else – programmed to kill. However, to stop me you must kill me. Attention all police: shoot me first – shoot to kill or else keep out of my way or you will die. Papa Sam is old now. He needs some blood to preserve his youth. He has too many heart attacks. 'Ugh, me hoot, it hurts, sonny boy.' I miss my pretty princess most of all. She's resting in our ladies house. But I'll see her soon. I am the 'monster' – 'Beelzebub' – the chubby behemoth. I love to hunt. Prowling the streets looking for fair game – tasty meat. The women of Queens are prettiest of all. I must be the water they drink. I live for the hunt – my life. Blood for papa. Mr Borelli, sir, I don't want to kill any more. No sur, no more but I must, 'honour thy father'. I want to make love to the world. I love people. I don't belong on earth. Return me to yahoos. To the people of Queens, I love you. And I want to wish all of you a happy Easter. May God bless you in this life and in the next. And for now I say goodbye and goodnight. Police: Let me haunt you with these words: I'll

be back! I'll be back! To be interpreted as – bang, bang,
bang, bank, bang – ugh!!
Yours in murder, Mr Monster

As disturbing as the letter was, it was the strongest lead the authorities had. They passed it on to psychiatrists, who determined they were possibly looking for a paranoid schizophrenic. Either way, it at least offered the police hope that they may soon find the serial killer.

The next victims were shot outside the Elephas nightclub in Queens on 26 June 1977. Sal Lupo and 17-year-old Judy Placido were having a conversation about how scary the Son of Sam murders were, when three shots ripped through their car window. Both Lupo and Placido were hit, but neither suffered serious injury.

Police sketches that had been made with information supplied from various witnesses or victims of the ongoing shootings seemed to suggest that there were actually two culprits. One image was of a man of average height who ran to overweight, with short, curly dark hair. The description fitted Berkowitz, at least superficially. The other image, though, had the shooter as taller, thinner and having lighter hair. The second image suggested someone with the image of a hippie. Still, the authorities were convinced they were only seeking the one suspect, and that he possibly wore a wig at times.

By this time, *New York Daily News* reporter Jimmy Breslin had received a letter from someone claiming to be the killer. Representatives of the newspaper spoke to the police and, after they received their approval, the letter later appeared, though with vital sections withheld from the public. The letter spoke of the gutters of New York being filled with 'dog manure, vomit, stale wine, urine and blood'. It also noted that 29 July would mark a year to the day of the first killing.

Despite Breslin publicly urging the murderer to turn himself in, the Son of Sam struck again on 30 July 1977. Even though the authorities were on high alert, with many officers secretly patrolling the area around the Bronx and Queens where most of the attacks had occurred, 20-year-olds Stacy Moskowitz and Robert Violante were both shot in the head while they sat in their parked car. Violante lived but was blinded by the bullet. Moskowitz, however, died.

Two days later, a woman named Cecilia Davis phoned the police. She had remained quiet until then out of fear that the Son of Sam would shoot her as well, but her conscience finally got the better of her. Just minutes before the most recent shooting, she had seen a man remove a parking ticket from the window of his yellow Ford Galaxie. The car had been parked too close to a nearby fire hydrant. The police checked their records and found that the ticket had been issued to Berkowitz. It was determined that he was at the very least an important witness. A police officer from Yonkers also revealed that they already had suspicions about Berkowitz being involved with other crimes in the area. These crimes were also mentioned in letters from the Son of Sam. Berkowitz became the prime suspect. On 10 August 1977, officers were sent to his address, on Pine Street, Yonkers, where his car was parked out the front on the street. In the backseat sat a hunting rifle. The vehicle was searched, and a .44 Bulldog pistol was also found, as well as a letter addressed to Deputy Inspector Timothy J Dowd of Operation Omega, and maps of the areas where the Son of Sam attacks had occurred. Realising they had their man, the police waited until Berkowitz emerged from his flat. As they took him into custody he asked why it had taken them so long to find him.

A search of Berkowitz's apartment revealed that the dwelling was in disarray. It also uncovered a diary where the killer had detailed several arson attacks around the city of New York. There was also occult-related graffiti covering the walls. Berkowitz quickly confessed to his crimes, and added that he would be keen to plead guilty in return for a sentence of life in prison, rather than receiving a death penalty. He was then questioned for half an hour, during which time he said that the 'Sam' mentioned in the first letter he had sent was a former neighbour of his named Sam Carr. He then said that he believed Carr's dog had been possessed by a demon, and that it was Harvey that had told Berkowitz to embark on his killing spree. Berkowitz had even tried to shoot the dog at one point, but claimed supernatural forces had spoiled his aim.

Berkowitz later claimed to have been a practising Satanist when he committed the murders, saying that he had been involved with a group of occultists who sacrificed animals to the devil and had dealings in child pornography.

Berkowitz was sentenced to six life terms on 12 June 1978. He was sent to Attica Correctional Facility for a maximum of 365 years. He had only been inside for a year, though, when his throat was cut in a murder attempt. Berkowitz refused to identify his attacker, but claimed the group of Satanists he had been involved with had ordered him to be killed. He later became a born-again Christian and stressed that his interest in the occult and pornography had led him down his murderous path. He now offers counselling to his fellow inmates, and is deeply committed to the prison ministry. He has come up for parole several times, and has said that he doesn't want to be released. Even though he has a good record inside, where he is considered a model prisoner, the authorities also believe that his crimes were too brutal for him ever to be released. It is most likely that David Richard Berkowitz will die in prison.

CHRISTIAN   REESE   WILLEM   CHLOE   SAMANTHA
BALE   WITHERSPOON   DAFOE   SEVIGNY   MATHIS

AMERICAN PSYCHO

...no introduction necessary

www.americanpsycho.com

AMERICAN PSYCHO

(2000)

DIRECTED BY MARY HARRON
SCREENPLAY BY MARY HARRON AND GUINEVERE
TURNER

FEATURING

Christian Bale as Patrick Bateman
Justin Theroux as Timothy Bryce
Reese Witherspoon as Evelyn Williams
Willem Dafoe as Detective Donald Kimball
Josh Lucas as Craig McDermott
Bill Sage as David Van Patten
Chloë Sevigny as Jean

Depending on who you're listening to, Mary Harron's screen adaptation of Brett Eason Ellis's 1991 bestseller *American Psycho* is either a masterpiece or a mindless blood fest. The jury, it appears, is still out. But one thing is for certain: if you hated the book, you will like the movie even less. If you loathed Patrick Bateman, the narcissistic, coke-snorting, designer-label, serial-killing snob on the printed page, wait until you get a load of him in the flesh.

Bateman is a stereotype of the successful yuppie, that strange creation of the late 1980s. A very successful young man, he was much admired by his peers within the acquisition and merger firm for which he worked and for whom he made lots of money. And with the money come the spoils. Designer label everything. European cars. The latest electronics. And always the best table at New York's unbookable restaurants. And the women are, of course, glamorous.

Patrick is such a good sort that if he hadn't been a whiz on Wall Street he would have been one of the world's top male models. He is obsessed with his looks and preens himself to the point where he has become dangerous to anyone who happens along and threatens his peace of mind. But that situation is easily fixed. He kills them.

Ellis's 1991 abattoir novel had everyone outraged because it described Patrick Bateman's serial killings in endless detail. It was as if Jack the Ripper was giving an after-dinner talk. But people, apparently, like that stuff and it sold lots of books. Or maybe it was just the publicity. There was a time there when it was very fashionable to have *American Psycho* in the house. Maybe it was the cover. Whether folks actually read it is debatable.

In the movie, director Mary Harron has turned the murders into fantasy killings that almost certainly only occur in Patrick's coke-addled brain. In doing so, she eliminates the hideous tortures and despicable acts that made the book such a talking point.

Perhaps Mary Harron would be upset if her movie was referred to as black comedy, but it's difficult to describe it as anything else, given that the main character, the most beautiful male on the planet, who lives in a palace and only sneezes when the line of coke is too big, or the Dom Perignon bubbles go up his nose, is in fact a serial killer. Then again, Mary might simply be sending up Ellis' absurd novel. Or perhaps it's a murderous analogy for the dog-kill-dog world in which Patrick Bateman exists – casting aside people instead of possessions?

Christian Bale is terrific in the role, but any one of a hundred young Hollywood spunks could have done the same job. Future

Oscar winner Reese Witherspoon is terribly miscast as our hero's fiancée, besides he is so much in love with himself it's surprising there's room for anyone else in his life at all. Willem Dafoe's detective does nothing but appear occasionally, allegedly providing jeopardy, but he just smiles stupidly and disappears again. Chloë Sevigny is excellent as Bateman's secretary who, along with every other female in New York, has a crush on her boss.

I hated what I read of the book. To this day there is a dent in the bedroom wall where I threw it at about page 98. I know, I hadn't got to the good bits, but I'm afraid life's too short. This movie is as bad as the book.

But then again, if you read some of the reviews it is a masterpiece. Maybe I missed something. According to the box office I missed the mark by a hundred miles. It cost only $8 million to make *American Psycho*, which took $34 million at the box office around the world. Hardly a failure, in business terms, at least.

HANNIBAL

(2001)

DIRECTED BY RIDLEY SCOTT
SCREENPLAY BY DAVID MAMET AND STEVEN ZAILLIAN

FEATURING
Anthony Hopkins as Hannibal Lecter
Julianne Moore as Clarice Starling
Gary Oldman as Mason Verger
Ray Liotta as Paul Krendler
Frankie Faison as Barney Matthews
Giancarlo Giannini as Pazzi
Francesca Neri as Allegra Pazzi

The long-awaited sequel to 1991's *The Silence of the Lambs* isn't in the same class as the original, but only the world's greatest optimist could have hoped it would be, given that Jodie Foster and Jonathon Demme vetoed the project.

It seems that after Thomas Harris finished writing the novel *Hannibal* he sent copies to the principals of *The Silence of the Lambs*: director Jonathan Demme, screenwriter Ted Tally and lead performers Anthony Hopkins and Jodie Foster for approval to go ahead and commission a screenplay. They all expressed their interest. But even after the screenplay was re-written as many as 15 times it couldn't satisfy director Demme or lead Foster and they, along with screenwriter Tally, opted to bail out. When Jodie Foster declined to resurrect her Oscar-winning part of FBI agent Clarice Starling, Julianne Moore ultimately won the hotly contested part over Angelina Jolie, Hilary Swank, Cate Blanchett, Helen Hunt and Gillian Anderson.

But Anthony Hopkins stayed on and he is brilliant once again in the role that he seems to have been born for, the evil Dr Hannibal Lecter; scholar, teacher, intellectual and bon vivant of exquisite taste.

And as if Dr Lecter isn't terrifying enough, in *Hannibal* we get to meet arguably the most grotesque screen villain of them all: billionaire paedophile, disgruntled out-patient and long-time Lecter nemesis, Mason Verger, who wants to have a word with the good doctor about the time Lecter filled him full of mind-altering substances and encouraged him to shave his own face off with slivers of broken mirror. As a result, Mason looks like Cyclops who's had all of the skin from his ass grafted onto his face by a surgeon on a bad acid trip. Actor Gary Altman's name isn't mentioned in the opening credits, but you will spot him in the closers.

While in lots of folk's eyes only Jodie Foster will ever be Clarice Starling, Julianne Moore turns in a stellar performance as the boots-and-all FBI agent in pursuit of the dreaded Lecter. She is attempting to regain her job with the FBI after being discredited by Verger cohort FBI agent Paul Krendler, played by Ray Liotta.

Set in America and France, *Hannibal* bowls along at a ripper pace and while it doesn't stick too closely to the book, it is still an excellent film for the genre. With more twists and turns than a bucket of blood worms, viewers shouldn't be dissatisfied with *Hannibal*. But you must stop yourself from comparing it with the original. And while it cost a whopping $87 million to make, *Hannibal* is the biggest grossing serial killer movie in history taking over $US350 million worldwide.

Here's one for the trivia buffs: Who is the only actor to have been in all of the Hannibal Lecter movies? Answer: The wonderful character actor Frankie Faison, who seems to have been around in the background forever. Faison played Lieutenant Fisk in *Manhunter* (1986) and Barney, the kindly asylum gatekeeper, in *The Silence of the Lambs* (1991), *Hannibal* (2001) and *Red Dragon* (2002).

Hannibal is a must in every serial killer movie library.

More than the legend will survive.
JOHNNY DEPP
HEATHER GRAHAM
A HUGHES BROTHERS FILM
FROM HELL
OCTOBER
R RESTRICTED
www.fromhellmovie.com

FROM HELL

(2001)

DIRECTED BY ALBERT AND ALLEN HUGHES
SCREENPLAY BY TERRY HAYES AND RAFAEL YGLESIAS

FEATURING

Johnny Depp as Inspector Frederick Abberline
Heather Graham as Mary Kelly
Ian Holm as Sir William Gull
Robbie Coltrane as Sergeant Peter Godley
Ian Richardson as Sir Charles Warren
Katrin Cartlidge as Dark Annie Chapman

The Hughes brothers have every reason to be proud of their movie, *From Hell*. Unfortunately for them, however, it will always be compared with the greatest Jack the Ripper movie of them all, 1979's *Murder by Decree*.

But *From Hell* is far from a bad movie. It is merely the Ripper murders told in a different style and featuring actors of a different calibre. The next generation might well prefer *From Hell* over the stuffier and more traditional 1979 Sherlock Holmes version.

From Hell sticks to the theory that a person in a very high place is carrying out the Ripper butcherings, covering up a scandalous conspiracy that could see a commoner on the throne and bring England to its knees. It's a great yarn and beats the alternative: a lunatic with a long knife and a medical journal taking out a personal grudge on the disease-riddled harlots of Whitechapel.

And while *From Hell* isn't a Sherlock Holmes movie, it may as well have been. Johnny Depp is Inspector Frederick Abberline, a Sherlock Holmes–type character who keeps his job by solving crimes through the dreams he gets while he is zonked off his face in an opium den. The real-life Inspector Abberline didn't have a drug problem, but rumour had it that Holmes was partial to a snort of cocaine from time to time.

Inspector Abberline's sidekick is another real-life adaptation, the Dr Watson–style Sergeant Godley, brilliantly played by Robbie Coltrane of *Cracker* and *Harry Potter* fame. Apart from the normal doting chores, Godley's main job is to drag his flyblown boss away from the bong to tell him that there's been yet another murder.

The striking beauty of Heather Graham as Mary Kelly, the key prostitute, is a welcome relief among a tsunami of grotesquely visual disembowelments and bush-pig ugly whores. She always looks as though she's just spent all day at the beauty parlour, but a strange thing is that no-one seems to have sex with her, even though that's what she does to pay the rent. You would have thought they would be queuing up around the block.

And, given that Ray Charles could have seen it coming from a hundred miles away, it's no surprise that the inspector and Mary Kelly fall in love. Ripperites know only too well what happened to poor Kelly in real life, so it isn't difficult to predict the demise of the besotted, opium-addicted policeman. The real Abberline's demise was entirely different.

Though slow in parts, *From Hell* should hold your interest until the end, which is worth waiting for. The acting is excellent, the sets, which were painstakingly built to scale, are authentic and the age-old plot a beauty. One big tip, though: if you haven't seen *Murder by Decree*, don't watch it before you watch this. Rent them both together, watch *From Hell* first and then compare the differences.

CLINT EASTWOOD
BLOOD
WORK

HE'S A HEARTBEAT AWAY FROM CATCHING THE KILLER

WARNER BROS FICTURES PRESENTS

A MALPASO PRODUCTION CLINT EASTWOOD "BLOOD WORK" JEFF DANIELS WANDA DE JESUS TINA LIFFORD PAUL RODRIGUEZ DYLAN WALSH AND ANJELICA HUSTON
JOEL COX HENRY BUMSTEAD TOM STERN LENNIE NIEHAUS JUDIE G HOYT ROBERT LORENZ MICHAEL CONNELLY
BRIAN HELGELAND CLINT EASTWOOD

BLOOD WORK

(2002)

DIRECTED BY CLINT EASTWOOD
SCREENPLAY BY BRIAN HELGELAND

FEATURING

Clint Eastwood Terry McCaleb
Jeff Daniels as Jasper 'Buddy' Noone
Angelica Huston as Dr Bonnie Fox
Wanda De Jesus as Graciella Rivers
Mason Lucero as Raymond
Tina Lifford as Jaye Winston
Dylan Walsh as Detective John Waller
Paul Rodriguez as Detective Ronaldo Arrango

Meet Dirty Harry Callahan 31 years down the track. That is assuming that Harry was Clint Eastwood's real age of 41 in the original *Dirty Harry* movie in 1971. That made him 72 in real life when *Blood Work* was made, though according to the movie he's only just past retirement age, in his mid- to late 60s. And Clint can get away with it.

But Clint isn't Harry any more. This time he's Terry McCaleb, retired FBI serial killer profiler and heart transplant recipient. The movie opens with Terry hot on the heels of a terrible bit of work known as the Code Killer. The killer murders and leave messages all over Los Angeles. Some of the notes taunt McCaleb, the celebrity cop, by name. Then, at a murder scene, Terry spots who he thinks is the killer in the crowd. He gives pursuit only to collapse with a heart attack just as he is about to nail the villain. Terry ends up with a heart transplant and now spends his life living on his unassuming boat on a Long Beach marina reading books, fishing and taking it easy.

One day he is visited by the stunning Graciella (Wanda De Jesus), who tells him that her sister was murdered and she would like Terry to find the killer. Terry isn't the least bit interested until he finds out that he is carrying the deceased woman's heart in his chest. Graciela now looks after Gloria's terrific 10-year-old son Raymond (Mason Lucero), with whom Terry immediately bonds.

Of course, now Terry agrees to help and, with the capable assistance of his yachty neighbour, Buddy Noone (Jeff Daniels), to drive him around and gopher for him, the three of them set out to solve the murder. Terry's cardiologist, Dr Bonnie Fox (Angelica Huston), is not impressed with his new venture and the dialogue between these two veterans is great. But Terry has made up his mind, whether it kills him or not, and that's where our story really starts.

Naturally the local cops aren't too fussed about an ancient ex-FBI profiler digging up one of their old cases for fear he'll show them up, and they make Terry's life as hard as possible. Fortunately for Terry there's an old FBI colleague and former romantic interest, Jaye Winston (Tina Lifford), in the office, and she slips him confidential information. On the other hand, Detective Arrango (Paul Rodriguez) doesn't hold back with the insults amd Terry's responses provide some comic relief in an otherwise humourless, albeit very entertaining, movie.

Will Terry catch the killer of the woman who donated his heart? More importantly, will the craggy old Terry make a move on the spectacular Graciella, who is at least 30 years younger than him.

When they eventually get around to it – even though Eastwood is in stunning nick for his age – it is cringe-worthy in the extreme. It's not just the age difference. You can't help thinking of Terry whispering something like, 'I love you with all of your sister's heart.' Still, under the circumstances they make the ideal family unit: Terry, Graciella, young Raymond, and his mum's ticker beating away in his new de facto step-uncle's chest.

There are some dismal oversights, such as skilled police forgetting to jot down a fleeing killer's licence number, but Michael Connelly, the author of the original 1998 novel of the same name, and his legion of fans should be pleased with the film adaptation, and Clint Eastwood's oh so cool direction.

RED DRAGON

(2002)

DIRECTED BY BRETT RATNER
SCREENPLAY BY TED TALLY

FEATURING

Anthony Hopkins as Dr Hannibal Lecter
Edward Norton as Will Graham
Ralph Fiennes as Francis Dolarhyde
Harvey Keitel as Jack Crawford
Emily Watson as Reba McClane
Mary-Louise Parker as Molly Graham
Philip Seymour Hoffman as Freddy Lounds
Anthony Heald as Dr Frederick Chilton
Frankie Faison as Barney Matthews

Movie remakes that are as good or better than the original are rare and *Red Dragon* isn't one of them. Not that *Red Dragon* isn't a good serial killer movie. It's just that it has a hard act to follow. *Manhunter*, the original movie of Thomas Harris' novel *Red Dragon*, was made in 1986. While *Manhunter* was about as good as it gets, *Red Dragon* will always be its poor relative and it is in the comparison that it is found wanting.

By 2002 the Hannibal Lecter bubble had just about burst. You couldn't be blamed for thinking that *Red Dragon* was put together in a hurry to catch the end of the phenomenon and make a few (million) quick bucks. In that sense it worked a treat. Of the Anthony Hopkins/Hannibal Lecter trilogy at the box office, *The Silence of the Lambs* (1991) took $272 million, *Hannibal* (2001) became the biggest grossing serial killer movie in history with $350 million and the revived *Red Dragon* took just over $200 million. No-one was surprised. After all, *Red Dragon* is well directed and scripted and has a brilliant cast. It was always going to be a hit. But, as far as quality goes, it wasn't in the same class as the original.

Way back in 1986 *Manhunter* had no competition. It really was the first of the serial killer profiler movies. Everything we watched was new and exciting. *Red Dragon* is more of the same, just not as good. Having said that, if you haven't seen *Manhunter*, there's every chance you will love *Red Dragon*.

Red Dragon is the story of a retired criminal psychologist and serial killer profiler, Will Graham (Edward Norton). He is enticed against his young family's wishes by his old boss, Jack Crawford (Harvey Keitel), to go back and solve one more ongoing series of horrific murders. But this is no ordinary serial killer. This fiend specialises in butchering whole families, then re-arranges their bodies and replaces their eyes with mirrors so he can look at himself while they are looking at him. His other calling card is that he leaves nasty bites all over his victims, and for this reason he has been dubbed the 'Tooth Fairy'.

If anyone can stop him, it's Will. His claim to fame is that he caught the serial killer psychiatrist Hannibal 'the cannibal' Lecter by getting inside Lecter's head. The trouble was, after Lecter was locked up Will couldn't stop thinking like him and wound up in the rubber room at the state mental facility. Not surprisingly, he then retired. In *Manhunter* we didn't know much about Lecter's past, or how Will caught him. That is all revealed in *Red Dragon*.

But now it seems that Dr Lecter is in touch with the Tooth Fairy from his asylum cell, and no-one is safe – especially Will's family, who Lecter would love to have murdered. Will visits Lecter to try to solicit his help, only to realise that it's game on, and that he must find the Tooth Fairy before he kills again.

We meet the serial killer, Francis Dolarhyde (Ralph Fiennes), and watch him go about his daily routine which includes a relationship with a blind girl, Reba (Emily Watson), who he's met through his work at a film laboratory. It's probably best that Reba can't see because if she got a good look at the tattoo of William Blake's famous painting of the *Red Dragon* that covers the best part of Francis' body, she'd be out of there at a million miles an hour.

You'll recognise a couple of familiar characters from *The Silence of the Lambs*. Hopkins as Lecter, of course, as well as Anthony Heald as Dr Frederick Chilton, Lecter's tormentor (and dinner), and Frankie Faison as Barney, the gatekeeper to the asylum and the only actor to feature in all four movies; he was Lieutenant Fisk in the original *Manhunter*.

Red Dragon is a fast-paced thriller with a feast of class actors and a fabulous plot. But it will always live in *Manhunter*'s long shadow. Rent them both, watch them back-to-back and make up your own mind. It's probably best to watch *Manhunter* first and let *Red Dragon* fill you in on all the juicy Lecter bits.

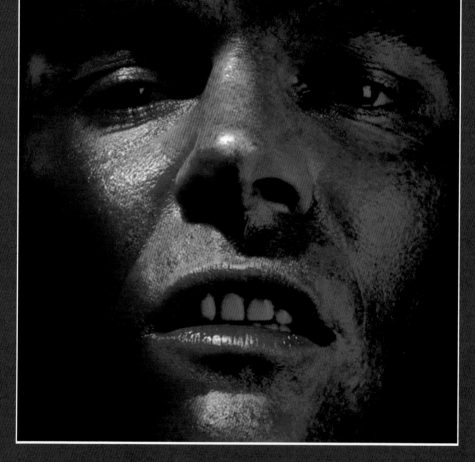

TED BUNDY

Based on the true story of America's most infamous serial sex killer.

TED BUNDY

(2002)

DIRECTED BY MATTHEW BRIGHT
SCREENPLAY BY STEPHEN JOHNSTON
AND MATTHEW BRIGHT

FEATURING
Michael Reilly Burke as Ted Bundy
Boti Bliss as Lee
Julianna McCarthy as Professor
Jennifer Tisdale as Pretty Girl
Steffani Brass as Julie

It's unlikely that there is a serial killer enthusiast anywhere in the world who hasn't heard of Ted Bundy, the charismatic and intelligent murderer of at least 33 young women across the US. Bundy was a monster capable of a level of depravity that most human beings cannot comprehend. Apart from violently battering and stabbing them to death, Bundy severed the arms and heads from at least 12 of his victims and kept them in his room. He spent hours in the forest applying make-up to the remains of his decomposing victims and performed acts of necrophilia on their putrefying remains.

Making a movie about Ted Bundy was never going to be easy. The American press had portrayed him as the all-American college boy, just with a few problems. The movie is basically a bloodbath, providing no explanation as to why this young man with movie star looks would do such terrible things. Michael Reilly Burke portrays Bundy as a below-average college student with a dopey girlfriend, played by Boti Bliss. From the outset we are told that he is a thief, and that his relationships with women are anything but what we would consider normal. He has a lot of snakes and spiders in the closet and one day he lets them all out to go on a raping and killing spree – not necessarily in that order – across the USA.

Ted Bundy the movie doesn't tell us anything that we didn't already know about the real-life man that isn't in any of the many books written about him. It's worth a look, but don't expect much.

Other Ted Bundy movies that were made for TV and may be available in your local DVD store and for sale on the internet include *The Deliberate Stranger* (1986), *The Stranger Beside Me* (2003) and the TV documentary *Serial Killers Great Crimes of the Century: Ted Bundy* (1996), which includes live footage of Bundy conducting his own defence in one of his murder trials.

Ted Bundy: The Co-ed Killer

Even though he eventually confessed to killing more than 30 females, raping and then bludgeoning and strangling them to death, during his four-year reign of terror between 1974 and 1978, Theodore Robert 'Ted' Bundy may well be responsible for the murders of many more victims. The actual number is still the subject of debate. Indeed, it is believed he may have committed his first murder in 1961 when he was just 15 years old. What is known is that at the peak of his killing spree Bundy was so depraved he was biting into the flesh of his victims, and having sex with their decomposing bodies.

THE MANY FACES OF TED BUNDY

A handsome man who was considered both smart and charming, Bundy was born on 24 November 1946 in the US town of Burlington, Vermont. No-one knows who his father was. His mother worked in a department store. As a child, Bundy often had violent outbursts, and family members thought he might have been mentally unstable. When he was just three years old, he surrounded a sleeping aunt with knives and stood at the foot of her bed smiling until she awoke, terrified and confused. He also spent most of his formative years believing that his mother was actually an older sister, and the pair lived with his grandparents, who he believed were his actual birth parents.

Bundy would later describe his grandfather – the deacon of his local church – as a volatile man who would often scare those around him with his fiery temper. The man held a deep prejudice against Italians and African-Americans. He also hated Jewish people and Catholics. On top of that, neighbourhood animals bore the brunt of his ill will, with cats being swung around by their tails and the family dog often receiving harsh beatings. Besides this violent behaviour, Bundy's grandfather also provided the young boy's first introduction to pornography, via the sizable collection stashed in his greenhouse. Bundy and a cousin would spend hours in there poring over the naked images. The killer would later point to the influence of pornography as just one of the many factors that led him down his deranged path.

Bundy's grandmother was the antithesis of her husband. A quiet, timid woman, she obeyed the tyrant's every command and suffered from such severe depression she would often be checked into hospital to receive shock treatment. Things got so bad for the elderly woman that she would later find it impossible to leave her own house.

Even though Bundy was quick to learn at school and college, he was a shy outsider, having no basic understanding of how to get along with others. Getting his start in crime by shoplifting while still in high school, he also developed a fascination with sex and violence at an early age. He recognised the part of himself that hungered for these images and gave it a name – 'The Entity'. He kept 'The Entity' a secret from everyone except for his unfortunate victims.

The young Bundy also learnt how to manipulate people to get what he wanted. Of the few friends he had, most were females and he developed methods to get what he wanted from them.

As he grew older, the articulate young man campaigned for the Washington State Republican Party, and volunteered at a Seattle suicide crisis centre. He developed a fondness for gourmet French food and fine wine. He also had an avid interest in sailing and skiing, and would often go for long hikes. Still, Bundy favoured material possessions, rather than people, and craved objects over affection. Despite this, he soon embarked on his only serious relationship with a female, a first-year college student who was later given the pseudonym Stephanie Brooks to protect her identity.

Displeased with Bundy's immature nature, Brooks severed ties with the future serial killer after they had been seeing each other for a while, but he took to courting her again two years later. Seemingly a changed man with a professional attitude, Bundy proposed marriage and Brooks accepted, only to have him call off the engagement by phone two days later. He would later explain that he had only asked her back in an effort to prove to himself that he could have her if he wanted. Soon after this, Bundy embarked on his murder spree, targeting mainly young women with straight long hair worn with a part down the centre; the same style favoured by Brooks.

Not long after midnight on 4 January 1974, Bundy bludgeoned sleeping 18-year-old student Joni Lenz with a metal bar after sneaking into her bedroom. He then sexually assaulted her with a gynaecological instrument, which he left stuck deep inside her vagina. Lenz lived through the ordeal although, after waking from a coma, she had permanent brain damage and no memory of the attack.

On 31 January, Bundy struck again, breaking into the basement room of Lynda Ann Healy, a student at the University of Washington, and the roommate of one of his friends. He knocked her out and took her away wrapped in a sheet. Her decapitated remains weren't found until a year later.

Bundy found his next victim, 19-year-old student Donna Gail Manson, on 12 March. She was walking to a concert at Evergreen State University when he kidnapped and murdered her.

The killer didn't lash out again until the early hours of 11 June. While waiting in the parking lot behind the Kappa Alpha Theta sorority house on the campus of the University of Washington, Bundy spotted student Georgeann Hawkins as she returned from her boyfriend's nearby dorm. Stumbling along on crutches he didn't need – using them as a ruse to appear helpless – he asked the student to assist him with his briefcase. Hawkins agreed and once they reached his Volkswagen beetle, Bundy grabbed a crowbar he had earlier stashed and hit her across the head, rendering her unconscious before handcuffing her and driving away. She woke up while he drove through the mountains on his way to killing her, so he knocked her out again. He later strangled her to death with a length of cord while the sun came up.

Bundy was on a roll, killing eight women in the first half of 1974. His violence was escalating and he grew bolder, kidnapping Janice Ott and Denise Naslund from a Seattle state park in broad daylight. He had been loitering in the area with his arm in a sling (again unneeded) and wearing white tennis gear, and asking women to help him unload a sailing boat from his car. Five women would later testify that a man calling himself Ted had approached them with the same story, while two others said they saw Janice Ott walk from the beach with the man in white. Ott was never seen alive again, but at least the authorities now had a description of the man stalking the women of Washington, as well as his brown Volkswagen car. They released it to the public and Ted Bundy's was just one of many names they received as possible suspects.

–Bundy's next murder occurred in Salt Lake City on 2 October, where he had moved to attend law school. His victim, 17-year-old Melissa Smith, the daughter of a respected police chief, was raped and strangled. It was nine days before her body was found.

Later that month, Bundy lashed out again, beating 17-year-old Laura Aime until she couldn't be recognised, then sodomising her and strangling the young woman with a sock after she left a Halloween party.

Little more than a week later, on 8 November 1974, Bundy was at it once more. Pretending to be a police officer, he managed to coax Carol DaRonch into his Volkswagen, but she was lucky enough to escape with just head wounds. Still, the killer would not be thwarted. Only hours later he kidnapped and murdered 17-year-old Debbie Kent. The student had just left a school play, and her body has never been found.

Bundy changed the location of his killing field once again in 1975. Though he was still attending law school in Utah, he began to hunt victims in Colorado. The first, Caryn Campbell, went missing on 12 January while on a holiday with her husband. It would be more than a month before her body was located. Next came Julie Cunningham on 15 March and Denise Oliverson on 6 April. Neither body has ever been found. After that, Lynette Culver was the next female reported missing person on 6 May, before Bundy shifted his killing spree back to Utah, snatching Susan Curtis on 28 June.

The authorities finally caught up with Bundy in Salt Lake City on 16 August 1975 when he failed to stop for a police officer. His car was searched, and several suspicious items were found – among them were handcuffs, a crowbar and a ski mask. Following his arrest the police managed to connect his car with the DaRonch case, as well as the women who were missing in both Colorado and Utah. On 1 March 1976, Bundy was convicted of kidnapping Carol DaRonch and found himself sentenced to 15 years in Utah State Prison. In the meantime, the authorities in Colorado wanted to convict Bundy for murder.

They had their chance on 7 June 1977 when Bundy was taken to the Garfield County Courthouse before a hearing for the murder of Caryn Campbell. But on a visit to the library during a court recess, he jumped out a second-floor window, injuring one of his ankles. He was caught a week later, but escaped again after cutting a hole in the roof of his cell with a contraband hacksaw. Bundy strolled out the front door of his Colorado jail on 30 December 1977, before stealing a car and making his getaway.

Thanks to more than $500 that he had been given by various friends who had visited him in jail, he bought a plane ticket to Chicago, and then caught a train to Michigan. From there he stole a car and drove to Atlanta where he caught a bus to Tallahassee, Florida, and rented a room in a boarding house. Six days later, on 15 January 1978, he entered a sorority house at Florida State University and bludgeoned and strangled Lisa Levy and Margaret Bowman to death while they slept. There were bite marks on Levy's buttocks where Bundy had ripped into her bare flesh in a murderous frenzy, leaving behind imprints that would prove vital in the prosecution's case against him at a later trial.

It wasn't long before Bundy was on the move again, kidnapping 12-year-old Kimberley Leach from Lake City, Florida, on 9 February 1978. He raped and murdered the child, then dumped her body under a shed. Thankfully she was his last victim, as Bundy was pulled over while driving a stolen orange Volkswagen at around 1am on 15 February.

He struggled with the arresting officer, David Lee, but was soon overpowered. On the way to the station, Bundy said that he would rather Lee kill him.

Bundy was later taken to Miami, where his trial began on 25 June 1979. He was appointed five defence lawyers by the court, but the former law student decided to represent himself. It did him no good, and he was sentenced to death on 31 July.

Still, the legal system wasn't finished with Bundy. In 1980 he was again tried and found guilty for murder, this time for the killing of Kimberley Leach. Again he acted as his own legal consul. Again he was sentenced to death, and it was this ruling for which he would eventually be executed. In sentencing Bundy to die in the electric chair, Judge Edward Cowart said:

> It is ordered that you be put to death by a current of electricity, that current be passed through your body until you are dead. Take care of yourself, young man. I say that to you sincerely; take care of yourself, please. It is an utter tragedy for this court to see such a total waste of humanity as I've experienced in this courtroom. You're an intelligent young man. You'd have made a good lawyer, and I would have loved to have you practice in front of me, but you went another way, partner. Take care of yourself. I don't feel any animosity toward you. I want you to know that. Once again, take care of yourself.

On the morning of 24 January 1989, at 7.06 o'clock, Bundy had 2000 volts shot through his body while sitting on the Florida electric chair known as Old Sparky. He was 42 years old at the time and his last words were declarations of love to his family and friends.

In his years on death row, though, Bundy would come to give more details of his gruesome murders, as well as admitting to other killings, all in an effort to prolong the inevitable – his execution. He admitted to cutting up at least 12 of his victims with a hacksaw, and said he had kept severed hands and heads in his room for periods of time. He also revealed that he had repeatedly revisited Taylor Mountain, where he had dumped several bodies, to spend hours with the decomposing corpses, applying make-up to them. As the date of his execution grew nearer he said that he had performed necrophilia on the rotting body of Georgeann Hawkins.

Around this time he also contacted former King County homicide detective Robert D Keppel and confessed to eight further murders in the Washington area. Keppel later described Bundy as 'born to kill', adding: 'He is just totally consumed with murder all the time.'

Bundy himself placed the blame for his sexually-based violence on pornography. In a television interview the night before his execution, he told the head of evangelical Christian group Focus, Dr James Dobson, that while his consumption of pornography wasn't the direct cause of his violent acts, it helped 'shape and mould' his antisocial behaviour. He warned that sexual violence in the media would lead others down the same dark path he had taken.

Bundy used other interviews to reveal how lucky other potential victims had been, admitting that for every female he had murdered, several others had escaped due to a variety of random circumstances, mostly unaware of the horrors to which they could well have fallen prey.

Though Bundy himself once said his murder tally ran to 35 victims, when the authorities put it to him once that they believed he was responsible for 37 he said, 'Add one more digit and you'll have it.' There is still speculation whether the number he was talking about was 38 dead females, or 137.

It's interesting to note that in the 1991 movie *The Silence of the Lambs*, serial killer Buffalo Bill uses Ted Bundy's techniques as he lures his victims into his van by asking them to help him lift an item of furniture as he can't lift it alone because his arm is in (fake) plaster. Once in the van the victim is knocked unconscious and whisked away to Bill's dress-making dungeon to become a part of his wardrobe.

DAHMER

(2002)

DIRECTED BY DAVID JACOBSON
SCREENPLAY BY DAVID JACOBSON

FEATURING

Jeremy Renner as Jeffrey Dahmer
Bruce Davison as Lionel Dahmer
Artel Kayàru as Rodney
Matt Newton as Lance Bell
Dion Basco as Khamtay
Kate Williamson as Grandma

How do you make a movie about a man who is deemed to be sane, yet drugs, murders, rapes and then dismembers young men before having sex with their body parts and eating them? Not easily. But most of us already knew about Dahmer's ghastly crimes. How could we not? They are among the most publicised in history. So director David Jacobson has the distinct advantage that he doesn't have to revisit the horror. Instead, he looks at the make-up of the handsome young chocolate factory worker who committed crimes so abhorrent that he became a household name around the world. And we are shown how Dahmer's quiet demeanour saw to it that he got away with murder for so long

Jacobson compiles a picture of Dahmer's past and present and lets us form our own opinions about the man and what drove him to such terrible crimes. Thus most of the actual horror is taken out of the film. As well, he avoids falling into any one of the million or so psychological theories that could encourage such complex crimes.

Jeremy Renner (*SWAT*, *North Country*) is excellent as the creepy loner Jeffrey Dahmer, and Bruce Davison (*Runaway Jury*, *LA Law: The Movie*) supports him well as his long-suffering dad who can only despair and wonder how such a beast came from his loins.

The opening montage shows the chocolate factory, where Dahmer worked in the 1990s. Following this we find him bringing home a victim to drug, torture, kill, rape and eat. This is the famous victim, the one who escapes into the arms of the cops who then release him after Dahmer explains that it is just a lovers' tiff and that the lad will be all right once he gets him home. Of course he is not.

Through a series of flashbacks we find out about Dahmer's faulty younger family life, which doesn't seem all that out of the ordinary except, perhaps, for his unhealthy fetish for mannequins. But so what? There must be plenty of blokes with similar preferences who didn't go on to become serial killers.

Moving on a few years we find young Jeffrey picking up a man in a knife store before going to a gay bar, where he is identified as the same man who had drugged and raped many of the clubs patrons over the years. We are then privy to his first killing, committed while he was still living at home.

Knowing what Dahmer did, and how he was eventually caught, doesn't make the movie any the less suspenseful. Jacobson keeps the jeopardy going without the slightest hint of sensationalism, and it flows to its anticipated conclusion. It's doubtful that it could have been done any better.

Jeffrey Dahmer: The Milwaukee Monster

With at least 17 murders of young men and boys to his name, perverted serial killer Jeffrey Lionel Dahmer was racking up a victim a week at the height of his 13-year murderous rampage between 1978 and 1991. But the terror didn't stop at sexual torment and death. Once he had despatched the males he would perform necrophilia upon them before dismembering them and performing sickening acts of cannibalism.

His usual method of murder started with inviting the victims to his apartment in the US city of Milwaukee to watch pornographic videos or pose for photos. Once he had them in his lair, he would surreptitiously crush sedatives into a drink and serve it to them, before strangling them to death. He would then have sex with the corpse before masturbating upon it.

Once he had defiled the corpse, he would take Polaroid photos of his work to preserve the memory, before cutting into the torso, getting sexually aroused once again by the lingering body heat escaping into the dank air around him. After that he would dismember the body, once again taking step-by-step photographs, and often keeping the head and genitals as trophies, preserving the genitalia in formaldehyde, and boiling the head until the flesh came away, then painting the skull grey so that it looked like plastic. Dahmer would also eat parts of the flesh, later claiming that he believed his victims would come alive again inside of him. He also became sexually aroused by eating the flesh, which he experimented on by using various tenderisers and seasonings to achieve different flavours. He tried to drink the human blood as well, though he wasn't fond of the taste.

To dispose of the remaining body parts, Dahmer tried a variety of acids and chemicals, turning the flesh into revolting, thick black sludge to be flushed away in the toilet or poured down the sink.

The monster responsible for these horrific acts was born on 21 May 1960 in Milwaukee and welcomed into the world by his loving parents Lionel and Joyce Dahmer, who were just happy to have a healthy and happy son after a very difficult pregnancy.

Dahmer has been described as a bubbly youngster, who enjoyed playing with his toys and spending time with his dog Frisky, though he did suffer from a high number of throat and ear infections.

In hindsight, though, Dahmer's father sees there may have been warning signs early on. When the boy was four, for example, Lionel swept up the remains of some small animals from under their house. Wild cats had killed the animals, and all that was left were their bones. The young boy dug his hands into the pile of bones, and seemed 'oddly thrilled' by the sound the crunching remains made.

When Dahmer was six he needed surgery to repair a double hernia. According to Lionel, the child never truly bounced back, and seemed 'more vulnerable' from then on.

By the time he reached first grade, Dahmer lacked self-confidence and seemed afraid of his peers. His outward joy had been replaced by a distant shyness that made him scared to even go to school.

By 1967, though, Dahmer had made a friend named Lee. He had also grown found of one of his teachers. So fond that he caught some tadpoles and gave them to her as a gift. But when Dahmer found out the teacher had given the tadpoles to Lee, the boy killed them by pouring motor oil into their water.

As Dahmer grew older, he became stiffer in both personality and posture. A tense youth, he spent much of his time at home alone watching television. Around the age of 15, he started to collect animal remains in plastic bags for a private cemetery he had created, stripping the flesh from the road kill.

In the coming years the uncommunicative young man would become overwhelmed with sick fantasies revolving around his sexual desires for the dead. He became unmotivated and began to shut himself off from the outside world. Though he maintained decent grades through high school and worked on the school newspaper, he started to develop an alcohol problem, even drinking liquor in class.

Shortly before Dahmer turned 18, his parents divorced and just months later Lionel married a woman named Shari, who was quick to notice her stepson's drinking problem. Lionel and Shari convinced Dahmer to go to college, and he enrolled at Ohio State University in 1978, but dropped out after just one semester, unable to maintain his studies due to his increasingly heavy drinking. Lionel told him to get a job or join the army, so Dahmer enlisted in January 1979. At first it seemed like he was comfortable in the service, and he was stationed in Germany, but he was discharged after a couple of years because he was always drunk. As it would transpire, he may have been trying to forget something horrible that he had done just before signing up.

Not long out of the service, in October 1981, Dahmer was arrested for public drunkenness and disorderly conduct. It was the first of the string of worsening arrests that would eventually escalate from indecent exposure to child molesting. Of course, by this time, Dahmer had already started down his dark path as a serial killer.

In June 1978, not long after finishing high school, Jeffrey Dahmer picked up hitchhiker Steven Hicks. The pair had a few beers and sex, but when Hicks said he had to be on his way, Dahmer felt like he was being abandoned. He picked up a barbell and hit the hitchhiker in the head with it. Hicks died as a result, and Dahmer cut up the body before placing the various parts in plastic bags and burying them in woodland. After he was discharged from the army, Dahmer dug up the decaying remains and broke them up with a sledgehammer before scattering the residual pieces throughout the forest.

Besides the disorderly conduct arrest, Dahmer managed to keep things mostly in check. There was one incident where he dropped his pants in front of a group of people while drunk, but he had no further run-ins with the law until September 1986, when he was arrested for masturbating in front of two boys and placed on a year's probation.

Around the time this probationary period finished, Dahmer took the life of his second victim, Steven Toumi. The pair had been drinking together in a gay bar. Heavily inebriated, they then went back to a hotel room together and, although he later claimed to have no memory of the event, when Dahmer awoke Toumi was dead. Noticing blood on his own mouth, Dahmer stuffed the corpse into a large suitcase and took it to the basement of his grandmother's house (where he was living at the time), and had sex with it before masturbating on it, cutting it up and placing it in the garbage.

Victim number three was 14-year-old Native American boy Jamie Doxtator. Dahmer came across him several months after murdering Toumi, hanging outside a gay bar. He lured the boy back to his grandmother's basement and repeated his by now regular pattern. The same thing happened with his fourth victim, young Mexican man Richard Guerrero, who he murdered in March 1988.

With his grandmother complaining about the drunken noise coming from her basement whenever he would bring a friend home, Dahmer realised he had to find a new place to live. He moved into an apartment on North 24th Street Milwaukee on 25 September 1988. The next day he found a 13-year-old Laotian boy with the surname Sinthasomphone and gave him $50 to pose for some photos. Back at the apartment, Dahmer drugged the child and fondled him, though he stopped short of rape or murder. Coincidentally, the boy was the older brother of a future victim of Dahmer's, one who wouldn't get away alive.

When the Laotian returned home, his parents sensed that something was amiss. After a hospital examined him and said he had been drugged, the story came out and the authorities picked up Dahmer. He was arrested for sexual exploitation of a child and second-degree sexual assault and later pleaded guilty.

Moving back to his grandmother's while waiting for his sentence to be handed down, Dahmer went out one night to a gay bar. While there he met a 24-year-old African-American man named Anthony Sears. He took him back to his grandmother's where he followed his by-now familiar pattern of drugging the young gay man before strangling him to death, defiling the dead body and then dismembering it. After boiling the flesh from the head, he kept the skull for two years.

Dahmer's trial for assaulting the young Laotian boy began on 23 May 1989. The prosecution recommended he be sent to prison for five years, but after presenting himself as articulate and repentant, and placing the blame for his behaviour on his escalating alcoholism, Dahmer got off with only five years of probation, though he was ordered to spend a year on work release at the House of Correction. This meant he could go to work during the day as long as he returned at night. He proved such a model prisoner that he was granted early release after 10 months.

After a stint back at his grandmother's, Dahmer moved into apartment 213 at 924 North 25th Street Milwaukee on 14 May 1990. This was the place where he would commit most of his atrocities in a 15-month killing spree following his drug/kill/defile/dismember modus operandi, with the focus of his actions being to feel a sense of control over the victim.

As he continued killing, he started to become more depraved in his actions. In several instances he drilled a hole in the skull of his drugged victims and shot muriatic acid into their brains. He also started to get involved in Satanism, hatching a plan to make a shrine out of the various body parts he had collected, and then use it to obtain 'special powers and energies to help him socially and financially'.

The beginning of the end for Dahmer came when he took 14-year-old Konerak Sinthasomphone to the rancid-smelling apartment 213. As usual, he drugged the boy but had to leave the flat for a moment. As he walked out, Konerak awoke naked and fought through his lethargic state to make it outside. He started to run blindly in whatever direction his feet were taking him, and was immediately spotted by Dahmer's 18-year-old neighbour Sandra Smith and her cousin Nicole Childress, also 18. Smith rang the emergency line to report the nude, injured boy running around outside and before the authorities arrived she also saw Dahmer struggling with Konerak, trying to drag the boy back inside.

Down at the station, Dahmer told the authorities that Konerak was his 19-year-old lover. He said Konerak had been drinking heavily, hence his incoherent state. He said that they had argued and Konerak had stumbled out of the apartment. Unable to talk for himself, Konerak was in no position to deny the story. The police believed Dahmer's version of the events, though they went back to apartment 213 with the pair anyway to make sure everything was above board. The room they found was neat, but there was a bad smell permeating throughout. They saw photos of Konerak in skimpy black underwear and listened while Dahmer apologised for the mistake and assured them the disturbance was all over. The police assumed it was just a domestic situation that had got out of hand and accepted Dahmer's story that it would never happen again. They left the pair to their own business. As soon as they were gone, though, Dahmer strangled Konerak and had sex with his still warm corpse. This would be his last unfortunate victim.

Around midnight on 22 July 1991, two police officers on patrol were driving through the hot, sticky night when they saw a short man on the street with one end of a pair of handcuffs hanging off his wrist. The man's name was Tracy Edwards and he told the officers that some 'weird dude' had cuffed him at an apartment block that he had taken him to. Edwards led the policemen back to Dahmer's flat and the blond man who answered the door appeared the picture of calmness. He admitted that Edwards was wearing his handcuffs and said he would get the keys from the bedroom. At this point Edwards said Dahmer had threatened him with a knife that was also in the bedroom. One of the officers went to check out the story, and that's when Dahmer's luck ran out. In the bedroom the officer was shocked to find photos of Dahmer's previous victims. The photos showed bodies in various states of dismemberment. He yelled out to his partner to apprehend the blond man, and Dahmer started to fight the other officer as he tried to handcuff him. With the suspect subdued the men started to investigate the apartment. The first thing they found was a head in the fridge. There were three more in the freezer compartment. In a pot in a closet they found rotting hands and a penis. On another shelf sat two human skulls. A further search of the closet revealed male genitals and more of Dahmer's collection of Polaroids. The officers were sickened by what the photos showed. Dahmer was taken into custody and the next phase of his story began when he went to trial.

As stories leaked out about the atrocities the tall blond man had committed, public interest – and disgust – reached fever pitch. So intense was the scorn directed at the monster that sniffer dogs checked the courtroom for explosives before Dahmer was placed in a barrier made out of bullet-resistant glass and steel. In the room sat 34 family members of his victims. On 13 July 1992, Dahmer admitted his guilt, but pleaded insanity. As the case dragged on, the jury heard of increasingly despicable acts that made everyone present wonder how a human being could behave in such a way. Detectives read from a 160-page confession Dahmer had made detailing his actions and admitting that he felt a deep sense of guilt over what he had done.

At the end of it all the jury took five hours to find Jeffrey Dahmer guilty. They also decided that he had been sane at the time of the murders, which meant he would be sent to prison for a total of 15 consecutive life terms – the equivalent of 957 years.

Installed in Columbia Correctional Institute in Portage, Wisconsin, Dahmer was at first kept isolated from the general population. He seemed to adjust to his new life, and at his own request was eventually allowed more contact with other prisoners. He was attacked by a Cuban inmate on 3 July 1994 while attending a service in the prison chapel, but soon after was allowed to eat in the mess hall and do some janitorial work. For this work detail he was teamed with two other murderers – Jesse Anderson, who had murdered his wife and blamed it on another man; and schizophrenic Christopher Scarver, who suffered from delusions that he was the son of God. It was a situation that was never going to end well.

The three men were left alone on the morning of 28 November 1994. When the guard on duty returned just 20 minutes later, Anderson had been beaten to death with a broom handle, and Dahmer was dead, his head crushed to a bloody pulp.

MONSTER

(2003)

DIRECTED BY PATTY JENKINS
SCREENPLAY BY PATTY JENKINS

FEATURING
Charlize Theron as Aileen Wuornos
Christina Ricci as Selby
Bruce Dern as Thomas
Lee Tergesen as Vincent Corey
Annie Corley as Donna

The enduring attraction of *Monster* is the casting of an exquisitely beautiful actress as the grotesque highway hooker, Aileen Wuornos. While Charlize Theron would be better suited on the catwalks of Paris, Aileen Wuornos looked as if she lived in one of the garbage dumpsters, alongside the bikie bars where she flogged her saggy wares.

Yet as if by miracle, beauty becomes the beast in a performance that is acknowledged as one of the best in movie history. The likeness is quite uncanny. The rhetoric mesmerising. Theron really is the Aileen Wuornos we have seen howling abuse at the court. It was enough to win Theron the 2004 Best Actress Oscar, and another 18 Best Actress awards around the world. It's fair to say that without Theron's performance it is unlikely that punters would have queued up around the world to see a grubby little movie about such a despicable person.

During 1989 and 1990 Aileen Wuornos shot dead six men on separate occasions after they picked her up at truck stops and along the highways of Florida, where she worked as a prostitute. At the time of the serial murders Aileen was in a lesbian relationship with Selby (Christina Ricci), to whom she eventually confessed the killings. Aileen had professed that she wanted to settle down and live a normal lifestyle in a loving relationship, but when she eventually found love, it didn't change her one bit.

Director Patty Jenkins gives Wuornos the human face of a violent woman, one who is to be pitied because of her horrendous upbringing and the sexual depravity committed upon her since she was a child.

Or was it really that Charlize Theron's magnificent performance in *Monster* was our excuse for a voyeuristic journey into another world that we know little about? The world of a woman at home in the pig-swill lifestye of bikie bars, violent sex, cheap drugs, truck stops, itinerant prostitution and, eventually, serial murder. To her it's all in a day's work.

The first thing I did after seeing *Monster* was have a long, hot shower. I've never seen it again. And that's how I judge a good serial killer movie. By the number of times I watch it. Just the once with Aileen was enough for me, thank you.

Aileen Wuornos:
America's Most Notorious Female Serial Killer

Even though Aileen Wuornos was not America's first female serial killer, as is widely believed, she is probably the most notorious. Where most female murderers seem to favour more passive methods of despatching their victims, such as poisoning, Wuornos killed her male victims by shooting them. At first she claimed that she acted in self-defence after they tried to rape, assault or sodomise her. The itinerant truck stop prostitute prone to violent outbursts eventually received six death sentences for her crimes and was executed by lethal injection in 2002.

Wuornos was born Aileen Carol Pittman on 29 February 1956. It's probably for the best that she never got to know her biological father, Leo Dale Pittman, a crazed child molester who committed suicide by hanging himself in prison in 1969. Pittman was known to beat his own grandmother. Aileen's mother, Diane Wuornos, divorced the psychopath just months before Aileen was born. She had an older son named Keith with Pittman, but left him because she was scared of his violent behaviour.

But life as a single mother was a huge burden on Diane and, unable to handle the responsibility, she abandoned her two young children in 1960. They were adopted by her parents, Lauri and Britta Wuornos, who raised them in Michigan. However, Lauri and Britta never told the children that they were actually their grandparents, not their parents, and Wuornos didn't discover the truth until she was 12. The news inflamed an already difficult situation and caused Wuornos – who was already scarred on her face as the result of playing with lighter fluid at the age of six – and Keith to rebel even further.

Lauri was a strict disciplinarian who drank to excess. He would often take a leather belt to his granddaughter's bare bottom, viciously whipping her while she lay face down on her bed or bent over the kitchen table.

The troubled child, who most people simply called Lee, was pregnant by the age of 14, and her son was adopted out in 1971. Wuornos would also later say that she'd had sexual encounters with her own brother from an early age, though there is doubt that this is the truth.

Britta Wuornos died in July 1971 from liver failure, but Diane Wuornos has alleged that Lauri killed her. Other family members say that the stress Aileen and Keith put her through with their increasingly bad behaviour made her turn to alcohol more heavily, bringing about her demise. It wasn't long after this that Wuornos dropped out of school and took up prostitution, plying her trade wherever she found herself while hitchhiking.

The next few years were a whirlwind. When he was 21, Keith died of throat cancer, and Lauri Wuornos committed suicide. Aileen made her way to Florida where, at the age of 20, she was picked up while hitchhiking by rich 69-year-old Lewis Fell, the president of a local yacht club. The older man fell for the young prostitute immediately and they were married in 1976. But even though the news was splashed across the Florida social pages, Aileen was still wild at heart. She would go to bars and get in fights, and treated her aging husband terribly. After a month – during which time she was jailed for assault – Fell had the marriage annulled.

For the next decade, Aileen drifted aimlessly, falling in and out of destructive relationships and supporting herself through prostitution, forgery and even armed robbery. She was drinking heavily and taking drugs to numb her emotional pain. Lonely and mad at the world, Aileen was stuck in a spiralling circle of self-destruction when her life finally took an apparent turn for the better when she met 24-year-old Tyria Moore in 1986 at a gay bar in Daytona.

The pair quickly became close and Tyria quit her job as a maid at a motel. Aileen supported her new younger lover with the money she made through prostitution, and the couple moved from one cheap hotel room to the next. But money was tight and they would sometimes have to bed down in barns or woodland. The honeymoon period didn't last for very long. It was around this time that male bodies started to turn up around the outskirts of Daytona, shot, robbed and dumped.

Aileen's first victim was Richard Mallory, the owner of a Florida electronics repair company who was known to go on sex and alcohol binges that lasted several days. That's why no-one thought much of it when the middle-aged man didn't open his shop for a few days in early December 1989. But when his car turned up abandoned, alarm bells started to ring. Mallory's body was then found on 13 December. He had been shot three times with a .22 pistol and dumped near a dirt road close to a busy highway. Despite a thorough investigation of Mallory's shady private life, the authorities soon came to a dead end and it looked like the case would remain unsolved.

Then another dead naked male was discovered in the woods of Citrus County, Florida on 1 June. This second victim was 43-year-old heavy-equipment operator David Spears, last seen on 19 May. A used condom was found near his body and he had been shot several times with a .22 pistol.

Another body turned up on 6 June. This victim was badly decomposed and was later determined to be a man named Charles Carskaddon. The corpse had nine .22 bullets in it.

A month later, on 4 July, Aileen and Tyria were drinking, driving and arguing when the car they were using veered off the road in Orange Springs, Florida, and stopped in some scrub near the house of Rhonda Bailey, who was sitting on her porch at the time. Rhonda watched as the two women got out of the automobile, swearing at each other and throwing away beer cans. Rhonda noted that Tyria wasn't saying much, and that Aileen's arm was bleeding as a result of the crash. Rhonda was about to call the police, but Aileen begged her not to.

Aileen and Tyria managed to get the car free of the bush it had landed in, but didn't get far before it broke down. They left it where it had stopped and walked off down the street. By this time, local volunteer fireman Hubert Hewett had made it to the scene in response to a call about the initial accident. He asked Aileen and Tyria if they had been driving the car, but Aileen swore at him and said no. They walked off again and he left them to it.

Deputies from the local Marion County sheriff's department were next on the scene. Examining the abandoned grey 1988 Pontiac, they noted that the windshield was smashed, the licence plate was missing, and there was blood throughout the inside of the automobile. Computer records showed the car belonged to a 65-year-old Christian named Peter Siems, who had been missing since 7 June. Police sketches of both Aileen and Tyria were sent around to US police departments in relation to the case.

The next of Aileen's victims was deliveryman Troy Burress, who was last seen starting on his rounds early on 30 July. When he didn't return that afternoon, his manager rang around and found out that Burress hadn't made the last of his scheduled deliveries. His truck was found at 4am the next day, abandoned and unlocked but with the keys missing. His already decaying body was found in a clearing about 12 kilometres away five days later. The cause of death was two .22 bullet wounds – one in the chest and one in the back.

The bodies kept coming. Dick Humphreys was the next to be shot to death. Disappearing on 11 September (the day after his 35th wedding anniversary), the 56-year-old private investigator's body turned up on 12 September in Marion County, shot seven times with a .22.

Then, on 19 November, the body of 60-year-old truck driver Walter Gino Antonio was found on a quiet logging road. His car turned up dumped on the other side of the state five days later.

By this time, Captain Steve Binegar of the Marion County Sheriff's Criminal Investigation Division was noticing the similarities between the rash of murders throughout the state. His prime suspects were the two women who had crashed missing man Peter Siems's car. Soon there were police sketches of Aileen and Tyria in papers all around Florida. By mid-December, the authorities had received several leads as to their whereabouts, as well as their names, though Aileen was using a variety of aliases, including Lori Grody, Susan Blahovec and Cammie Marsh.

As detectives came closer to catching the killer, it was found that Aileen had pawned a set of tools taken from David Spears' truck, as well as a camera and radar detector belonging to Richard Mallory. An outstanding warrant on a weapons charge (under the name Lori Grody) gave the police a copy of her fingerprint. It matched one left in blood in Peter Siems' car. Now all the authorities had to do was find Aileen Wuornos.

On 8 January 1991, undercover police officers Mike Joyner and Dick Martin were posing as drug dealers named Bucket and Drums when they found Wuornos drinking at the Port Orange Pub. They started talking to her and were soon buying her beer, but Aileen left the establishment at 10pm, turning down their offer of a lift. She made her way to a biker bar called the Last Resort. Bucket and Drums turned up there as well, and the drinking and conversation continued. The undercover detectives left the bar at midnight, and Aileen stayed the night where she was, sleeping on an old car seat after the place had shut for the evening.

Bucket and Drums returned to the Last Resort the next afternoon. This time they were wearing wires. The plan was to arrest Aileen later that evening after gathering more intelligence. But then they heard the bar was having a barbecue that night. The place would be full of drunken bikers. They decided they had to make their play right away. The men offered Aileen the opportunity to use their motel room to clean herself up in, and as they left the bar Larry Horzepa of the Volusia County Sheriff's Office came up and arrested her on the old weapons charge as Lori Grody. The murder charges weren't mentioned, as the police still needed time to find both the weapon used and Tyria Moore.

It turned out that Tyria had left Aileen and was living with her sister in Pennsylvania. Two officers flew out to interview her, and she soon admitted that she had known about the murders from the day Aileen came back to their cheap hotel room with Richard Mallory's Cadillac. Her lover had confessed to killing the man but Tyria simply told her that she didn't want to know about it.

The next day, Tyria went back to Florida to help the authorities with the case. The idea was to get Tyria to talk to Aileen over the phone, in taped conversations, telling her she was back in Florida to get her remaining belongings, and that the police had been talking to Tyria's family about the murders. Tyria was to tell Aileen that she was afraid she would be blamed for the shootings. The authorities believed that if Aileen thought Tyria would go to jail for her actions she would confess to save her.

Tyria made her first call on 14 January, but Aileen – assuming she was merely being held for what she called 'that concealed weapons charge in '86 and a traffic ticket' – told her not to worry about it.

Tyria made further calls over the next three days, insisting that the police were after her, and Aileen seemed to understand what she had to do. She told Tyria to tell the police whatever she felt she needed to in order to stay out of trouble. She added that, 'I'm not going to let you go to jail. Listen, if I have to confess, I will.' That confession came on 16 January.

When she finally admitted to the killings around the Florida area, Aileen was quick to stress that Tyria had played no part in them whatsoever. She also claimed that all had happened as self-defence, that the victims had all assaulted her or threatened to, or raped her. She told the police that she had been raped several times while working as a prostitute and that she had decided she wouldn't take it any more. She added that fear had driven her to murder.

The media set upon the story with gusto, and soon everyone involved in the case was fielding offers for books and interviews. The case was big news around the country, with the public becoming infatuated with the female serial killer. As time went on, Aileen refined her story until she seemed more like a folk hero than a murderer. She was receiving masses of mail. One of these letters was from 44-year-old born-again Christian Arlene Pralle, who told Aileen that Jesus had told her to get in contact with her. Pralle included her contact details in the letter, and on 30 January Aileen called the woman collect. Before long Pralle became the killer's confidante and started helping her case from outside the jail. She even described their relationship as 'a soul binding', and stressed that anyone who knew 'the real Aileen Wuornos' would never convict her of the crimes of which she was accused.

Pralle arranged strategic interviews for Aileen, as well as telling her story for her on numerous talk shows. The pair made much of Aileen's troubled upbringing as a reason for her later crimes. Then, on 22 November 1991, Pralle and her husband adopted Aileen as their legal daughter, explaining that God had told her to do so.

Aileen went to trial for Richard Mallory's murder on 14 January 1992. She entered a plea bargain that would have seen her receive six consecutive life terms if found guilty – though there was still one state attorney pushing for the death penalty. The damning evidence against her didn't help. A medical examiner pointed out that Mallory would have been in intense pain for as long as 20 minutes before he died. Then Tyria took the stand to say that Aileen had not appeared to be upset or nervous when she admitted to the murder.

Against the advice of her legal team, Aileen took to the stand herself, telling the court that Mallory hadn't just raped her but sodomised and tortured her as well. But when the prosecution cross-examined her they were able to point out several inconsistencies in her story. Aileen became visibly angry. On 25 occasions she used her constitutional right not to answer.

On 27 January it took the jury less than two hours to find Aileen Wuornos guilty of the first-degree murder of Richard Mallory. The killer was incensed, screaming out her innocence and reasserting that she had been raped. She called the jury 'scumbags' and said that she hoped they too were raped. The next day the men and women of the jury unanimously recommended that Aileen be executed. The judge agreed.

When it came time to face court for the murders of Dick Humphreys, Troy Burress and David Spears, Aileen pled no contest. She read a statement to the court saying that while Mallory had violently raped her, the other men had only started to before she killed them. She then turned to Assistant State Attorney Ric Ridgeway and said, 'I hope your wife and children get raped in the ass!' She received three more death sentences.

In June 1992 Aileen pleaded guilty to the murder of Charles Carskaddon and received yet another death sentence. Her sixth death sentence, for the murder of Walter Gino Antonio, came in February 1993. Because the body of Peter Siems has never been found, she was not charged for his murder.

At 9.47am on 9 October 2002, Aileen Wuornos was executed by lethal injection at Florida State Prison near Starke, Florida. She was the 10th woman to be put to death after the penalty was re-introduced in 1976. Before she died, she recanted her statement that she had shot her victims in self-defence after being raped, explaining that she wanted to be at peace with God before her execution.

THE HILLSIDE STRANGLER

(2004)

DIRECTED BY CHUCK PARELLO
SCREENPLAY BY STEPHEN JOHNSTON
AND CHUCK PARELLO

FEATURING

C Thomas Howell as Kenneth Bianchi
Nicholas Turturro as Angelo Buono
Allison Lange as Claire Shelton
Marisol Padilla Sánchez as Christina Chavez
Jennifer Tisdale as Erin
Kent Masters King as Gabrielle

We can only wonder at what would make two men act together to rape and murder 12 women and girls. The movie of *The Hillside Strangler* attempts to find some reason for the madness. Couples who kill, be they same or opposite sex, are usually driven by the more dominant personality in the relationship. Psychiatrists report that one wouldn't have done it without the other. That seems to be true in the case of cousins Kenneth Bianchi and Angelo Buono.

From the outset it is clearly apparent that while the 17-years-younger Bianchi was a drunk and a woman-basher, it is highly unlikely that he would have resorted to brutal murder without his misogynistic cousin urging him on. If you are really interested in trying to work out why serial killers do what they do, then *The Hillside Strangler* is worthwhile viewing. But, given the amount of swearing, grunting and legs all over the place, you could be forgiven for thinking you had just walked in on an R-rated porno. *The Hillside Strangler* is not a pleasant look and you wouldn't be blamed for turning it off.

Nicholas Turturro, brother of actor John Turturro, is well cast as the instigator Angelo Buono. If his face seems familiar it's because he's been around a lot, mainly as Detective James Martinez in a hundred episodes of *NYPD Blue*. He generates the required malevolence, convincing us that this is one bad dude who is more than capable of unprovoked murder. C. Thomas Howell as Kenneth Bianchi is equally as effective in making us hate his character. Curiously, in the end, it is the victim Bianchi who leads to their demise by murdering two girls on his own.

What is intriguing about *The Hillside Strangler* is how this pair of dumb asses kept getting away with murdering women, and dumping their bodies all over Los Angeles, for so long. They spend most of their nights cruising for street prostitutes to pick up and kill yet, even after at least half a dozen murders, they are still cruising the streets looking for victims, without any apparent fear of being questioned. Only in America.

The Hillside Stranglers

Though they had actually started their sadistic murder spree a month earlier, the first victim attributed to tandem serial killer cousins Angelo Buono and Kenneth Bianchi was found in an out-of-the-way section of hills in Los Angeles, between the suburbs of Eagle Rock and Glendale, on 20 November 1977. Called on to the scene to investigate, LAPD homicide detective Sergeant Bob Grogan stumbled up to the site where the body of 20-year-old student Kristina Weckler was dumped, all the while thinking that whoever had left the corpse in such a remote spot in a middle-class section of the city must have known the area well. As it turned out, he was right.

When Grogan finally located Weckler's lifeless body lying in the grass, the first thing he noticed were the ligature marks on her neck, wrists and ankles. There was bruising on her breasts, and when he turned her over blood flowed from her rectum. She had been raped before she was murdered. He also made note of two needle pricks on her arms, but discounted the idea that she was a drug addict due to the absence of telltale track marks.

The authorities later found out that she had died as a result of gas asphyxiation. The young woman's head had been placed in a plastic bag along with a gas pipe that was then turned on. It would have taken up to 90 minutes before she finally passed away.

The dumpsite showed no sign of disturbance, and Grogan reasoned that the murder must have occurred at a different location and the body carried there later after her death, perhaps by two men.

That same day, Grogan's partner Dudley Varney was called to another section of the same hill-lined LA area,

ANGELO BUONO

where the bodies of two young girls had been found by a nine-year-old boy playing in a garbage heap. The bodies were in a state of decay and insects had eaten away much of their flesh. As with the earlier gruesome discovery, it was apparent that the two girls – 12-year-old Dolores Cepeda and 14-year-old Sonja Johnson – had been murdered elsewhere and dumped in the quiet area. Again, it seemed like the work of two men rather than one.

Investigations revealed that the girls had been missing for a week. Their last reported sighting had been getting off the school bus and then going over to a car and talking to someone on the passenger side.

The next strangled victim was found on 23 November, near an off-ramp for the Golden State freeway. The maggot-infested body belonged to attractive 28-year-old Jane King. She had been lying rotting there for around two weeks. With four corpses turning up within a week, the LAPD realised

KENNETH BIANCHI

something serious was happening and were quick to set up a 30-man task force. It wasn't long before they were called upon.

Detective Grogan was sent in to the hills around the Mount Washington area of Glendale on 29 November, where the naked body of 18-year-old Lauren Wagner had been dumped. Once again, the corpse had ligature marks on the neck, wrists and ankles, and had been raped, but this time it looked as though there were also burn marks on the palms of her hands. It seemed that whoever had killed her had also tortured her.

It turned out that Lauren lived in the San Fernando Valley with her parents, who had gone to bed the night before and were shocked in the morning to find their daughter's car outside their house, but no sign of the young student. The door of her car was slightly open, and her father asked their neighbours if they had seen or heard anything. Beulah Stofer, whose house Lauren had parked in front of, told Mr Wagner that she had seen Lauren pull to a stop at about 9pm. Two men then pulled up in a car beside her and, after a short argument, the young girl got into the car with the men and they all drove off.

Around this time, the task force connected the Hillside Stranglers to three earlier murders. Tall prostitute Yolanda Washington's naked body had been found strangled, raped and dumped near Forest Lawn Cemetery on 17 October 1977. Two weeks later, a detective sergeant with the Los Angeles County Sheriff's Department named Frank Salerno was called to La Crescenta, north of Glendale, where a female teenager's naked body had been found in the middle-class neighbourhood. It was obvious that the victim had been raped and sodomised, and there were ligature marks around the neck, wrists and ankles. Interestingly, a small piece of fluff sat on an eyelid. Salerno was sure to bag the fluff for investigation by the forensics team. It would prove a small but vital clue when it came time to bring the killers to justice.

A week after that grim discovery, on 6 November, the nude body of 21-year-old Hollywood waitress Lissa Kastin was found near the country club at Glendale. She had been raped and familiar ligature marks indented the skin on her neck, wrists and ankle. Combined with the other murders, this totalled eight rapes and killings in just two months. But there were more to come.

The body of Kimberly Diane Martin was found dumped on a vacant lot on a steep hill in mid-December bearing all the hallmarks of the Hillside Stranglers. The next victim was 20-year-old clerk Cindy Hudspeth. Her raped and strangled body was found on 16 February 1978, stashed in the boot of her Datsun car and pushed off a cliff. An eager and attractive young woman, Cindy had last been seen leaving her apartment building at 800 East Garfield Avenue – across the road from the home of Kristina Weckler. Both detectives Grogan and Salerno reasoned that there was a chance at least one of the men they were looking for lived in the Glendale area. But just as it seemed like a breakthrough was on the cards, the trail grew cold and there were no more murders for almost a year.

It wasn't until 12 January 1979 that police in the town of Bellingham, Washington received a report that two female roommates and students at Western Washington University – Karen Mandic and Diane Wilder – had gone missing. Karen's boss was concerned when the otherwise reliable woman didn't show up for work. Not knowing what to do, he recalled that a security guard friend of hers had offered her a position house-sitting in the wealthy suburb of Bayside. He called the police, who contacted the security company. The company asked their man about the situation, but he told them he had never even heard of the two missing women.

The security guard's name was Kenneth Bianchi, a tall, trim, intelligent father of a baby boy named Sean who lived with his long-term partner Kelli Boyd. The thought of the gentle, well-groomed Bianchi being involved in the disappearance of the two women seemed ludicrous to both his boss and girlfriend. Especially when he explained to his boss that he had been at a Sheriff's Reserve meeting on the night they went missing.

But the authorities checked Bianchi's story and it transpired that he had not been at the meeting. When questioned about it, the friendly man explained to the police that they were right, he had skipped the meeting after all, because it was about first aid, a subject he was already well versed in. Sensing they were about to reach a dead end, the Bellingham chief of police Terry Mangan went to the house

Karen and Diane shared. If they had merely gone away for a while and forgotten to tell Karen's boss, why was their starving cat left unattended? He searched the house and found the address of the Bayside house. Something didn't fit, so Mangan had the records of the security firm checked. Bianchi was listed as being responsible for looking after the house. Then the police found out that he had used a company truck on the night of the women's disappearance.

Mangan then gave a report to the media containing a description of the missing females and the car they would be driving. It wasn't long before Karen's automobile was located, dumped in dense woodland. Inside were the strangled bodies of Karen Mandic and Diane Wilder. Bianchi was brought in for questioning while the police started an in-depth examination of the forensic evidence they had found, such as loose pubic hairs found on Diane's body and on the carpet at the Bayside residence.

In the meantime, Mangan noticed similarities between his case and the Hillside Strangler murders months earlier. He contacted the authorities in Los Angeles and was eventually put in touch with Frank Salerno. A quick check revealed that Bianchi had lived near Cindy Hudspeth and Kristina Weckler at the time of their murders, and near where Kimberly Martin had been headed on the day of her murder. Things were finally starting to fall into place, and the case only got tighter when jewellery found in Bianchi's house matched items that had belonged to Yolanda Washington and Kimberly Martin.

Then the authorities released a photo of Bianchi to the media. Before long a lawyer named David Wood called them with a story of rescuing a girl named Becky Spears from Bianchi and his cousin Angelo Buono. The men had been using threats and physical violence to make the teenage runaway and a friend prostitute themselves. It was clearly time for detectives to look into Bianchi's past.

Born in New York on 22 May 1951, Kenneth Alessio was adopted out by his alcoholic prostitute mother at birth, and taken in three months later by the Bianchi family. A temperamental child with a mean temper, Bianchi's grades at school fluctuated wildly, despite an IQ of 116. He simply didn't apply himself to his studies.

He married a woman his own age not long after finishing high school, but the relationship ended when she filed for an annulment eight months later, leaving Bianchi feeling bitter and betrayed. He applied for work within the sheriff's department but was turned down and eventually found a job as a security guard. He started to steal from the places he worked at, passing the pilfered goods on to girlfriends as gifts.

In 1975, at the age of 26, Bianchi moved to Los Angeles, where he lived with an older cousin, Angelo Buono. Even though Bianchi embraced the free sex and drugs attitude of 1970s California at first, he soon turned his back on it and – after once again failing to gain employment in law enforcement – he found a job working for a title company. He also bought a 1972 Cadillac and moved into an apartment in Glendale.

At his job Bianchi soon met Kelli Boyd. The pair got along well and in May 1977 she broke the news that she was expecting his baby. Five months later the Hillside Strangler slayings started.

At around the same time, Bianchi lied to Kelli that he had lung cancer and had to undertake chemo and radiation therapy. He started taking time off work, using his fake sickness as an excuse, and his relationship with Kelli grew strained. It got better for a while after Sean was born in

February, but Bianchi was soon back to his irresponsible ways, taking time off work to play poker with his cousin Buono and missing payments on his car. With their life in shambles, Kelli could take no more, so she returned to her hometown of Bellingham, Washington. Bianchi felt that he had been betrayed by a woman once again but endeavoured to win Kelli back by writing to her over and over again. He wore her down in May 1978 and he went to live with her in Bellingham.

While detective Salerno was in Washington putting together the story, his partner Peter Finnigan joined detective Grogan in investigating Angelo Buono in LA. Buono seemed the most likely candidate as Bianchi's partner in the Hillside Strangler murders. It turned out that Buono was something of a ladies' man, describing himself as the 'Italian Stallion' despite being quite unattractive, with a mean, sadistic streak to match. He had several ex-wives, and was known to have abused his children both physically and sexually.

Born in Rochester, New York, on 5 October 1934, Buono's parents later divorced and he moved to Glendale, Los Angeles with his mother and older sister in 1939. A Catholic upbringing did little to instill a sense of morality in the boy. He would often call his mother a whore to her face, and he started raping and sodomising girls in the neighbourhood when he was as young as 14.

He did a stint at a boys home at an early age for grand theft auto, and got a girl at his high school pregnant in 1955, but left her a week later, refusing to pay any form of child support. Indeed, the day his first son was born, Buono was doing his second run of incarceration for auto theft.

Another marriage followed in 1957, as well as several children, but his new wife, Mary Castillo, filed for divorce in 1964, tired of the physical and emotional violence, as well as

Buono's ever stranger sexual desires. Buono again refused to pay child support and Mary had to go on welfare. At one point she tried to get back together with him, if only for the sake of their offspring. But Buono handcuffed the woman and threatened to murder her while pointing a gun at her stomach.

Buono's next relationship started in 1965 with 25-year-old Nanette Campina. The pair had two children together, but when he started to abuse her 14-year-old daughter from a previous relationship in 1971, Nanette decided to risk the death threats and leave the callous child molester.

Buono moved on to Deborah Taylor next. He married her in 1972 but never actually lived with the woman. They never bothered to get a divorce, either.

By the time Bianchi appeared on the scene in 1975, Buono was running an auto upholstery business and keeping himself otherwise occupied with tacky clothing, loud jewellery and any number of too-young and impressionable girls. With Bianchi in need of money, they decided to embark on a career as pimps, but after their first attempt was foiled when Becky Spears and her friend Sabra Hannan managed to get away from them. Instead they found another girl and bought a list of names of men known to sleep with hookers from a prostitute named Deborah Noble.

The list, however, turned out to be worthless. Bianchi and Buono decided to make up for the deception by killing Noble. But as they couldn't find her, they settled for her friend, Yolanda Washington. This was the start of their killing spree, a spree that wouldn't end until Bianchi was locked up.

In jail and sensing that things could go badly for him, Bianchi decided an insanity defence was his best bet, and started to pretend he had a multiple personality disorder, telling any doctor that would listen that an alter ego named Steve Walker had told him to strangle Karen Mandic and Diane Wilder in Bellingham. At least the concocted story helped to implicate Buono in the crimes.

Eventually a deal was struck – if Bianchi pled guilty to the murders in Washington, as well as some of those in Los Angeles, he would dodge the death penalty and receive a life sentence with the possibility of parole instead. As an added incentive, the jail time would be served in California where the penal system was nowhere near as harsh as that of Washington at the time. In return, though, he had to testify against Buono. Given the choice of life in prison with at least the possibility of eventual freedom, or certain death, Bianchi chose life. He started to tell Salerno how he and Buono masqueraded as policemen, complete with fake badges, to lure their victims into their car before raping and killing them. Other important details came out during these interviews. Salerno asked about the fluff found on Judy Miller's eyelid. It turned out the men had used foam from Buono's upholstery business to blindfold the woman. Every piece of evidence would help.

Bianchi eventually offloaded all of the horrible details of the brutal murders he and his cousin had perpetrated, and received double life sentences in Washington, before being transferred to California, where he faced 35 years in prison.

Buono was arrested on 22 October 1979, but as Bianchi had already given the police information against him in order to receive a lighter sentence, there was little reason for him to help the authorities. Bianchi, too, was rethinking his position; feeling guilt for informing on his cousin and worrying that if other prisoners heard that he was an informer life would be made very difficult for him in jail. He started to feign mental illness, and invented a story where another person was responsible for both the Washington murders and those of the Hillside Strangler.

Still, the prosecutors went about making their case against Buono. Besides linking him to the fibres found on Judy Miller's eyelid, they found that animal hairs found on Lauren Wagner's hands were from Buono's pet rabbits. They also found the imprint of a fake police badge in his wallet.

When the case against Buono for 10 counts of murder finally went to trial in November 1981, around 250 witnesses took the stand. Bianchi was also brought back to answer to the killings he admitted responsibility for. In the end both men found themselves sent to prison for life with no possibility of parole. On 22 September 2002 Angelo Buono died in his cell of natural causes. He was 67 years old.

THE CASTLE
THE MURDERS
THE MONSTER

H. H. Holmes

AMERICA'S FIRST SERIAL KILLER

A John Borowski Film

"The Ultimate Horror Story" Film Threat.com

Narrator TONY JAY   Music DOUGLAS ROMAYNE STEVENS
WILLY LASZLO   AUDREY WELLING   RACHELLE VILLARREAL   ED BERTAGNOLI   CARY CALLISON
Voice Talents of TOM CIAPPA   BEKA   SARAH MILLS   Sound Design and Editing JOHN MURRAY
Directors of Photography FREY HOFFMAN   JOHN BOROWSKI   5.1 Surround Mix AARON/STOKES LTD.
5.1 Mix Engineer DARIN HEINIS   Associate Producer DIMAS ESTRADA
Producer - Writer - Director JOHN BOROWSKI

DOLBY
DIGITAL

www.hhholmesthefilm.com

WATERFRONT
PRODUCTIONS
© 2004 Waterfront Productions

H.H. HOLMES: AMERICA'S FIRST SERIAL KILLER

(2004)

DIRECTED BY JOHN BOROWSKI
SCREENPLAY BY JOHN BOROWSKI

FEATURING

Tony Jay as Narrator
Willy Laszlo as HH Holmes
Rachelle Villarreal as Alice Pitezel
Thomas Cronin as Himself
Harold Schechter as Himself
Marian Caporusso as Herself

While it is debatable that HH Holmes was in fact America's first serial killer, this drama/doco is an excellent look at a man whose actions well justify the claim. Reading about the terrible crimes of HH Holmes is bad enough. But watching them is much worse. You get to see what actually went on in this evil fiend's Castle of Horrors: his madhouse of trapdoors, asphyxiation devices, body chutes, and acid vats that were purpose built for murder right in the middle of Chicago.

John Borowski does a terrific job with actors and memorabilia. Without all that much to work with – given his small budget and the fact that the crimes took place more than a century ago – he goes a long way towards letting us know who this mad man was. But while the movie admirably captures Holmes' crimes, it never really solves the riddle of why this doctor committed such atrocious crimes as gassing children to death in a locked trunk with a gas pipe leading through the lid. We find out that he derived pleasure from listening to the youngsters scream and kick as they tried to escape. And we are given some explanations: authoritative opinions come from Harold Schechter, the author of the book on Holmes' life *Depraved*, as well as from serial killer profiler Thomas Cronin, and from the Illinois State Police Forensic Science Center's Marian Caporusso.

For serial killer movie enthusiasts *H.H. Holmes: America's First Serial Killer* is both informative and entertaining viewing and a welcome addition to your library. While it may not be readily available through DVD stores and libraries, if you are finding it hard to get a copy you will find it on mail order on www.hhholmesthefilm.com.

HH Holmes: America's First Serial Killer

A born schemer and con man, with a black heart and a silver tongue, serial killer HH Holmes was capable of manufacturing a story upon demand, then twisting it like a child caught with his hand in the lolly jar as circumstances changed. His criminal career may have started out with bigamy and insurance scams but before he was served with the death penalty in 1896 and sent to the gallows, it was estimated that Holmes was responsible for the deaths of as many as 150 men, women and children. The monster himself admitted that he had done enough to be hanged '12 times over', and eventually confessed to 27 murders and six attempted murders, though just as he was about to drop through the trapdoor on his hanging day, the killer who could lie so effortlessly downplayed his murderous achievements to just two victims. No-one believed the criminal whose career was based around fraud and forgery.

Holmes was born Herman Webster Mudgett in the town of Gimmanton in the US state of New Hampshire in 1861. He claimed to have had a poor but ordinary childhood, despite having an alcoholic father. Still, the young boy was prone to being bullied, and later pointed to an early incident at a local doctor's office when older children forced him to confront a skeleton up close as being a deciding factor in his choice to pursue a career in the field of medicine. Calling it 'a wicked and dangerous' act to pull on a youngster, he added that it put an end to any fears he may have been harbouring. It apparently wiped him of a conscience as well.

Holmes gained his medical certificate at the University of Michigan and soon opened his own practice. It was then that he started on a life of crime and deception by pulling an insurance scam by helping someone fake their own death using a stolen cadaver. After that he worked in a mental asylum, a position that didn't exactly help his own mental state, with memories of the traumatic conditions plaguing him for years to come.

It was after working with the insane that the doctor changed his name to HH Holmes and moved to Chicago. By this time he was already married to two women, without divorcing his first wife. He would later marry another woman as well.

When Holmes arrived, the city was busy preparing for the World's Fair of 1893, also known as the Great Exposition. With around 27 million people flooding through the fair site,

called White City, through its six months, Chicago was rife
with opportunity for anyone with even a half-decent scam to
pull. But Holmes had plans on a far grander scale than
merely duping tourists out of a few dollars.

He first found employment as a prescriptions clerk at a
pharmacy, but when the woman who owned it moved away
abruptly, supposedly to California with her daughter,
Holmes took charge of the business – it is, of course, widely
believed that he defrauded and then murdered the woman.

Before long he bought a property across the road from the
pharmacy on 63rd Street. Using money he gained through
dodgy rackets killing the innocent, he proceeded to build a
three-level monument to murder that he called The Castle.
With more than 100 rooms, the building was akin to an
intricate maze, impossible for the uninitiated to navigate.
Holmes even changed builders several times during the
construction so that there could be no exact record of its
design. While the ground floor housed shops and Holmes'
own office, the upper two levels were a confusing mess of
windowless rooms, stairways that led nowhere, and doors
that opened to reveal nothing but brick walls. There were
sliding walls and false floors, secret walkways, and hidden
ladders leading to smaller enclaves. Adding to the horror was
a complete surgery, and rooms full of torture equipment,
including a rack used to stretch victims.

With his masterpiece complete, Holmes started filling the
rooms with his mostly female victims. Some were employees,
others were lovers. Many were simply random women or
other transients who had come to the city to witness the
spectacle of the World Fair and were seeking accommodation
while they were there. Either way, they would soon find
themselves locked inside asbestos-lined soundproof gas
chambers that Holmes controlled from the comfort of his

own bedroom, releasing deadly poisons into the air to asphyxiate the helpless victims. The bodies were then sent down greased chutes to the basement, where they were either stripped of their flesh and sold as skeletons to medical schools, or cremated in one of two huge furnaces and then dumped into lime pits. There were also containers of acid used to dissolve the corpses.

Once the World Fair had finished and creditors started closing in on Holmes, he decided to bring his ghoulish operation to an end, and went on his way, travelling around the country, murdering people as he went until the killing of an associate and his children finally saw Holmes brought to justice.

The Castle mysteriously burnt down about a month after Holmes left Chicago, but not before investigators searched the macabre site, finding a number of skeletons, as well as several separate bone fragments, one of which was the pelvis of a 14-year-old boy. The newspapers ran sensationalist headlines such as: 'The Castle is a tomb!' while the police carted out the evidence. But, by that time, Holmes had already moved on to the next sadistic chapter of his twisted life.

In October 1894 a man named Marion Hedgepeth told the authorities about a scam he had heard about from a man named HM Howard. Howard – an alias Holmes had been using – and a man he worked with named Benjamin Pitezel had supposedly taken out life insurance on Pitezel for $10,000. They then faked his death in an explosion, leaving a medical cadaver in the laboratory in its place, much like the insurance scam that sent Holmes down his dark path in the first place. The idea was for Pitezel and Holmes to split the cash later, but Holmes ran off with the ill-gotten proceeds of the scam.

Even before the police had been told Hedgepeth's story, though, the insurance company had their suspicions that something was amiss about the claim. The body found in the laboratory at 1316 Callowhill Street, Philadelphia, was already in an advanced state of rigor mortis, and had been so badly damaged that identification was impossible. Nonetheless, Holmes – accompanied by one of Pitezel's three children – stated categorically that it was his colleague. He then collected the money from the insurance policy and disappeared with Pitezel's children – Alice, 15, Howard, 8, and Nellie, 11.

Agents from the Pinkerton National Detective Agency were put onto the trail and they pieced together Holmes' dodgy path of deceit, finding out about a seemingly endless run of scams and swindles through the years.

Holmes was finally arrested in Vermont on 16 November 1894, about to leave the US on a steamship. He soon declared that the body he'd identified as Pitezel was in fact a medical cadaver. When asked what had happened to the children he had been seen leaving Philadelphia with, Holmes said they were with Pitezel in South America, or possibly Florida.

The authorities next questioned Pitezel's wife Carrie, who admitted that she knew about the scam but added that she had no idea where her husband and children were – only that she would hopefully see them soon. The woman was arrested for conspiracy, even though the authorities believed she had no idea of the depth of what was going on. They believed that her husband and children were already long dead.

Holmes was then transported back to Philadelphia and placed in Moyamensing Prison, where he was housed in a small cell. The smooth-talker convinced the guards to bring him the daily newspapers, and as he saw the ongoing investigation of his horrible acts in Chicago made public, Holmes realised he had to change his story. He began to scheme on the best possible way to get himself out of trouble, as he had done so many times before. By December he was saying that the body found in the explosion was indeed Pitezel's. The revised story saw Pitezel devising the scam along with Holmes, his wife and two other men, but before they could carry it out, Pitezel became depressed and committed suicide, using chloroform while drunk. Holmes merely staged the explosion in order to get the insurance money and then left town, telling Carrie Pitezel that the children were safe in England with an associate of his, a woman named Minnie Williams.

Holmes pleaded guilty in court to conspiracy to defraud the insurance company on 3 June 1895. But while he was awaiting sentencing, questions were raised about the children's whereabouts. No-one could locate them. A detective named Frank Geyer was given the job of finding them. He soon found out that not only were the children missing, but so was the mysterious Minnie Williams, as well as her sister Nettie. The fact they were both former associates of Holmes made the case seem all the more sinister. Even the London street that Holmes had said the women lived in didn't exist. What Geyer did have in his possession, though, were a series of letters the children had written to their mother while travelling with Holmes, which had been found unmailed in the scam artist's possession when he was taken into custody. Geyer set off using the places where the letters were written as a guide.

After trekking around the US, he eventually located a house in Toronto, Canada, that Holmes had rented. The house had a dark cellar under a trapdoor, and buried in the ground Geyer found the naked rotting corpses of Nellie and

Alice Pitezel. But Geyer's work hadn't finished; he still had to locate Howard Pitezel. Through sheer persistence he eventually followed the clues to the town of Irvington, where, on 27 August, five weeks after he uncovered the sisters, Geyer found the young boy's cremated remains in the chimney of a property Holmes had rented. In his later confession Holmes admitted to locking the children in a large trunk and killing them slowly with a gas pipe into a hole through the lid.

With the evidence stacked against him, Holmes was indicted for the murder of Benjamin Pitezel on 12 September. Meanwhile, the dark terrors of what he had been up to in Chicago were coming to light through the press in articles that Holmes continued to keep up to date with in prison. To counteract the obvious and growing public opinion against him, he decided to release his memoirs, in which he painted himself as a battler who had been hard done by, and denied playing a part in any of the deaths surrounding him. It's fair to say that very few readers believed a word of what he wrote. His silver tongue was starting to fail him as he got deeper and deeper into trouble.

The trial began in Philadelphia on 28 October with Holmes opting to defend himself. It was the first time anyone accused of murder had done so in the US. The skilled con man played up to the judge while attacking the prosecution. But at the end of the first day it still looked like he was guilty. At this point Holmes decided it would be for the best to have professionals take over his case, but the damage was already done in the eyes of the jury. The case became a simple matter of going through the motions.

In the prosecution's closing statements, they described Holmes as 'the most dangerous man in the world'. The judge and jury agreed and he received a sentence of death.

HH Holmes ate a final meal of coffee, eggs and toast on 7 May 1896. He was then taken to the gallows where he was hung by the neck until death and the trapdoor beneath him was flung open. The man who had caused so much pain to so many random victims through deceit and murder struggled with the noose around his neck for a quarter of an hour before the life was finally choked out of him.

WOLF CREEK

(2005)

DIRECTED BY GREG MCLEAN
SCREENPLAY BY GREG MCLEAN

FEATURING

John Jarratt as Mick Taylor
Cassandra Magrath as Liz Hunter
Kestie Morassi as Kristy Earl
Nathan Phillips as Ben Mitchell

'Based on a true story' the opening credits tell us. Well, not quite, but this Australian thriller certainly does have links with two famous Australian murders cases. The most recent case is the disappearance of British tourist Peter Falconio in the Northern Territory in July 2001. Bradley John Murdoch was subsequently convicted for his murder. The second is the most notorious case of serial murder in Australia's history, the Backpacker Murders, for which Ivan Milat was convicted of seven murders between 1989 and 1992 in the Belanglo State Forest on the outskirts of Sydney.

In *Wolf Creek* John Jarratt plays Mick Taylor, the ocker outback loner who befriends two girls and a young bloke who have broken down in the middle of nowhere. Kind Mick offers them a tow – to a graveyard of luckless young tourists and their vehicles. All of this peripherally relates to both Peter Falconio's disappearance, and the real-life murderer Murdoch could be likened to the make-believe Mick.

The similarity to the Backpacker Murders comes when Mick refers to one of his victims as 'a head on a stick', after severing her spine with a huge Bowie knife. This was the method used by Ivan Milat to render his victims helpless, but leave them still alive, so he could have his way with them without any interference.

Both the Falconio disappearance and the Backpacker Murders are featured in this chapter.

Wolf Creek is a very scary movie. But what is scariest of all is that it is very believable. There could very well be a Mick Taylor, or several for that matter, out there preying on kids in their $2000 Holden station wagons and kombis. And I guess it's Aussies who would have the best understanding of this, given our knowledge of the vastness of the outback – the hours or even days that can pass before seeing another vehicle, and the huge distances between outposts of civilisation. So it is little wonder the film was panned unmercifully by the US critics, who couldn't get past the blood and guts to soak up the reality. The doyen of them all, Roger Ebert, gave it zero stars and said, '*Wolf Creek* is more like the guy who bites the heads off chickens at the carnival sideshow. No fun for us, no fun for the guy, no fun for the chicken. In the case of this film, it's fun for the guy.' Another said: 'It made me want to vomit and cry at the same time.' Yet another: 'It must be giving Australia's outback tourism industry a bad case of heartburn.'

Still, at a cost of about $A1 million and with worldwide box office takings of over $US24 million, I guess the producers couldn't care less. I thought it was great.

The Peter Falconio Murder

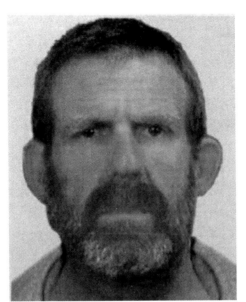

BRADLEY MURDOCH

On 14 July 2001 English tourists, Joanne Lees and Peter Falconio, both from Huddersfield, Yorkshire and in their late 20s, were heading up the Stuart Highway for Darwin in their 30-year-old kombi that they had bought in Sydney specifically for touring the outback. They had been travelling the world together for six years and had been in Australia for about six months, starting with a working stint in Sydney where they had both made many friends.

It was their intention to drive to Darwin and then over to Brisbane, where Peter would fly out to Papua New Guinea and Joanne would go back to Sydney to catch up with friends. They then planned to meet up again after two weeks and travel on to New Zealand, Fiji and the US.

A couple of hours earlier they had taken a break from cruising the lonely highway while listening to music and had shared a marijuana joint at a stop called Ti Tree. They had cuddled and watched the sun set spectacularly on the desert. But in a couple of hours their plans would change for ever in the worst possible way.

Their orange kombi was about 10km north of Barrow Creek when a white Toyota Land Cruiser ute overtook them. The driver waved his hand to flag them down, indicating that there was something wrong with the back of the vehicle. Joanne didn't want to stop, but Peter was driving and he pulled over to the side of the road where he got out and went to the back of the kombi with the stranger, while Joanne stayed in the cabin with the engine running. A few moments later she heard a bang like a car backfiring and then the strange man appeared at her window holding a silver handgun.

The tall, thickset stranger got into the driver's side of the kombi, pushed her forward and, despite her violent struggling, tied her hands together behind her back. He dragged Joanne out of the kombi, loosely bound her feet, threw her into the back of his ute and left her there – she wasn't sure for how long.

Realising that her partner had most likely just been murdered and soon it would be her turn, Joanne struggled. She managed to untie her feet and, with her hands still tied behind her, she dropped from the back of the ute and fled into the pitch black undergrowth along the side of the highway until she stumbled into a large bush and hid beneath it, not daring to breathe.

There she stayed, curled up and crouching forward with her head on her knees, terrified to make the slightest sound as the killer frantically searched for her. Time and again he passed nearby and she could hear his dog panting. She heard him dragging something along the ground. She saw the headlights of a vehicle scan the bushes in search of her. How the reflector strips on her shorts were never caught in the headlights, or the man's dog never smelt her fear, is a miracle.

Almost five hours later at about 12.45am and still not certain whether the killer had gone, Joanne plucked up enough courage to run in front of a road train. She was rescued by driver Vince Millar and his co-driver Rod Adams. Almost in disbelief at finding a distraught young lady in the middle of nowhere telling a tale of murder and abduction, the truckies cut the hand-ties from Joanne's wrists and drove her to the nearby Barrow Creek pub, where they rang the police.

When the police arrived several hours later they found Peter and Joanne's kombi driven off the road and blood on the highway. Joanne was able to give them a positive description of the man who had apparently killed her partner in cold blood. Seeing as he had made no attempt to cover his face, they could only assume that she would have been murdered also. Joanne also had some tiny specks of blood on her T-shirt that could not be eliminated by DNA and could be assumed to belong to the killer.

Within months a Broome diesel mechanic, Bradley John Murdoch, 46, came under suspicion when several people told police that Murdoch had gone to great lengths to change the appearance of his vehicle and had shaved off his distinctive Merv Hughes moustache, as well as shaving his head. Police questioned Murdoch, but he claimed that he was hundreds of kilometres away on his way home from a marijuana drug run in South Australia when the incident at Barrow Creek took place. They couldn't disprove this, but the times and places he was allegedly at didn't quite add up as the perfect alibi.

Unfortunately for the police investigating the case, the law of the Northern Territory at the time didn't allow for them to take Murdoch's DNA or illegally acquire it and compare it against the blood on Joanne Lees' T-shirt, which would either eliminate him or allow them to charge him with attempted abduction and murder.

Then in August 2002 the police got the break they desperately needed. Bradley Murdoch, who was said to be highly agitated about the search for Peter Falconio's killer and couldn't stop telling people that he was a prime suspect, was arrested and charged with the abduction and multiple rapes of a woman and her 12-year-old daughter in rural South Australia.

It was alleged that after a 25-hour drive, in which the mother and daughter were chained together and repeatedly raped at gunpoint, Murdoch dumped them at a Port Augusta service station, gave the mother $1000 and told her: 'You could make some money out of this if you went to the media.' The woman eventually went to the police who arrested Murdoch on 28 August 2002 in a nearby Woolworths store. He was carrying a loaded gun in a shoulder holster and another in the waistband of his trousers. In his vehicle police found a shotgun, a rifle with telescopic sights, ammunition, a crossbow, night-vision goggles, several knives, a cattle prodder, handcuffs made from cable ties, rolls of tape, gloves, tins of cannabis and a large amount of cash.

Murdoch was well known to police. He was a drug-runner who took large amounts marijuana from state to state concealed in the spare petrol tank of his car. Murdoch knew every back road in the bush and desert, and could travel extraordinarily distances without going near a main road, high on amphetamines.

Murdoch was a big, tough, foul-mouthed bully who had his front teeth missing. He had a fascination with guns and owned a big collection of rifles and handguns. He made no secret of his hatred of Aboriginals and one of his many tattoos was of an Aboriginal man hanging from a noose.

Murdoch's most notorious crime was on the day of the 1995 football grand final in the far north Western Australian town of Fitzroy Crossing. Several hundred Aboriginal people celebrating their team's victory refused to move and allow Murdoch to cross the bridge across the Fitzroy River. Unable to get past, Murdoch turned around and drove 25km back to a cattle station, where he was working at the time, and collected a .308 rifle and .22 lever-action magnum. He returned to the bridge and opened fire on the revellers cars, narrowly missing women and children in the process. He got 15 months in jail for the shootings and another six months for stealing the guns.

Aware that Murdoch was a prime suspect in the Falconio case, the South Australian police legally took his DNA and sent it on to the Northern Territory police. When matched with the DNA from the blood found on Joanne Lees' T-shirt it was found to be 150 quadrillion times more likely to have come from Murdoch than any other person in the Northern Territory. The DNA from the hand ties was 100 million times more likely a match. They had their man. Trouble was he looked liked spending the next 20 or so years in a South Australian prison for the abduction and assaults on the mother and daughter. But, incredibly, that was not to be.

Murdoch was acquitted of all charges on the grounds that the woman, a former prostitute, and her daughter did not go to the police earlier. The rumours were rampant that because the Northern Territory police couldn't get a sample of Murdoch's DNA they had planted the woman and her child in South Australia near Murdoch, and then the woman had encouraged him to commit a crime so the police could test his DNA legally. But that's all it was, just a rumour.

Murdoch was extradited to the Northern Territory where he was charged and tried for the murder of Peter Falconio and the attempted abduction of Joanne Lees. When asked if the man who assaulted her was in the court Joanne Lees pointed to Murdoch and said: 'Yes. I'd recognise him anywhere.'

Despite driving 1800km in the 18 hours following the Barrow Creek incident to create an alibi, the DNA and other evidence was too overwhelming. In December 2005, Bradley John Murdoch was found guilty and sentenced to life imprisonment with a nonparole period of 28 years, despite Peter Falconio's remains having never been found.

After Murdoch's sentencing, his girlfriend, Jan Pittman, had the final say on the Nine Network: 'My man is innocent,' she said. 'He loves to go fishing, have a few drinks and light the barbie. He's very good at the barbie.'

Ivan Milat: The Beast of Belanglo

Australia's most prolific convicted individual serial killer of the 20th century, Ivan Robert Marko Milat, was born in Sydney on 27 December 1945, the fourth child in a family of nine brothers and four sisters. At 17, he received his first criminal conviction, for stealing, and was placed on probation. Later that year he served six months in a juvenile institution for breaking and entering. Two years after his release he was charged with two counts of breaking, entering and stealing and sentenced to 18 months.

In 1965, Milat was convicted of auto theft and sentenced to two years. In April 1967 he was charged with multiple counts of larceny and auto theft and sentenced to three years, with an 18-month nonparole period. He was released in 1969 and began a series of armed robberies with his brother Michael and other accomplices. Ivan was soon charged with an armed hold-up at a bank in Canley Heights.

In April 1971 he was charged with the rape of two girls who had left a mental institution and were hitchhiking to Melbourne. Milat fled to New Zealand while on bail. Three years later he returned and the court found there was insufficient evidence to convict him for armed robbery. He defended the rape charges by saying the girls had consented.

On 25 January 1990, English tourist Paul Onions was at Liverpool, on the southwestern outskirts of Sydney, looking for a lift. He was approached by a man sporting a drooping moustache. The man introduced himself as Bill. After an hour and a half on the road, Bill turned nasty. Onions later told *60 Minutes* reporter Charles Wooley of his scrape with death:

His speech became aggressive, and instead of being a friendly kind of guy he changed all of a sudden ... then he pulled over to the side of the road and got out and started messing round with the seat. I was a bit nervous and I thought I'd just get out and stretch my legs and try to suss things out.

Milat was furious. He ordered Onions back in the car. Moments later Onions was staring down the barrel of a revolver. He said:

Next thing he had produced a coil of rope, and when I saw it I thought, that's it, I'm getting out of here. With that I undid my seatbelt, opened the door, jumped out and ran up the road for my life.

Milat chased, firing several shots. Onions tried to flag down passing cars. None would stop. Milat grabbed Onions. Again he broke free. He recalled:

I turned round and faced the traffic, and when the next vehicle, a family van, came across over the rise I put both my hands out in front for it to stop. And as soon as it did I pulled around to the side and opened the sliding door on the passenger side and got in and locked it. There were two women and five children inside and they were all yelling at me to get out and I was saying, 'He's got a gun, he's got a gun.'

The driver could see Milat walking back to his vehicle. She drove Onions to Bowral police station, where he provided a thorough description of his assailant and of his assailant's vehicle. It was filed away and forgotten.

On 19 September 1992 two orienteering enthusiasts found the remnants of a black T-shirt in the Belanglo State Forest in the New South Wales southern highlands. Both recoiled in horror when they saw the heel of a shoe protruding from a stack of branches and leaves. Police cordoned off the area. The next day, they found a second body. Forensic evidence established the victims as British backpackers Caroline Clark, 22, and Joanne Walters, 22. They had last been seen in Kings Cross in December 1989 and they were planning to hitchhike to Melbourne.

Joanne had been stabbed in the chest, neck and back 14 times. Five of the wounds had severed her spine and broken two ribs. There were no defensive wounds to Joanne's hands or arms, indicating that perhaps she had been tied up. The zip on her jeans was undone, which signalled the possibility of sexual assault, but the top button was still done up.

Caroline had been stabbed just below her neck once with the same knife and shot 10 times in the head. It appeared she had been tied to a tree, with her head used for target practice.

On 5 October 1993 a man collecting firewood in Belanglo came across partially buried human remains. Detectives were called again and another body was found. The bodies were later identified as Deborah Everist and James Gibson, friends who had last been seen on 30 December 1989 on the Hume Highway, looking for a lift to Melbourne.

Deborah had been stabbed in the spine and had numerous fractures to the skull. Pantyhose and a black bra were found nearby. The bra had been slashed. James had multiple stab wounds to his spine, breastbone and chest. As with the previous victims, one stab wound had penetrated his mid-thoracic spine, slicing upwards, effectively paralysing him. The zip on his trousers was open, but the top button remained closed.

Authorities conducted a search of the whole area. On 31 October 1993 the body of German hitchhiker Simone Schmidl was found. She had been stabbed numerous times in the chest. Again there was a downward stab wound in her upper back, severing her spinal cord.

Two days later the bodies of Anja Habschied and Gabor Neugebauer were found. The German backpackers had disappeared on Boxing Day 1991. It took three police officers to lift a heavy log off Gabor's body. There were six bullet wounds to his skull. The zip on his jeans was undone but the top button was done up.

Anja had been decapitated, and her clothing had been pulled above her chest. Her head had been removed with a long, sharp instrument such as a sword. It appeared she had been forced into a kneeling position and then beheaded.

Most of the seven victims had been paralysed by a knife to the spine. They would still have been alive, but unable to move a muscle except their head. This is the reference in *Wolf Creek* to 'a head on a stick' an expression that is believed to have originated in the Vietnam war in reference to a torture and murder procedure of prisoners. All these victims been tortured and probably sexually assaulted. Investigators believed the killings were linked. The huge log on the body of Gabor Neugebauer was almost certainly placed by more than one man.

A woman came forward, telling of a man named Ivan Milat, who lived near Belanglo. Detectives turned up at a worksite that was his last-known address. Ivan's younger brother Richard also worked there. They found that Richard had been working on the days the backpackers had disappeared. Ivan hadn't. Most interestingly, he had been charged with rape in 1971. Although he was acquitted on that charge, statements indicated that the two girls had been hitchhiking when offered a lift by Milat.

Workers at a concrete manufacturing company also came forward about one of their workmates, Paul Miller. When the bodies of Joanne Walters and Caroline Clarke were discovered in 1992, Miller told co-workers: 'There's more bodies out there. They haven't found the two Germans yet. Oh yeah, I know who killed those two Germans.' Later, Miller said: 'Stabbing a woman is like cutting a loaf of bread.' He also told workmates: 'You could pick up anybody on that road and you'd never find them again. You'd never find out who did it either.' A check revealed that Paul Miller was Richard Milat.

Now back in England, Onions heard of the discovery of the seven bodies. He went to authorities and told them what had happened to him. Onions was flown to Australia in April 1994. Shown a video line-up of 13 men, he identified Ivan Milat instantly.

In dawn raids on 22 May 1994 more than 300 police officers hit Ivan Milat's home in Eaglevale, as well as the homes of his brothers Richard, Walter and Bill, a property owned by two of the Milat brothers in the southern highlands and the Queensland home of Alex Milat. The raids provided a horde of evidence. A dismantled Ruger .22 was found, as was a drinking bottle belonging to Simone Schmidl, and Caroline Clarke's camera. A photo was found of Milat's girlfriend in which she was wearing a windcheater that belonged to Caroline Clarke. Sleeping bags belonging to Simone Schmidl and Deborah Everist were found.

In the other raids, police found ammunition and weapons, as well as camping gear belonging to the victims. At the home of Milat's mother, a long curved cavalry sword was found. Police believed it to be the weapon used to decapitate Anja Habschied.

On Saturday 27 July 1996 Ivan Milat was found guilty of seven counts of murder and one count of attempted murder. He will spend the remainder of his life behind bars.

While there has been much debate over the years that Ivan Milat didn't act alone in some of the killings, there has never been any evidence produced to substantiate these suspicions. But police have good reason to believe that Ivan Milat is responsible for more than just the seven backpacker murders. In 1987 an unclothed female skeleton believed to be that of a female backpacker who went missing while hitchhiking around Australia, was found in bush near Taree in northern New South Wales. At the time of her disappearance it is believed that Ivan Milat was working for the Department of Main Roads as part of a resurfacing gang. Milat is also suspected of knowing about other mysterious disappearances in the district.

In January 1988 the body of 18-year-old hitchhiker, Peter Letcher, who had gone missing around 14 November 1987 was found in the Jenolan State Forest, 160km west of Sydney. He had been shot in the head with five .22 bullets and his head was wrapped in material in an identical fashion to that of Caroline Clarke. Letcher had gone missing on the weekend before Milat's road crew was due to start roadwork nearby. Police have little doubt that the teenager was murdered by Milat. He is also suspected to be involved in the disappearance of two hitchhikers, Alan Fox and his fiancée Anneke Adriaansen, who went missing between Sydney and the New South Wales north coast in January 1979.

THE HUNT FOR THE BTK KILLER

(2005)

DIRECTED BY STEPHEN T KAY
SCREENPLAY BY TOM TOWLER AND DONALD MARTIN

FEATURING

Robert Forster as Detective Jason Magida
Gregg Henry as Dennis Rader
Joey Campbell as John
Maury Chaykin as Robert Beattie
Andrew Church as Kevin Bright
Michael Fox as Officer Rodriguez

Made for television and now available in DVD stores as a movie, *The Hunt for the BTK Killer* presents the hunt for one of the most cunning serial killers in America's history. It's filmed in a dramatic documentary style, and is an accurate depiction of the events. But while the hunt for the BTK killer went for 31 years, his eventual capture came as an anticlimax. He was caught because of a monumental blunder on the part of the killer, rather than brilliant detective work.

With that in mind, *The Hunt for the BTK Killer* looks at the murders, the frustration of the investigators and the serial killer acting in tandem with police without them knowing who (as yet) he is. It makes for interesting viewing. The film gives us insights into BTK's bizarre character – one minute confiscating and putting to death a lady's pet and the next accepting the presidency of the congregation of his local church.

In his usual craggy style, veteran Robert Forster (*Mulholland Drive*, *Jackie Brown*) plays the frustrated cop in charge of the investigation. He follows the case right up to the capture of BTK, when he finally gets a look at the killer who has been living and working among the citizens of the city of Wichita, Kansas, for more than three decades. While Forster does a very capable job as the detective Jason Madiga, Madiga was not a real person – but it makes no difference to the movie. Gregg Henry's performance as BTK is chilling; he has captured both his likeness and mannerisms. The now famous video confession of BTK is available on the internet, if you'd like to draw a comparison.

Part of the BTK killings – the Otero family murders – have been covered on page 167 in this book. Here is the full story.

The BTK Serial Killer

When he arrived home from school in Wichita, Kansas, in the mid-afternoon of 15 January 1974, 15-year-old Charlie Otero came across the dead bodies of his mother and father in their bedroom. His father Joseph, 38, was lying face down on the floor at the foot of the bed with his wrists and ankles bound together and he had a plastic bag tied over his head. Charlie's mother, 34-year-old Julie Otero, was tied up on the bed where she had been gagged and strangled. Charlie fled to a neighbour's house to get help, not realising that he had only witnessed the half of the horror.

The neighbour tried to call the police, but the Otero home phone line had been cut. He went home and rang the police while Charlie waited outside. When the police arrived and searched the house they found Charlie's brother, nine-year-old Joseph Jr face down on the floor in his bedroom. The boy's wrists and ankles were also bound and there were three plastic bags over his head. In the basement police discovered the dead body of Charlie's 11-year-old sister, Josephine. She had been sexually assaulted, strangled and hanged. Joseph Otero's watch was missing and Julie Otero's purse was rifled and dumped nearby. Outside of that there was no evidence of a break and enter, robbery, or any sort of a struggle. After the murders the killer then brazenly drove off in the Otero family car and parked it to be found near Dillons grocery store, only a few blocks away.

With absolutely nothing to go on, police dug deep into Joseph and Julie Otero's past. Joseph Otero was born in Puerto Rico and emigrated to the United States, where he joined the military services. He was a well-regarded flight instructor and mechanic in peak physical condition and he was an excellent boxer and a loving husband and father. His beloved wife Julie was a devoted mother with lots of friends. Like her husband, she knew how to look after herself in the event of trouble after many years of training in judo.

So how could this possibly happen? Was it a contract hit? If so, why? There was no possible reason. Was it a random killing? If so, then why a whole family? To be carried out without so much as a living witness in broad daylight required surveillance, planning and precision timing. And how could one person subdue so many people who were skilled in martial arts? That's if it was just the one killer?

But it was just the beginning. After the Otero family killings, over the next four years three more women were

FAMILY ALBUM PHOTO OF DENNIS RADER

brutally tied up, tortured, asphyxiated and murdered, unmistakably by the same killer. And, as the death toll mounted, the killer taunted police with a barrage of appalling poems of death, and letters complaining that his murders weren't getting enough publicity. In the letters the killer said that he reasoned it was because he didn't have a nickname like other multiple murderers and, seeing as the local police or paper wouldn't give him one, he would come up with one himself.

After giving police such alternatives as 'the Wichita Strangler', 'the Poetic Strangler', 'the Wichita Hangman' and 'the Asphyxiater' the serial killer settled on 'BTK' as the nickname for himself. It stood for 'BIND, TORTURE, KILL' because this was how he murdered his victims. And then, in 1978, with seven murders to his credit, BTK disappeared without a trace or the slightest clue as to who he may be.

MUG SHOT OF DENNIS RADER SOON AFTER BEING CAUGHT AND CHARGED WITH THE BTK KILLINGS

Wichita police never gave up the hunt for BTK but every new investigation came to nothing. Then, in 2004, almost 26 years after his last murder, Wichita police received a letter containing information that only the killer could have known about: a murder committed in 1986 in nearby Park City, a death that investigators hadn't connected with the BTK slayings.

Over the next 12 months BTK corresponded regularly with police and left packages all over town containing items that he had souvenired from each victim, along with graphic descriptions and photos of each murder scene. Becoming more brazen as each week passed, BTK decided to use a computer for his correspondence and, in his ignorance of modern technology, in one of his letters asked the detectives if he sent them a floppy disk, would they be able to read anything else on the disk other than the file he addressed to them. Naturally, in their response via the local newspapers, they said no.

When the disk arrived and the investigators saw what was on it, they couldn't believe their eyes. Apart from the usual BTK diatribe of torture and death, there were other files which provided information showing the disk had originated from the local Lutheran Church. On 26 February 2005 Wichita police arrested 59-year-old Dennis L Rader, Wichita's ordinance inspector and dog-catcher, former boy scout leader and president of the Wichita Lutheran Church congregation. Rader was a happily married, highly respected member of the city's religious community with two grown-up children. BTK had been living right there among them all of those years. Rader confessed to all of the BTK murders and another three murders in nearby Park City in 1985 and 1991, bringing his total to 10.

Dennis Rader explained to police what had most puzzled them for years. How did a single man overpower the four members of the Otero family, all of whom were experienced in martial arts? Rader explained that when he entered the house by the open back door at around 7 o'clock on the morning of 15 January 1974, he bailed up Julie and Joseph Otero and the two children with a .44 handgun and told them that he had just escaped from jail and all he wanted was money, food and their car. The God-fearing Oteros took him at his word and let him tie them up. But Rader had different plans. Knowing that the other children had left for school he set about slowly torturing and murdering them one at a time. (See page 172 for the full confession)

At the first day of his trial on Monday 27 June 2005, Dennis Rader pleaded guilty to the murder of 10 people. When asked by Judge Waller if he had anything to say, such as apologise to the victim's families or ask forgiveness, it was as if this was Dennis Rader's moment of glory and he wasn't going to miss a beat.

To the court's astonishment – and an audience in the tens of millions watching live on Court TV across America – Rader stood up and proudly described in horrific detail every murder he had committed, and the ones he almost had, which were equally as terrifying. Prompted by the judge, Rader went on and on for hours with what must be the most extraordinary confession ever broadcast on live television anywhere in the world.

Dennis Rader, the BTK serial killer will die in jail. The whole story of the BTK serial murders is available in the extraordinary book *Unholy Messenger* by Stephen Singular. It is not for the faint hearted.

A JOHN BOROWSKI FILM

ALBERT FISH

IN SIN HE FOUND SALVATION

NARRATOR TONY JAY   MUSIC COREY A. JACKSON

STARRING OTO BREZINA DEREK GASPAR NATHAN HALL COONEY HORVATH GARRETT SHRIVER KASEY SKINNER

FEATURING THEODORE BERNSTEIN JOE COLEMAN KATHERINE RAMSLAND, PH.D.

VOICE TALENT BOB DUNSWORTH HARVEY FISHER DONNA RAWLINS DAVID SHERMAN RONNI TRANKEL

SOUND DESIGNER/SOUND EDITOR JARED K. NEAL CO-PRODUCER DIMAS ESTRADA

PRODUCER – WRITER – DIRECTOR JOHN BOROWSKI

WWW.ALBERTFISHFILM.COM

NR | NOT RATED
themes of torture and murder
sexually explicit language

WATERFRONT PRODUCTIONS
feature and documentary films
© 2007 Waterfront Productions

ALBERT FISH

(2007)

DIRECTED BY JOHN BOROWSKI
SCREENPLAY BY JOHN BOROWSKI

FEATURING
Oto Brezina as Albert Fish
Joe Coleman as Himself
Derek Gaspar as Young Albert Fish
Nathan Hall as Kedden
Cooney Horvath as Jesus Christ
Kasey Skinner as Grace Budd

The main story of Albert Fish centres around the abduction and murder of 10-year-old Grace Budd in New York in 1928. When Fish was caught six years later in 1934 it was revealed that he was, and still is, one of the most evil serial killers of all time. Having said that, it appears that in *Albert Fish* the movie, the director has set out to make this the most evil serial killer *movie* of all time. Let's face it, he certainly had a lot to work with.

In this classy docudrama, award-winning director John Borowski (*H.H.Holmes: America's First Serial Killer*) doesn't tread lightly through the life and times of Albert Fish. Instead he accentuates almost every vile act this beast ever performed. And then he adds a few more for good measure. The viewer is spared nothing. Stabbings and mutilations, flagellation, self-flagellation, preparing children for the oven, children's body parts roasting in the oven or sizzling in the frying pan, explicit explanations of murdering and eating children, living bodies with arrows protruding from them. And on and on it goes.

But apparently it is all for a very good reason, and that is to find out why Albert Fish did what he did. And to do that the movie takes an unconventional look at Albert's life and the things that allegedly drove him to commit the worst imaginable crimes.

For all his shortcomings, Albert was very religious. A good Catholic, he could read and he believed in the Bible. And the Bible is full of the most terrible deaths, as the movie shows us: conventional and upside-down crucifixions, beheadings and stabbings galore. Could the Bible have set Albert on his life of debauchery? Or could it be the boy Albert had an affair with in his youth who beat Albert to a pulp before they had sex?

But, apparently, Albert wasn't all bad. The movie points out that Albert was very proud of the fact that he didn't 'fuck' the child – as he so gracefully put it in the letter to Grace's parents – before he strangled her to death and cooked and ate her, thus saving her from the terrible sexual experiences that lay ahead. Perhaps, the movie asks, in Albert's kind, loving and fatherly mind, sex was obviously much worse than being murdered and eaten.

And while all of these visual theories are being thrown about we are randomly subjected to the opinions of an artist of the bizarre, named Joe Coleman, who owns and runs a place in New York named the Odditorium. In this menagerie of the macabre, Joe's prized exhibit is the original letter that Albert Fish wrote to Grace Budd's parents telling them of their daughter's terrible demise.

Joe proudly points out how, due to a clerk's error, he wound up with the original and that it is now where it rightly belongs – in his Odditorium – and that because of this he is an authority on Albert Fish. And he talks accordingly. Joe and his colourful dialogue sprinkled with obscenities fits perfectly as an almost comic interlude into the horror that is going on around us.

And every so often we are jolted back to reality by Katherine Ramsland PhD, author of 25 books on crime and serial killers and one of the world's most respected serial killer authorities. What Katherine has to say gives *Albert Fish* an even balance between the esoteric, the bizarre and the outright horror.

And with that going for it *Albert Fish* is interesting viewing as we watch him progress from the orphanage to the electric chair. Not everyone's cup of tea, and I have to admit that without Katherine Ramsland's many contributions I would have gone home a lot sooner. *Albert Fish* the movie may not be readily available through DVD stores and libraries and if you are finding it hard to get a copy you will find it on mail order on www.albertfishfilm.com.

Albert Fish:
The Most Evil Serial Killer of Them All

No crimes in history were more abhorrent than those of deranged 64-year-old house painter Albert Fish. Passing himself off as an innocuous, benevolent little old man, Fish abducted, molested, tortured, castrated, killed and ate as many as 25 children and teenagers in New York and all over the US in the 1920s and '30s.

What made Fish's crimes so ghastly was that he was a prolific writer and his jottings included a letter to the parents of a little girl telling them in detail how he murdered, dissected, cooked and ate their daughter. This letter would be his undoing.

Born in 1870, young Albert spent most of his early life in an orphanage where he experienced daily beatings for the

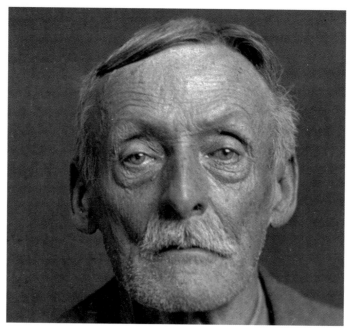

ALBERT FISH

most minuscule misdemeanors. After a while he came to love being beaten and whipped. He also got off on watching the other boys being beaten, especially when they bled from the wounds around their buttocks.

Albert Fish grew up in New York to become a devout Christian who married in 1898, and fathered six children. A house painter with a long record of minor crimes and a jail term for embezzlement, Fish travelled all over America in search of work, only returning home for short periods. He practised his perversions with young men wherever he was at the time, and when it got too hot he moved on, never to return to the same town twice for fear of retribution. He later boasted to have killed a child in each of the states he visited.

When his wife left in 1917, Albert's perversions boiled to the surface and he began indulging in coprophilia (eating human excrement), inserting alcohol soaked cotton wool balls in his anus and lighting them, getting his children to beat him bloody with a nail-studded paddle and inserting needles into his genitals.

In 1928, in response to an advertisement that 18-year-old Edward Budd had placed in the paper looking for work, Fish, calling himself Frank Howard, called on the Budd family taking with him cheese and strawberries. He had the intention of interviewing Edward, pretending to be offering him employment on his farm outside New York, but instead he planned to murder and eat the boy at the first opportunity.

But while Edward's 10-year-old sister Gracie was sitting on the 58-year-old Fish's lap, he was fantasising about eating her instead. Fish convinced the Budds to let him take their daughter to a local children's party that afternoon. That was the last they would ever see of her. Six years later, in 1934, the Budd family received what would become the most infamously cruel letter in the history of murder anywhere in the world. This is that letter in its entirety:

Dear Mrs. Budd,
In 1894 a friend of mine shipped as a deck hand on the Steamer Tacoma, *Capt. John Davis. They sailed from San Francisco for Hong Kong, China. On arriving there he and two others went ashore and got drunk. When they returned the boat was gone. At that time there was famine in China. Meat of any kind was from $1–3 per pound.*

So great was the suffering among the very poor that all children under 12 were sold for food in order to keep others from starving. A boy or girl under 14 was not safe in the street. You could go in any shop and ask for steak – chops – or stew meat. Part of the naked body of a boy or girl would be brought out and just what you wanted cut from it.

A boy or girl's behind which is the sweetest part of the body and sold as veal cutlet brought the highest price. John staid [sic] there so long he acquired a taste for human flesh. On his return to N.Y. he stole two boys, one 7 and one 11. Took them to his home stripped them naked tied them in a closet. Then burned everything they had on. Several times every day and night he spanked them – tortured them – to make their meat good and tender.

First he killed the 11 year old boy, because he had the fattest ass and of course the most meat on it. Every part of his body was cooked and eaten except the head – bones and guts. He was roasted in the oven (all of his ass), boiled, broiled, fried and stewed. The little boy was next, went the same way.

At that time, I was living at 409 E 100 St. near – right side. He told me so often how good human flesh was I made up my mind to taste it. On Sunday June the 3, 1928 I called on you at 406 W 15 St. Brought you pot cheese – strawberries. We had lunch. Grace sat in my lap and kissed me. I made up my mind to eat her. On the pretense of taking her to a party. You said yes she could go.

I took her to an empty house in Westchester I had already picked out. When we got there, I told her to remain outside. She picked wildflowers. I went upstairs and stripped all my clothes off. I knew if I did not I would get her blood on them. When all was ready I went to the window and called her. Then I hid in a closet until she was in the room. When she saw me all naked she began to cry and tried to run down the stairs.

I grabbed her and she said she would tell her

mamma. First I stripped her naked. How she did kick
– bite and scratch. I choked her to death, then cut her
in small pieces so I could take my meat to my rooms.
Cook and eat it. How sweet and tender her little ass
was roasted in the oven. It took me 9 days to eat her
entire body. I did not fuck her tho [sic] *I could of had*
I wished. She died a virgin.

It was to be Albert Fish's undoing. The envelope had a
small emblem with the letters 'NYPCBA' in it, which led
police to a rooming house at 200 East 52nd Street. The
landlady informed them that an elderly man with grey hair,
who answered the description of the man who was last seen
with Grace Budd, had vacated only days earlier. But as luck
would have it, she was holding some money for the man
and expected him back at any time. When Albert Fish
returned he was arrested and readily confessed to the
murder of Grace Budd. He stated that he had originally
gone to the Budd household with the intentions of killing
her brother, Edward, but chose Grace instead after realising
that Edward was a tall, strapping lad who could have easily
defended himself against an old man.

In custody, investigators asked Fish if he knew anything
about the disappearance of a boy named Billy Gaffney who
went missing in Brooklyn in 1927 in the company of a man
who answered to Fish's description. Fish admitted that he
had abducted the boy and after he gave this full confession,
some of the police regretted that they had ever asked. This is
what Albert Fish told them:

I brought him (Billy Gaffney) to the Riker Avenue
dumps. There is a house that stands alone, not far from
where I took him. I took the boy there. Stripped him
naked and tied his hands and feet and gagged him with

*a piece of dirty rag I picked out of the dump. Then I
burned his clothes. Threw his shoes in the dump. Then
I walked back and took the trolley to 59 Street at 2
a.m. and walked from there home.*

*Next day about 2 p.m., I took tools, a good heavy
cat-o-nine tails. Home made. Short handle. Cut one of
my belts in half, slit these halves in six strips about 8
inches long. I whipped his bare behind till the blood
ran from his legs. I cut off his ears, nose, slit his mouth
from ear to ear. Gouged out his eyes. He was dead
then. I stuck the knife in his belly and held my mouth
to his body and drank his blood.*

*I picked up four old potato sacks and gathered a
pile of stones. Then I cut him up. I had a grip with
me. I put his nose, ears and a few slices of his belly in
the grip. Then I cut him through the middle of his
body. Just below the belly button. Then through his
legs about 2 inches below his behind. I put this in my
grip with a lot of paper. I cut off the head, feet, arms,
hands and the legs below the knee. This I put in sacks
weighed with stones, tied the ends and threw them
into the pools of slimy water you will see all along the
road going to North Beach.*

*I came home with my meat. I had the front of his
body I liked best. His monkey and pee wees and a
nice little fat behind to roast in the oven and eat. I
made a stew out of his ears, nose, pieces of his face
and belly. I put onions, carrots, turnips, celery, salt
and pepper. It was good.*

*Then I split the cheeks of his behind open, cut off
his monkey and pee wees and washed them first. I put
strips of bacon on each cheek of his behind and put
them in the oven. Then I picked 4 onions and when*

*the meat had roasted about 1/4 hour, I poured about
a pint of water over it for gravy and put in the onions.
At frequent intervals I basted his behind with a
wooden spoon. So the meat would be nice and juicy.*

*In about 2 hours, it was nice and brown, cooked
through. I never ate any roast turkey that tasted half
as good as his sweet fat little behind did. I ate every
bit of the meat in about four days. His little monkey
was a sweet as a nut, but his pee-wees I could not
chew. Threw them in the toilet.*

Although Albert Fish confessed to only one other killing it
was believed that he was involved in the deaths of more
than 25 young people who had either been murdered or
had gone missing in New York and 23 states across
America. He pleaded not guilty to murder on the grounds
of insanity but was found to be both guilty and sane at the
time he murdered Grace Budd and Billy Gaffney.

Fish was delighted to hear that he was to die in the electric
chair. He described it as the 'ultimate experience in pain' and
went to his death like a man going to a picnic, even helping
the warders strap him in.

The popular urban myth of the time was that the metal
pins and needles self-embedded in Fish's genitals and scrotum
caused the electric chair to short circuit and the first charge
failed to kill him. The myth described how he sat there
grinning as they cranked it up for another go. Not so.
Everything went as planned and, amid wisps of blue smoke,
it took just three minutes and Albert Fish was sent smiling to
his maker.

And, predictably, the newspaper headlines the following
day read 'Fried Fish'.

THERE'S MORE THAN ONE WAY TO LOSE YOUR LIFE TO A KILLER

MARK
RUFFALO

JAKE
GYLLENHAAL

ROBERT
DOWNEY JR.

FROM THE DIRECTOR OF SE7EN AND PANIC ROOM

PARAMOUNT PICTURES AND WARNER BROS. PICTURES PRESENT A PHOENIX PICTURES PRODUCTION A DAVID FINCHER FILM JAKE GYLLENHAAL MARK RUFFALO ROBERT DOWNEY JR. ANTHONY EDWARDS
"ZODIAC" BRIAN COX ELIAS KOTEAS DONAL LOGUE JOHN CARROLL LYNCH DERMOT MULRONEY MUSIC BY DAVID SHIRE MUSIC SUPERVISORS RANDALL POSTER AND GEORGE DRAKOULIAS EDITED BY ANGUS WALL
PRODUCTION DESIGNER DONALD GRAHAM BURT DIRECTOR OF PHOTOGRAPHY HARRIS SAVIDES, A.S.C. EXECUTIVE PRODUCER LOUIS PHILLIPS PRODUCED BY MIKE MEDAVOY ARNOLD W. MESSER BRADLEY J. FISCHER JAMES VANDERBILT CEAN CHAFFIN

WARNER BROS. PICTURES   PHOENIX PICTURES

ZodiacMovie.com

BASED ON THE BOOK BY ROBERT GRAYSMITH   SCREENPLAY BY JAMES VANDERBILT   DIRECTED BY DAVID FINCHER

COMING SOON

ZODIAC

(2007)

DIRECTED BY DAVID FINCHER
SCREENPLAY BY JAMES VANDERBILT

FEATURING

Jake Gyllenhaal as Robert Graysmith
Mark Ruffalo as Inspector David Toschi
Anthony Edwards as Inspector William Armstrong
Robert Downey Jr as Paul Avery
Brian Cox as Melvin Belli
John Carroll Lynch as Arthur Leigh Allen

If you don't know anything about California's Zodiac murders that occurred in the late 1960s, then this is the movie for you. If you do, then you're going to have to wait until about halfway through this 150 minute documentary/drama to find out anything new. But having said that, the meticulous research and presentation of the first half will keep you enthralled, no matter how up to date you are on the subject.

Zodiac tells the story of one of America's most enduring mysteries. Jake Gyllenhaal plays Robert Graysmith, a *San Francisco Chronicle* political cartoonist who became so obsessed with the Zodiac that, at dramatic cost to his personal life, he wrote two books on the subject – *Zodiac* and *Zodiac Unmasked*. Robert Downey Jr is brilliant as the *Chronicle*'s chain-smoking, alcoholic crime reporter Paul Avery who, at one stage, looks like being Zodiac's next target. Mark Ruffalo plays Dave Toschi, the detective leading the Zodiac investigation who is almost driven mad by the obsessed Graysmith, long after the case has gone cold. The wonderful character actor Brian Cox (who had the honour of being the very first screen Hannibal Lecter in *Manhunter*) features as Melvin Belli, the celebrity defence lawyer who was contacted live by the Zodiac on TV.

The police, with the *Chronicle* reporters in hot pursuit, finally narrow it down to one suspect – convicted paedophile Arthur Leigh Allen – a surly bit of work who looks and acts the part. A search of Allen's home comes up with all sorts of goodies which, if you don't know any better, will have you believing that Allen is our man and it's all over. But despite all sorts of circumstantial evidence that the cops keep throwing at us, Allen is legally exonerated and the case is allowed to go cold. Three years later Zodiac sends another letter and it's on again until Zodiac disappears forever.

Director David Fincher (*Se7en*) includes the viewer every step of the way. The first half of *Zodiac* is about the police investigation and the reporters, and it features some of the best big city newsroom banter since *All The President's Men*. The second half concentrates on the torment of the obsessed cartoonist Graysmith. We watch as he is eaten alive by his pursuit of the serial killer, and he loses his young family, his job and most of his friends. Hence the movie's tagline: 'There's more than one way to lose your life to a killer'. His consolation is watching his books become best-sellers. And *Zodiac* won't do him any harm by selling a few million more.

For a serial murder story that has no ending, David Fincher has created a masterpiece.

The Zodiac Murders

In northern California between December 1968 and October 1969 the Zodiac Killer murdered five people. Two others miraculously escaped with their lives. To this day, the identity of the Zodiac Killer remains a mystery. In letters to local newspapers, which were sent until 1974, he claimed responsibility for as many as 37 deaths – and there is definitely circumstantial evidence to suggest his tally is higher than the official one. The unsolved case was closed in April 2004, but reopened around the start of 2007 with the hope DNA evidence from the letters may eventually lead to an arrest. The families of both the confirmed victims and those believed to have been killed by the Zodiac Killer live in hope that the sadistic murderer will eventually be brought to justice.

The first victims attributed to the self-named Zodiac Killer were Betty Lou Jensen and David Faraday, murdered on 20 December 1968 in the small Californian town of Benicia. The couple were on a first date and had eaten at a local restaurant, before parking in a gravel patch on the side of Lake Herman Road at around 10.15pm. The Zodiac Killer is believed to have pulled up behind them not long after 11pm, and a witness later reported seeing two cars, though they couldn't confirm if anyone was in either of them. The witness also claims to have heard a sound as he drove past, which may have been a gunshot. But he couldn't confirm it as his car radio was on at the time.

Not long after that, a woman named Stella Borges, who lived in the area, found the two lifeless bodies. Faraday had died from a bullet wound to the head, while Jensen had been shot in the back five times as she tried desperately to escape from her attacker. Detectives were called in, but they didn't have a lot of evidence to work with and the case soon started to grow cold.

The Zodiac Killer struck again at around midnight on the evening of 4 July 1969, shooting Darlene Ferrin and Michael Mageau with a 9mm pistol while they sat in a car at the Blue Rock Springs Golf Course parking lot in Vallejo, which is only about six kilometres from the spot Jensen and Faraday had been murdered. The killer had parked his car behind their vehicle so that they couldn't drive away, then approached the car's passenger side, using a flashlight to blind them before pulling the trigger several times. Ferrin was dead before she reached the hospital, but Mageau survived even though he had been shot at close range in the chest, neck and face.

A little after half an hour later, an anonymous caller phoned the Vallejo Police Department claiming responsibility for the shootings, as well as those of Jensen and Faraday. The tip-off was traced to the public phone at a service station close to Ferrin's home, but again the police could find few leads.

The Zodiac Killer began his bizarre correspondence with the media by sending three virtually identical letters to the *San Francisco Examiner* on 1 August 1969. In the letters he again claimed responsibility for the shootings. He also included one third of a strange cryptogram comprised of 408 characters on each letter. He said that the characters contained his identity, if anyone was capable of deciphering them. He added that he wanted the letters printed on the front page of the newspaper or else he would go on a killing spree over the weekend and murder 12 more people.

Through the media, the chief of police in Vallejo asked the letter-writer for more details in order to prove his callous claims, and the *San Francisco Examiner* received another letter on 4 August. It read: 'Dear Editor. This is the Zodiac speaking…' And he signed off with a symbol of a cross inside a circle that would become his trademark.

Four days after that, a married Californian couple, Donald and Bettye Harden, cracked the bizarre cryptogram, but found that it did not contain the Zodiac Killer's identity as he had said it would. Instead it was a message that read:

I LIKE KILLING PEOPLE BECAUSE IT IS SO MUCH FUN IT IS MORE FUN THAN KILLING WILD GAME IN THE FORREST [sic] BECAUSE MAN IS THE MOST DANGEROUS ANAMAL [sic] OF ALL TO KILL SOMETHING GIVES ME THE MOST THRILLING EXPERENCE [sic] IT IS EVEN BETTER THAN GETTING YOUR ROCKS OFF WITH A GIRL THE BEST PART OF IT IS THAT WHEN I DIE I WILL BE REBORN IN PARADICE [sic] AND ALL THE [sic] I HAVE KILLED WILL BECOME MY SLAVES I WILL NOT GIVE YOU MY NAME BECAUSE YOU WILL TRY TO SLOI [sic] DOWN OR STOP MY COLLECTING OF SLAVES FOR MY AFTERLIFE EBEORIETEMETHHPITI

The seemingly random letters added at the end of the message have never been deciphered.

The Zodiac Killer struck out again on 27 September 1969 when he found Bryan Hartnell and Cecelia Shepard having a picnic beside Lake Berryessa. The relaxed couple were surprised to see a man wearing a black hood over his head, in the style of an executioner. The man had clip-on sunglasses over the eyeholes, and was carrying a gun in one hand. He told the pair that he had escaped from a prison in Montana, killing a guard in the process and stealing a car. He demanded they give him their car and money so that he could flee to Mexico. Then he produced some lengths of plastic cord and ordered Shepard to tie Hartnell up. When she had done so, he tied her up as well. Then he viciously stabbed them both and walked about half a kilometre to Hartnell's car where he used the knife to scrape the cross-and-circle symbol he had been signing his letters with on the door. Beneath that he scraped 'Vallejo 12-20-68, 7-4-69, Sept 27-69-6:30' and left.

The Zodiac Killer phoned the police in Napa, California, at 7.40pm that evening to tell them what he had done. The call was traced to a public phone at a car wash just a few blocks away from the station. But Hartnell and Shepard had already been found by a fisherman and taken to hospital. A traumatised Hartnell survived the ordeal, but Shepard died after being in a coma for two days.

The Zodiac Killer's next victim was taxi driver Paul Stine. He hailed down Stine's cab at the corner of San Francisco's Mason and Geary Streets on 11 October. After they had reached Cherry Street in Presidio Heights the Zodiac Killer produced a 9mm pistol and shot Stine in the head before taking the car keys, his wallet and ripping off the tail of his shirt. A group of teenagers watched the murderer exit the taxi and walk away. They phoned the police and told them that the killer was still in the area. The police arrived within minutes and started to comb the area but the murderer managed to elude them.

Still, the teenagers gave a detailed enough description of the man they had seen that police artists were able to create a composite sketch of the killer. The man they described was aged somewhere between 35 and 45 years old. The San Francisco Police Department assigned detectives Bill Armstrong and Dave Toschi to the case. The men would come to investigate more than 2500 suspects through the years, all to no avail.

The Zodiac Killer's next move was to send another letter

to the media. This time he included part of the shirt tail he had ripped from Stine as proof that he had murdered the helpless cab driver. He also threatened to start shooting school children.

He then sent a card on 8 November, which featured another cryptogram, this time featuring 340 characters. It has never been deciphered. Then, on 9 November he posted a seven-page letter that claimed a pair of police officers had stopped and spoken to him just minutes before he had murdered Stine.

On 20 December, the Zodiac Killer sent another letter, this time to prominent Californian lawyer Melvin Belli, asking the man for help. Included with the letter was another piece of Stine's shirt tail.

The Zodiac Killer kept up his correspondence with the police through 1970. In one letter, posted on 20 April, he taunted them by including a still-undeciphered 13-character cryptogram that he claimed held the key to his identity. He also said that he planned on using a bomb to blow up a school bus.

He repeated the threat in a letter to the *San Francisco Chronicle* on 28 April, adding that he wanted people to start wearing Zodiac badges. In his next letter, on 26 June 1970, he expressed his disappointment that he hadn't seen anyone wearing the badges, and said that he had shot a man 'sitting in a parked car'. He said he had used a .38 pistol for the slaying. It is thought that he was referring to the murder of San Francisco police sergeant Richard Radetich, who had been shot in the head with a .38 while writing a parking ticket, but there is no proof to back up the theory, and the case remains unsolved to this day.

By now, the Zodiac Killer had started to send messages directly to *San Francisco Chronicle* reporter Paul Avery, who had been covering the case for a while. Avery received a

Halloween card on 27 October that included the cross-and-circle signature, as well as the handwritten words 'Peek-a-boo, you are doomed'. The story made his newspaper's front page.

Not long after that, Avery received a letter from an anonymous sender. The letter pointed out similarities between the Zodiac murders and the unsolved killing of college student Cheri Jo Bates four years earlier at Riverside, California. Avery investigated the claims, and printed a story about it on 16 November 1970. Bates had been found brutally beaten and stabbed to death on 31 October 1966, not far from the campus library where she had spent the previous evening studying. A month later, the local police received a letter from a person claiming responsibility for the murder, adding that there would be more killings in the future.

Four months after Avery's piece ran, the Zodiac Killer sent a letter to the *Los Angeles Times* that spoke of his 'Riverside activity'. It also stated that 'there are a hell of a lot more down there', implying that Bates wasn't the only Riverside victim. Still, as there is no direct evidence that the Zodiac Killer was responsible for killing the young student, she isn't included in the official list of his victims.

Another slaying not on the official list was that of young couple Robert Domingos and Linda Edwards, who were found shot to death on a beach on 4 June 1963. In circumstances similar to the lake Berryessa incident, the lovers were thought to have been bound and then shot several times in the back and chest when they managed to escape. Their corpses were then left inside a small shack, which the murderer tried to burn down in an effort to hide the evidence.

The Zodiac Killer went quiet eventually, with no further

official murders or correspondence to the police or media for almost three years. It wasn't until 29 January 1974 that the *San Francisco Chronicle* received another letter, this one strangely praising the satanic horror film *The Exorcist* as the best satirical comedy he had ever seen. At the end of the letter he stated that he wrote 'Me = 37, SFPD = 0', implying that he had murdered 37 victims and that the San Francisco Police Department were yet to catch him. There have been no confirmed messages sent since, and while the case is still open, the Zodiac Killer is yet to be bought to justice.

INDEX